UNIVERSITY OF
WIN

OTHER PEOPLE'S ANTHROPOLOGIES

Ethnographic Practice on the Margins

edited by
Aleksandar Bošković

Berghahn Books
New York • Oxford

First edition published in 2008 by

Berghahn Books
www.berghahnbooks.com

©2008, 2010 Aleksandar Bošković
First paperback edition published in 2010

Library of Congress Cataloging-in-Publication Data

Other people's anthropologies : ethnographic practice on the margins / edited by Aleksandar Bošković. — 1st ed.
    p. cm.
Papers originally presented at a workshop at the 2004 EASA conference in Vienna.
Includes bibliographical references and index.
ISBN 978-1-84545-398-5 (hardback : alk. paper)
    1. Ethnology—Congresses. I. Bošković, Aleksandar. II. European Association of Social Anthropologists. Conference (2004 : Vienna, Austria)

GN302.0884 2007
305.8—dc22   2007042675

British Library Cataloguing in Publication Data

A catalogue record for this book is available from the British Library

Printed in the United States on acid-free paper

ISBN-13: 978-1-84545-398-5 hardback
ISBN-13: 978-1-84545-702-0 paperback

to our students

Contents

❧

Acknowledgements

The idea of organizing something about "marginal" anthropological traditions was suggested by Thomas Hylland Eriksen. His contribution to this book far exceeds the role of a contributor and a co-convenor of the workshop from which some papers were drawn. Part of the work on this book was done while I was supported by the JRC Research Grant at the Rhodes University in Grahamstown (South Africa). The "final touches" were done while I was enjoying the hospitality of the Max Planck Institute for Social Anthropology in Halle/Saale (Germany), for which I am most grateful to Chris Hann.

At various stages of this project, I benefited from the experience and expertise of the late Eduardo Archetti, James T. Clifford, and Han F. Vermeulen. My M.A. students at the Faculty of Social Sciences (Ljubljana, Slovenia) were keen to discuss some of the issues of global anthropological traditions during the courses I taught there in July 2004 and January 2005. Many thanks to my friends and colleagues from different parts of the world: William H. Fisher (USA), Henyo T. Barreto Filho (Brazil), the late W.D. Hammond-Tooke, Fiona Ross, Isak Niehaus, Robert Thornton (South Africa), the late Borut Brumen, Vesna V. Godina, Rajko Muršič (Slovenia), Sanja Potkonjak (Croatia), Jos Platenkamp (Germany), Ilana van Wyk, and Glenn Bowman (UK). Gašpar Petrač facilitated access to the chapters by all the contributors by putting them on the web. The anonymous Berghahn Books reader provided very useful suggestions and comments, and Dr. Marion Berghahn has been very helpful and supportive throughout this project.

Last but not least, my parents, Zlatka and Đorđe Bošković, and my friends, Jelena Stefanović, Branimir Stojanović, Snežana Mićić-Omerović, and Miran Lavrinc (with his family) provided important support at some personally extremely trying and challenging times.

List of Contributors

Aleksandar Bošković is Senior Research Fellow at the Center for Political Studies and Public Opinion Research of the Institute of Social Sciences in Belgrade (Serbia) and Visiting Professor of Anthropology at the Faculty of Social Sciences, University of Ljubljana (Slovenia). His research areas include ethnicity and nationalism, popular culture, and he has also published widely on the history and theory of anthropology. Bošković is the author or editor of several books in Serbo-Croatian, including *The Ethnology of Everyday Life* (Belgrade, 2005) and *Myth, Politics, Ideology* (Belgrade, 2006).

Magdalena Elchinova is Associate Professor and Head of the Department of Anthropology at the New Bulgarian University in Sofia (Bulgaria). Her research topics include folklore, ethnicity, discourse analysis, and semiotics. She is the author of, among other titles, "Ethnic Discourse and Group Presentation in Modern Bulgarian Society," *Development and Society* 30 (2001).

Thomas Hylland Eriksen is Professor of Social Anthropology at the University of Oslo (Norway). His research has focused on the dynamics of culture, politics, and identity in contexts of change, and he has published widely on ethnicity, nationalism, and globalization. He has also written several textbooks in English and numerous books spanning many genres in Norwegian. His most recent books in English are *A History of Anthropology* (with F. S. Nielsen, London, 2001), *Globalisation – Studies in Anthropology* (London, 2003), *What is Anthropology?* (London, 2004), and *Engaging Anthropology* (Oxford, 2005).

Jude Fokwang is Doctoral candidate in the Department of Anthropology, University of Toronto (Canada). He obtained his M.A. with distinction from the University of Pretoria. In 2001, he was a laureate of the Social Science Research Council's fellowship on African Youth in the Global Age. He contributed to several journals, including *African Affairs* and *African Anthropologist*.

Rosana Guber is Researcher at the Argentine Council for Scientific and Technological Research (CONICET), and at the Institute of Economic and Social Development (IDES), where she chairs the Center for Social Anthropology. Her current research deals with social memory, nation and nationhood, the Malvinas/Falklands War, and ethnographic methodology. She is the author of *El Salvaje Metropolitano* (Buenos Aires, 1991), *De chicos a veteranos* (Buenos Aires, 2004), *Etnografia* (Buenos Aires, Bogotá, 2001), *Por qué Malvinas?* (Buenos Aires, 2001), and co-editor of *Historia y Estilos de Trabajo de Campo en la Argentina* (Buenos Aires, 2002).

Ulf Hannerz is Professor of Social Anthropology, at Stockholm University, in Sweden. He has taught at several American, European, Asian, and Australian universities and is a former Chair of the European Association of Social Anthropologists and a Fellow of the American Academy of Arts and Sciences. His research has been focused especially in urban anthropology, media anthropology, and transnational cultural processes, and his most recent books in English are *Cultural Complexity* (1992), *Transnational Connections* (1996), and *Foreign News* (2004). He was the anthropology editor for the *International Encyclopedia of the Social and Behavioral Sciences* (2001).

Anatoly M. Kuznetsov is Professor and Chair of Social and Political Anthropology at the Far Eastern State University in Vladivostok (Russia). He edited the collection of the ethnographic works of S.M. Shirokogoroff (in Russian, 2001–2), and is the author of over fifty scholarly articles on the topics ranging from "Shamanism as an anthropological problem" (in Russian, 2001), to the influence of Shirokogoroff on the "ethnos" theory.

George E. Marcus is Chancellor Professor of Anthropology at the University of California in Irvine (USA). He is co-author with Michael Fischer of *Anthropology as Cultural Critique* (1986) and co-editor, with James Clifford, of *Writing Culture* (1986). More recently he has edited *Critical Anthropology Now* (1999), and authored *Ethnography Through Thick & Thin* (1998). Through the 1990s, he originated and edited the University of Chicago series of annuals, *Late Editions,* designed to document change at the turn of the century through ethnographic interviews. At present, he is working on a short book about the reinvention of the ethnographic process in graduate training.

Mwenda Ntarangwi is Associate Professor in the Department of Sociology, at Calvin College (Grand Rapids, MI, USA). With previous training in Swahili studies from the Kenyatta University (Nairobi, Kenya) and a Ph.D. in anthropology from the University of Illinois at Urbana-Champaign (USA), his main research interests are popular culture, gender, and cross-cultural studies. He is former President of the Pan African Anthropological Association, the author of *Gender, Identity, and Performance* (Africa World Press, 2003), and co-editor of *African Anthropologies* (London, 2006).

Mariza G. S. Peirano is Professor of Anthropology at the University of Brasilia (Brasilia, Brazil). She did research on the history of Brazilian anthropology, resulting in her Ph.D. from Harvard University (1981). She is the author of *Uma Antropologia no Plural* (1992), *A Favor da Etnografia* (1995), *Rituais Ontem e Hoje* (2003), and editor of *O Dito e o Feito. Ensaios de Antropologia dos Rituais* (2001). Her articles in English include "When Anthropology is at Home" (*Annual Review of Anthropology*, 1998) and "Otherness in context: A guide to anthropology in Brazil" (in press, D. Poole, ed., *Companion to Latin American Anthropology*, 2005).

Kaori Sugishita studied at universities in Japan and the United Kingdom. She obtained a Doctorate in anthropology from the University of Oxford in 2002 for her research on the development of traditional medicine in modern Zambia. After two years of postdoctoral fellowship at the University of the Witwatersrand in South Africa, she is currently teaching part-time in Japan.

Zerrin G. Tandoğan teaches in the Department of Political Science at Bilkent University (Ankara, Turkey). She received her Ph.D. in Social Anthropology from Hacettepe University (1991). She conducted fieldwork in Oslo, Norway (1989–91) focusing on the ethnocentric tendencies in cross-cultural human contact, and carried out an image research about Turks and Turkey in Raleigh, US (1985–86). Tandoğan's interest areas include cosmopolitanism, interculturalism, EU, transnational academics, and research ethics. She contributed to, among others, *European Journal of Intercultural Studies, City and Society,* and *Journal of Turkish Studies.*

Han F. Vermeulen is a cultural anthropologist from the University of Leiden, now working at the Max Planck Institute for Social Anthropology in Halle (Germany). He has conducted anthropological fieldwork in North Africa (Tunisia) as well as library and archival research in Europe (the Netherlands, Germany, Austria, and Russia). Vermeulen is currently interested in the history of ethnography and ethnology in Europe and Asia from the eighteenth century onwards. He is a co-editor of the two-volume research project *Tales from Academia: History of Anthropology in the Netherlands* (2002).

Introduction

Other People's Anthropologies

Aleksandar Bošković and Thomas Hylland Eriksen

ABOUT THIS BOOK

There were several formative moments in the creation of this book. First of all, the idea of organizing the workshop on "Other Anthropologies" at the 2004 EASA conference in Vienna was suggested by Thomas Hylland Eriksen, as we were walking through the High Street of Grahamstown (South Africa) on a windy Sunday morning in May 2003. The two day (10–11 September) and three session workshop in Vienna went extremely well, both in terms of attendance and the discussions. Many papers from this workshop (by Kuznetsov, Elchinova, Sugishita, and Guber) eventually made it into this book.

This book cannot be viewed in isolation from the earlier discussions of "indigenous" or "non-Western" (Fahim 1982; Asad 1982), "native" or "nativist" (Narayan 1993; Mingming 2002), "central/peripheral" (Hannerz and Gerholm 1982; Cardoso de Oliveira 2000), "anthropologies of the South" (Krotz 1997; Quinlan 2000), or "world anthropologies" (Restrepo and Escobar 2005; Ribeiro and Escobar 2006). Apart from the collection of articles in *Ethnos* (Hannerz and Gerholm 1982) and Fahim's book, we must also mention the edited volume dealing with the European anthropology and ethnology, by Vermeulen and Roldán (1995). The fact that all of these books have been out of print for a long time stands at odds with the growing interest in these issues. Last but not least, the leading Russian anthropological journal, *Etnografičeskoe obozrenie,* recently also devoted a special issue (2/2005) to "world" anthropologies, edited by Alexei Elfimov.

ONE OR MANY?

It would probably be safe to say that the issues of alterity and difference were crucial for the human questioning of different (and potentially threatening) others, at least from José de Acosta's[1] *Historia natural y moral de las Índias* in 1590.[2] It would also be safe to say that the quest for understanding others was at the same time defining for the (rarely explicit task of) understanding ourselves, and anthropology has contributed to this since its very beginnings. Naturally, there were different traditions and different theories; there were gruelling intellectual debates between advocates of the "monogenetic" and "phylogenetic" theories in the early nineteenth century, then there was the issue of the "psychic unity of mankind," so forcefully championed by Bastian and his followers (and Franz Boas was one of them); finally, the issue of the "cultural circles" and the spread of culture and civilization (with Rivers' 1911 address to the Section H of the British Association for the Advancement of Science as the defining moment),[3] and many more during the twentieth century. It has been argued that even some "great" or "central" traditions arose as a direct consequence of the encounter with the other (Brumana 2002, Latour 2004).

But just as anthropology never had a single point of origin, it also never had a single stream of development—and this becomes, perhaps, more pronounced than ever in our "post-colonial" or "post-industrial" times. Some projects focusing on particular (imagined) points of view therefore become a bit problematic—for example, the distinction between "Western" and "non-Western" anthropologies has been so described (Madan 1982, Asad 1982). On the other hand, anthropology as a discipline is usually defined in terms of the "centers" or "central" traditions (de Oliveira 2000 mentions the American, British and French traditions [Cardoso de Oliveira 2000]; one might add the German one as well)—the processes of marginalization go so far that, for example, it is practically impossible for non-members of the biggest anthropological association in the world (the AAA) to even submit papers to some AAA journals.[4]

The processes of decolonization, along with critical interrogation of the dominant narratives, led to much greater visibility of the non-central anthropological traditions. Of course, some of them (like India, for example) have been quite visible for many decades. Others, like the Russian one, have been around for a very long time, and along with the Japanese and the Brazilian traditions, are quite impressive when it comes to the numbers of professional anthropologists or ethnologists. However, there are some differences in the focus of research (Asad 1982: 285; Madan in Fahim, Helmer et al. 1980: 655, Fahim 1982: 265ff.), as "Western" anthropologists tended to

study societies "abroad," while their "non-Western" (or "peripheral") counterparts much more often opted (or had to, due to financial and/or political
constraints) to study "at home."

On the surface, this creates a very different situation: this anthropologist begins with considerable knowledge of cultural and social patterns, she
often does not have to learn a new language, etc. Yet, it can be argued that
this supposedly crucial difference between works of "Third World" or "non-
Western" anthropologists does not really affect the quality of work or research,
although the fact remains that the most influential anthropological works
today are published in English (and occasionally French).[5] Some questions
follow from this. Firstly, is this leading to a certain "auto-provincialization"
of anthropology? Secondly, how does this contribute to a "critical Third
World vision" (Cardoso de Oliveira 2000: 11)?

The work of anthropologists from non-metropolitan traditions displays
enormous variation, much of it poorly known in dominant, largely Anglophone anthropology. Some of these anthropologists have had extensive training
in the metropolitan schools, while others have been educated in a domestic
or regional intellectual environment. Some have done their fieldwork at
home, or among "others at home," making for a closer relationship to the
domestic public sphere and domestic politics; while others have worked overseas. Some publish chiefly in non-hegemonic languages (which increasingly
means any language but English); some depend on extensive consultancy
work to make ends meet, while others have a strong institutional base in
their national university system. Some may function as free intellectuals and
scholars, while others are expected to conform to strictly academic or ideological norms. In brief, the differences between "marginal anthropologies"
are just as pronounced as the similarities, and make comparisons both demanding and necessary—even more so as the stories of these anthropologies
may stimulate critical reflection on the basis for the assumed centrality of
hegemonic anthropologies.

In the introduction to their pioneering collection of peripheral anthropologies, Gerholm and Hannerz (1982) compared the center–periphery
relationship in anthropology with that of a mainland to the outlying archipelago. People living in the islands were variously connected to the mainland by ferry, bridges, etc., but their main point, which remains valid today,
is that the island people needed the mainland to survive, while mainland
dwellers did not even need to be aware of the existence of the islands. While
this discrepancy in symbolic power is well known in the "islands," it is rarely
noticed on the mainland. Majorities do not need to learn the minority languages; minorities are forced to learn majority languages. Majorities define
the terms of discourse, while minorities can either remain marginal or adapt.

Such basic insights into intergroup power relations, taught in Anthropology 101 courses everywhere (both on the mainland and in the archipelago, incidentally), are rarely brought to bear on anthropology itself. Do peripheral anthropologies create their own centers, or do they slavishly adapt to the latest fashions of the metropoles? Do they at all perceive themselves as peripheral? Do they represent alternative theoretical or methodological perspectives which should have been better known at the center, or is their work either second rate or similar to metropolitan anthropology?

In this Introduction, we ask these and related questions by drawing on eleven original, hitherto unpublished accounts from as many countries,[6] ranging from the huge to the tiny; from countries with an old, confident, and venerable tradition of anthropology, to countries where the subject was either developed during twentieth century colonialism or even more recently, that is, after the fall of the Berlin Wall. The stories cover Argentina and Brazil in the Americas, Cameroon and Kenya in Africa, Bulgaria, Russia, and former Yugoslavia in Eastern Europe, the Netherlands and Norway in Western Europe, as well as Japan and Turkey.

DIVERSE ORIGINS

British and French anthropology had partly overlapping origins with colonialism, although it would be preposterous to claim, as many have done, that they were "an extended arm" of the colonial endeavor.[7] The relationship with colonial authorities was much more complicated than that. Regarding the anthropologies that emerged outside the centers, their relationship with global power structures varies greatly.

Han Vermeulen traces Dutch anthropology back to the 1770s, arguing that it was institutionalized from the 1830s onwards—a generation ahead of Morgan and Tylor. In the Netherlands, the early interest in systematic studies of faraway peoples was quite clearly a result of colonialism, and early (proto-) anthropologists stood in a complex relationship to the VOC (the Dutch East Indies Company). Through most of its history, Dutch anthropologists have concentrated on the country's colonies, largely Indonesia. Independent theories of social and cultural dynamics have been developed by Dutch scholars in Dutch, and their awareness of metropolitan traditions naturally exceeded the metropolitans' knowledge of their work. Even more interestingly, scholars working seriously with Indonesian ethnology need to acquire a reading knowledge of Dutch.

Although there is a strong publishing tradition in Dutch, anthropology in the Netherlands is increasingly bilingual; even the central journal,

Bijdraagen, publishes articles in both English and Dutch. In the last decades, Dutch anthropology has become more diverse in terms of regional orientation, and it must by now be said to be fully integrated into the mainstream, as witnessed in the fully English language journal *Focaal,* which takes on topics such as immigration and "the Other" in Europe.

While Dutch anthropology quite clearly has colonial origins, this cannot be said to be the case with the other West European country in our sample, Norway. Although there was considerable scholarly interest in the Sami in the nineteenth century already, and although the pioneering Norwegian sociologist Eilert Sundt (1817–1875) wrote sensitively about traveling communities and rural customs, the impetus to a modern Norwegian anthropology in the twentieth century came wholly from abroad; initially from German, French, and Anglophone sources, but after the Second World War increasingly from Britain and the USA. Following a period of eclecticism with a strong base in museum anthropology, Norwegian social anthropology was institutionalized and professionalized in the 1950s under the leadership of a few individuals, foremost among them in the formative period the young rebels, Fredrik Barth and Axel Sommerfelt, who were both reputed to have said, at various times, that one ought to sell off the Ethnographic Museum's collections in order to fund fieldwork. Since this period, Norwegian anthropologists have prioritized publishing in English, but somehow opposite to the Dutch situation, Norwegian language anthropology has flourished since the early 1990s. The Norwegian story reminds us, relevantly in the present context, of the fact that a handful of individuals can make a great deal of difference.

Moving east, Russian anthropology shares its colonial origins with Dutch anthropology, but since its empire was contiguous with its center, the clear cut distinction between ethnology (local culture) and anthropology (faraway peoples) is more fuzzy in Russia than in the Netherlands. Kuznetsov shows that in their pioneering studies of the *ethnos,* Russian anthropologists included themselves, or Russians rather, as one of the ethnic groups. Informed by both German *Volkskunde* and, obviously especially after 1917, a particular brand of Marxism or "Diamat" (dialectical materialism), Russian anthropologists saw their research, according to Kuznetsov, as being superior to that carried out in the West. Before 1990, little anthropology was translated between Russian and the West European languages, in spite of efforts by people like Ernest Gellner (1980) to develop a dialogue. The post-1990 situation seems to be characterized by a dual desire to "catch up" (the self-proclaimed provincial's attitude) and to show the West that a powerful Russian anthropological tradition does exist.

Lacking the means to carry out fieldwork overseas, Russian/Soviet anthropologists were always forced to problematize the distinction between "self" and "other" in ways Western anthropologists began to do only in the 1970s, notwithstanding their dependence on a stifling evolutionist explanatory scheme. In Brazil, Peirano points out, the "self–other" distinction has also played itself out in a way shaped by local circumstances. While anthropological theory in Brazil has been heavily influenced by both French and North American impulses, its articulation with society is very different. Like in Russia, the peoples studied by Brazilian anthropologists live in areas contiguous with their own. They have often assumed the advocate's stance, and, as Peirano puts it, "guilt has not prospered in a context which has always demanded social scientists' commitment to the objects of their study."

The Japanese situation, again, is qualitatively different. Sugishita points out that Japanese made the "shocking discovery" already in the 1870s that they were the object of Western observation! Their first anthropological association was founded as early as 1884. Not a conventional colonial power, Japan nevertheless was a regional power in East Asia, and yet twentieth century Japanese anthropology has been truly global in its reach. Sugishita, in a critical assessment of anthropology in Japan, argues that it remains a neocolonial enterprise based to a great extent on an unquestioned contrasting of "self" and "other," lacking careful self-reflection on "the complicated relationship between Japan, the West and the rest of the world." In this, Japanese anthropology seems to mirror, oddly, concerns which have been at the forefront of Western anthropology for a long time.

Spanish language Latin American anthropology has stood in a more direct, and arguably more dynamic, relationship to Western anthropology than either Russian or Japanese anthropology. Many Mexican and Argentinian anthropologists received their training overseas, and their work has developed in close dialogue both with metropolitan anthropology and with foreign anthropologists working in their own regions. Argentina parallels Norway in that anthropology was for a long time oriented towards cultural history. Guber notes: "Until the late 1950s, Argentinian anthropology only dealt with the past and with what anthropologists and most state agents conceived of as survivals of pre-Hispanic and pre-modern times—archaeology, ethnology and folklore."

The Soviet/Russian case is unique. There exists a rich and theoretically significant research literature in Russian that goes back to the eighteenth century. Research was later curbed and shaped by Soviet authorities with an active ideological interest in ethnology, subsuming it under Marxist universal history, a fact which did not prevent Soviet scholars from developing sophisticated theories and amassing enormous comparative ethnographic knowledge. The USSR was at the same time a hub attracting students, many of them interested in the ethnology of their own country, from socialist countries worldwide.

Some "peripheral" anthropologies may in fact claim to represent "great traditions" in their own right, and this is clearly the case for the former Soviet Union and possibly for Japan and Brazil as well. The Russian anthropologist V.I. Kozlov wrote in 1992 that, "I often had to socialise with American scientists from the prestige universities, as well as from the average ones, and I must say that their 'doctors' and 'professors' are scientifically inferior to ours" (quoted by Kuznetsov).

Brazilian anthropologists would probably not go this far, but it is clear from Periano's account that Brazilian anthropology, chiefly Lusophone, never saw itself as marginal or peripheral. Ethnological research has been carried out in Brazil for many generations, and today it plays a social and political role rarely paralleled in the North. Although the indebtedness to European and North American anthropological theory is evident in Brazil, there appears to be no sense among Brazilian anthropologists of living in a backwater or running a remote branch office.

Geographically closer to the centers, Serbian, Turkish, and Bulgarian anthropologies have histories which perhaps justify the term "periphery" more easily than some of our other examples. The most extreme example is Bulgaria, where anthropology appeared, according to Elchinova, only after the fall of the Berlin Wall, and where it is still very much in the making. Anthropology lacks a domestic tradition and even singular prominent scholars like Holy, Stuchlik, Gellner, and Skalník (from the former Czechoslovakia), Gusti (Romania), and Malinowski (Poland). However, like in most Central and Eastern European countries, an ethnological research tradition existed long before this; yet, according to Elchinova, the academic interest in faraway places was almost nonexistent. (Interestingly enough, Bulgarian exiles like Julia Kristeva and Tzvetan Todorov, who have written superbly about cultural differences, are non-anthropologists.)

Tandogan dates the origins of Turkish anthropology to 1925, just after the establishment of the Turkish Republic in 1923. Significantly, it was founded not by foreigners, but by domestic scholars. In Turkey, rural sociology overlapped with anthropology and possibly still does. In Serbia, anthropology has been practiced (as part of the so-called "human geography") at least since 1884. Its history is fraught with political concerns, political factionalism, and a difficult relationship to the nationalist discipline of ethnology, but there has also for decades been a very active dialogue with foreign (largely Anglophone, but recently also German language) anthropologists who carried out research in Yugoslavia and in the neighboring countries.

In the two African countries included in our sample, anthropology was quite clearly established by foreigners or expatriates like the Leakeys (Kenya). In Cameroon, there are few domestic scholars; Kenya has more, but in both countries, most of the well-known ethnographies have been published by foreigners. In Brazil, by contrast, the vast majority of anthropologists working in the country are locals.

In spite of Jomo Kenyatta's early monograph, *Facing Mount Kenya,* foreigners have dominated Kenyan anthropology. The famous paleoanthropologist Louis Leakey's mounting presence for decades in Kenyan academic life may have influenced sociocultural anthropology in the country; it is nonetheless a fact that it appears to be much more interdisciplinary than in most other countries. Anthropology is taught at several Kenyan universities, and also has an institutional base at the country level that has produced some remarkable polyhistors, easily transcending the boundaries of social or cultural anthropology.

Anglophone Cameroonian anthropology has been shaped by a handful of engaged foreign anthropologists, from Phyllis Kaberry to Edwin and Shirley Ardener, who helped to institutionalize research in the country and to develop local research expertise. However, in spite of this, it is probably fair to say that no truly independent research paradigms with an overseas influence have seen the light of day in postcolonial African societies (with the possible exception of South Africa). The funding remains erratic and the institutional infrastructure remains poor.

These are our eleven cases. With the exception of the Netherlands, Norway, and Japan, research in these countries is largely carried out at home or in the library. One characteristic of "peripheral anthropology" may thus appear to be that one tends to do fieldwork "at home." However, this will clearly not work as a general description. Certainly in Russia and Brazil, but also in the other countries under consideration, the tendency has been to study "the others at home"—Amerindians in Brazil, ethnic minorities in Russia, and rural farmers in Kenya and Cameroon.

Nevertheless, the empirical focus and breadth of research in a country is obviously interesting. Conversely, it is just as relevant to look at the domestic impact of anthropology in a country, which may be inversely related to the extent of overseas fieldwork—a topic to which we will return.

The extent of foreign ethnographic interest is also relevant, not least for its contribution to the internal dynamics of the subject in the country. Foreign anthropologists have consistently studied, published about, and engaged in dialogue with local scholars in Africa and Latin America, to some extent in Japan and former Yugoslavia, but to a much lesser extent in Russia, the Netherlands, Norway, and Bulgaria. According to Elchinova, only two anthropological monographs have been written about Bulgaria, and to date, their influence on Bulgarian scholars has been modest.

The varying relationship to colonialism is also interesting. Some anthropologies developed in the nineteenth and twentieth centuries were connected, however tenuously and uncomfortably, to colonial expansion; others were subjected to colonial interests, while yet others developed independently of colonialism, sometimes in direct competition with the anthropologies of the centers. This kind of difference is an important dimension of comparison. The Japanese case is such an example. Japanese anthropologists followed the colonial expansion of the Japanese state in the early twentieth century by concentrating their research on Eastern Siberia, Southern China, and other regions of imperial interest. After the demise of Japanese imperialism in 1945, Japanese anthropology became more global, sometimes seeing itself as a competitor to Western anthropologies. With Cameroon, the situation is very different in almost every respect. Cameroonian anthropologists depend on external funding for their research, lack a firm institutional and publishing base at home, publish in the colonial languages, and rarely do fieldwork abroad. The contrast reminds us that there is no such thing as "peripheral anthropology," but many, arising from highly distinct historical circumstances, and functioning under extremely different institutional, financial, and intellectual conditions.

LANGUAGE ISSUES

Issues of language enter into the discussion in a variety of ways. Does it make an anthropological tradition peripheral if its main body of published work is in a non-metropolitan language? If this is the case, then Russian, Japanese, Portuguese, and Spanish must be considered peripheral languages. Arguably, Anglophone anthropologists are more parochial than their Brazilian counterparts. Brazilians read English language works, either in the original or in translation; the opposite takes place much more rarely.

In Cameroon and Kenya, anthropological works are published almost exclusively in the colonial languages—English and French. The Dutch, Turkish, Serbian, Slovenian, and Norwegian anthropologies tend to be bilingual, while Russian, Japanese, Brazilian, and Argentinian anthropology is chiefly published in a non-English language. Who is peripheral, he who emulates the language of the hegemon or he who opts for his own? There is obviously no answer to this question, and it hardly makes sense to raise it. When Eriksen began to write up his Mauritian fieldwork in the late 1980s, it was easy for him to decide to publish in English rather than Norwegian. Otherwise, it would have been impossible for him to take part in any well-informed professional dialogue about Mauritian culture and society. The point here is about scale, not about language as such, but it is worth noting that important anthropologies remain unknown to Western Europeans because of a lack of translations.

As a rule, anthropology is translated *into* these languages, mostly from English and French, and rarely *out of them*. Worldwide, the number of translations into English is much lower than the number of translations out of English. In fact, according to UNESCO statistics,[8] more books are translated in Finland (with five million inhabitants) than in the USA (with 300 million). Thus, it is not just in anthropology that the English-speaking world tends to isolate itself.

Naturally, the paucity of translations into English indicates the symbolic power and discursive hegemony of the Anglophone world. The majority rarely needs to learn the language of the minority. However, it could be the case that the majority sometimes has important lessons to learn from the minority!

As a result of globalization, there is currently a great pressure to publish in English among academics in a very many countries. In small country newspeak, the term "international publication" means "any grotty little piece that has been accepted by an English-language journal or edited volume." In this book, Japan appears to be the only country where it gives a scholar higher prestige to publish in the national language than in English.

Using the vernacular has its costs, but also its benefits, as it enables the writer to engage with the public sphere in his or her country. As Eriksen argues, the widespread use of the Norwegian language among the anthropologists of the country has given them considerable influence in the public sphere. The situation is somewhat similar in Brazil. When Tandogan describes anthropology in Turkey as "a silent discipline" in the greater public sphere, one cannot but ask if this has anything to do with the eagerness on the part of Turkish anthropologists to write in English. Bilingual publishing is probably the best solution, intellectually speaking, at least in smallish countries with a limited domestic public sphere. Significantly, there appears to be no anthropological publishing activity to speak of in African languages.

CONSTRAINTS

One of us remembers a job interview some years back, where the interviewee was a West African scholar who had applied for a research position in Western Europe. When asked why he wanted to move to the cold north, he simply answered that it was necessary for his academic work. At home, he had access to few journals, a slow and dated computer with an erratic Internet connection, a salary which made it impossible to support oneself, let alone a family, and no money to go to conferences.

The contrast between a West African country and a West European one is perhaps extreme, but anthropologists in many countries face serious constraints of an institutional, infrastructural or simply financial nature. In the UK, funding for anthropology was extremely limited in the 1980s, but the discipline survived due to its strong institutions and solid professional infrastructure. In less fortunate countries, sudden financial cuts may lead to the departure of the brightest stars and the end of anthropology at home. Both Elchinova and Bošković make this point in their essays. In Central and Eastern Europe after the transition, anthropologists have increasingly come to depend on international foundations since state funding has become less reliable. In general, anthropology is often precarious at the institutional level, with few tenured posts and small departments. Some eke out a marginal existence and have to supplement their income outside the academy. In the context of Kenyan anthropology, Ntarangwi talks about "the anthropology of short-time consultancies," where intellectual energy is deflected from research to better paid work. This is also rapidly becoming a major issue in South Africa, which has a much broader and larger anthropological tradition than Kenya.

In the Netherlands and Norway, where public funding for research is still available, the situation is fiercely competitive, but at the same time there are many potential sources of funding. Both national research councils and ethnographic museums may fund research, along with university departments in social and cultural anthropology, non-western sociology, and development studies. As a result, a large number of research projects are funded every year. This is also the case in Russia, Japan, and Brazil. Others depend on international foundations.

Varying degrees of academic freedom also create distinct opportunity spaces. In the so-called post-Communist world, academic agendas had for decades been shaped by ideological concerns and relatively fixed theoretical blueprints. Soviet ethnology was grafted onto universalist Marxist theory after the Revolution, but this was a controversial move among ethnologists and anthropologists who rejected unilinear evolutionism. According to Kuznetsov, ethnology, which was very nearly abolished in the 1920s because of its inherent un-Marxist tendencies, was rescued by the adoption, among Soviet ethnologists, of the principles of "stadialism." Since the early 1990s, Russian anthropology has partly been concerned with "catching up" and partly concerned with asserting its own identity.

The Turkish case is also a reminder of the ideological and political constraints on research. It was the formation of a state committed to modernization that led to the establishment of anthropology in the first place; later, the military coups of 1971 and 1980 led to a temporary curtailing of all social science research, including anthropology. Faced with such oppression, one may be forgiven for thinking that Thatcherism was a trifling annoyance.

Anthropology often struggles for its legitimacy, but it may also suddenly become fashionable. In Kenya, where social anthropology had been associated with a romantic view of the "tribals"—a difficult role to undertake in a country where modernization was the main political goal—Ntarangwi tells of a sudden change in the early 1980s. This was when the Moi regime decided that traditional cultural forms "ought to be preserved and documented." All of a sudden, anthropology became perfectly legitimate.

The role of individuals is always emphasized in standard histories of anthropology. Quite clearly, in countries with a fledgling academic structure, unpredictable funding for anthropological research, and uneven access to metropolitan publications, outstanding individuals may play an enormously important part. In remote Norway, Fredrik Barth was extremely important in establishing social anthropology as a high prestige academic discipline. But often, the heroes and heroines are less well known. In Argentina, Esther Hermitte, who studied in the 1950s at a Chicago department still heavily influenced by Radcliffe-Brown's research ideals, was decisive in shaping the subject at home. Guber also mentions eclectics like Eduardo Menéndez, whose politically engaged and anti-colonial views would shape students' perspectives through textbooks and lecturing. In fact, as mentioned above, Elchinova partly explains the poverty of anthropology in Bulgaria by mentioning the lack of one or two outstanding local scholars.

In the larger countries, individuals have played a less pronounced role as the subject slowly grew and became more solidly institutionalized. It may also have become more streamlined and standardized. Perhaps, by this token, it is from the anthropologies which can still properly be described as peripheral that real originality may be expected in the future.

That said, it may be a sign of true peripherality that one oscillates between trying to emulate the metropoles and to assert one's independence. In a critical characterization of Japanese anthropology, Sugishita speaks about a Japanese "we/here" that continues to reproduce similar us/them distinctions as those produced by Western anthropologists. In her view, Japanese anthropology "is inseparable from Japan's desire to join the West as the dominant socio-cultural entity" in the world. Lacking reflexivity, she adds, a major epistemological shortcoming of Japanese anthropology consists in its lack of reflection "on the complicated relationship between Japan, the West and the rest of the world." If truly original anthropologies are to emerge from one or several of the sprawling non-metropolitan traditions, she seems to imply, a mental decolonization must first take place. Perhaps the answer to Sugishita's concern can be found in one of the rich anthropological traditions concentrating on the study of cultural variation within the borders of one country, namely one's own.

ANTHROPOLOGY AT HOME

A tension running through anthropology in many parts of the world, but perhaps more strongly in Central and Eastern Europe than elsewhere, is that obtaining between ethnology (the study of local customs, often favoring material over ephemeral culture) and the study of faraway places. In Germany and many other countries, this is the contrast between *Volkskunde* (the study of one, usually one's own, people) and *Völkerkunde* (the study of peoples). Although the distinction was clear enough a few generations ago, it is more difficult to draw the boundary today. For example, Swedish ethnology has, under the leadership of scholars like Orvar Löfgren and Jonas Frykman, been transformed into a cultural anthropology of Swedish society. Moreover, social and cultural anthropologists increasingly write about their own society even if they have the means to pursue overseas fieldwork. Turkish anthropologists seem to have evaded the confrontation with nation-building ethnology by turning towards rural sociology.

Yet, there is something important in this distinction. Elchinova notes that young Bulgarian anthropologists strongly recognize the significance of their break with the earlier folklore and ethnological research, which was among other things encouraged by the Communists. In Serbia, as well as in several other countries, a similar tension exists, there is little contact between folklore/ethnology and anthropology; different sets of questions are being asked and different underlying political and intellectual agendas inform the research.

Nevertheless, anthropologists in most of the countries we consider here do the bulk of their research "at home," meaning in the country where they have academic jobs. Even in Norway, the Netherlands, and Japan, many anthropologists now write about their own majority society.

The question is when one does fieldwork "at home," and to what extent does this compromise one's ambition to contribute to a discipline with a global outlook rather than a nation-building ambition. There can be no simple answer to this huge question, but some of our cases shed light on it. In other cases, like the one discussed by Narayan (1993), the very positioning of the "native" scholar in her own cultural context becomes a very important issue.

The Latin American cases seriously question the notions of "remote areas" and "otherness," and the way they tend to be conceptualized in metropolitan anthropology. Guber and Peirano emphasize that their anthropologies have grown out of questions that arise from specific local circumstances and issues, and that their view is not as much from afar as from within. As an anthropologist working in one's own country, one is never insulated from domestic issues and can often be forced to take political positions. The intellectual detachment often praised, but just as often lamented, by commentators on anthropology does thus not present itself to anthropologists working "at home" like it does to those who choose to do fieldwork far away.

Yet there are varying degrees of being at home. The partly discredited Afrikaner *Volkekunde* tradition, which in its day was a main source of inspiration for *apartheid,* might credibly claim that its detailed, but often completely a-theoretical treatises about the customs of local African groups amounted to studying at home. However, it would not be fair to compare Brazilian anthropologists writing about Amerindians to Afrikaner intellectuals writing about Zulus. The ethical codes guiding anthropological research in Brazil are quite different from those that were informing *volkenkundige* ethnologists (for more details, see Bošković and Van Wyk 2005), and Brazil is an open society where people are made accountable in ways unthinkable under apartheid.

However, it is quite clear that there are centers and peripheries, not just globally, and not just between the metropolitan and the "peripheral" anthropologies, but also in a general way within each country. The anthropologists at the University of Brasília in Brazil are part of a center; the Xingu are part of a periphery. Who studies the elites or even urban middle classes? Few anthropologists in any country do, it must be granted.

Studying "the other at home" can be a virtue in itself, not just because it leads to valuable knowledge, but also because of its ideological implications. In many countries of the South, the modernization policies of the latter half of the twentieth century implied that cultural variation was undesirable, and especially that traditional cultures were inferior. Modernization was generally equated with "Westernization," and this view was naturally at odds with the aim of anthropology to value and appreciate non-western, non-industrial cultures. So anthropologists had an important ethical, and by implication political, role to play here. As a logical extension, anthropologists could—and do—propose models of modernity which are based on local customs. This can probably only be done efficiently and credibly by local anthropologists.

A peculiar form of domestic anthropology which has popped up in several countries is the ironic, but often quite illuminating anthropology of "one's own tribe," which implicitly and sometimes explicitly makes it clear that the "normal" way of life is to be found in the Trobriands or some such place. In Norway, there has been a great demand for this kind of self-satirizing anthropology in recent years. It can only be undertaken with credibility by local anthropologists, or by foreigners such as the late Eduardo Archetti, who had lived for many years in the country (see Eriksen 2005 for more details).

In a strong statement about the difference between the conceptualizations of "otherness" in metropolitan countries (where anthropologists go overseas for fieldwork) and countries where the bulk of research is carried out at home, Peirano states:

> [I]n Brazil, (i) otherness has been predominantly found within the limits of the country; (ii) research by a group of ethnographers has been quite common, especially in the case of Indian populations; (iii) salvage anthropology was never an issue—rather the study of "contact" between Indian and local populations as considered more relevant than preserving intact cultures; (iv) funds for research have come mainly from state agencies for advanced research.

The logical conclusion of Peirano's challenging analysis is, in fact, that the "metropoles" are being othered. *They* are the provincials.[9]

CONCLUSION: CRISIS, WHAT CRISIS?

The past changes really quickly. Article titles in Gerholm and Hannerz' 1982 collection read, for example, "Polish ethnography after World War II" (it would have been integrated into a radically different narrative now), "The state of anthropology in the Sudan" (with no mention of ethnicity or religion), "After the quiet revolution" (about Quebec; today, few speak about the quiet revolution—it happened such a long time ago), and "Through Althusserian spectacles: Recent social anthropology in Brazil." Peirano, unsurprisingly, does not mention Althusser in her review of Brazilian anthropology.

Claude Lévi-Strauss, writing almost five decades ago, specifically mentioned the "three sources of the ethnological reflexion," as the "discovery" of the Americas, the French revolution, and the beginnings of evolutionism in mid-nineteenth century France and the UK. These are all very political and deeply influential historical events. In recent years, his idea of anthropology (*ethnologie*) as a humanistic discipline has become increasingly influential even outside the French-speaking circles, as the boundaries (as well as genres) between social sciences, humanities, and "cultural studies" increasingly become blurred. The intersections of anthropology, politics, and history also become very apparent when one looks at the development of the discipline in the "peripheral" traditions. They were of course very much present in the "central" disciplines as well (Detienne 2002; a good example also being AAA's censure of Franz Boas in 1919, because he objected to American anthropologists serving as spies), but outside the centers, the very fact of conducting anthropological research could be seen as potentially subversive (as in Argentina), or part of the global nation-building endeavour (like in India or Brazil). Historical knowledge, experiences, and their interpretations traditionally formed important parts of considerations of different scholars (Archetti 2003, Augé 1989), but one should also note the dissatisfaction of some leading anthropologists from the "non-central" traditions for what they perceive to be lack of understanding of their culture on the part of more "central" scholars (for China, see Mingming 2002).

This lack of understanding can be easily remedied through increased and improved communication, which so far has mostly been surprisingly one-sided. "Third world" scholars are supposed to know everything that is going on in the "main" traditions, but their own work (regardless of its actual quality), even when it is published in English or French, mostly goes unnoticed. As noted above, there is a growing need for this type of communication to be increased and become less one-sided. Together with the authors around the "Other Anthropologies" project, we would like to argue for a pluralistic, multicentered discipline of a type suggested by Latour (2004).

It is striking to see the excitement of many "Third World" scholars at the international meetings, as well as the fervor with which they present their research results. This is very different from the frequent disillusionment and scepticism expressed by colleagues from "great" traditions, perhaps burdened with the idea of a discipline in crisis.

But how does one justify the general "crisis talk" when anthropology seems to be thriving in distant and extremely diverse traditions, such as Brazil, Norway, Japan, Kenya, or India. Russia is perhaps a slightly more complicated case, as already noted by Tishkov (1992). Even much smaller nations and newcomers to the global scene, such as Slovenia, invest in research and produce some very good and original work (for example, Brumen 2000). Even in countries without institutional backing, like Croatia or Serbia, the interest for studying other peoples and cultures is continuously growing. The generations of younger scholars throughout the world are coming out of the academic programs also armed with healthy doses of scepticism, but with the addition of important lessons learned from their predecessors and put in a very global contemporary context. The amount of research coming out in various forms is truly fascinating, so it is easy to agree with Peirano that there is no global crisis of anthropology.

Or, to put it differently, perhaps an old scholarly discipline that refused to change with the times is in crisis—as summed up wryly several decades ago by Diamond: "a study of men in crisis by men in crisis" (2004: 11). But anthropology as we know and practice it, along with many of our colleagues in the "developing countries," certainly is not!

NOTES

1. José de Acosta (1539–1600), Spanish Jesuit and at the time of his death, Rector of the University of Salamanca. He spent several years (1571–1576) in South America, then two years in Mexico. As a result, he published *De natura Novi Orbis et de promulgatione evangelii apud Barbaros* (Salamanca, 1588–1589), which was subsequently translated into Spanish. His book became an instant best-seller, and it is interesting to note that he assumed that the American Indians came from Asia (Mongolia) via land—and this was more than a century before Beringhia was "discovered" by the West Europeans.

2. Of course, it could be argued that the interest in explaining "the Other" pre-dates this—going as far back as the Herodotus' *Histories* in the fifth century BCE, or Diodorus and Pausanias also in the ancient Greece (Lévi-Strauss 1987: 37), or Ibn Khaldun's travel accounts in the twelfth century CE. Lévi-Strauss claimed these accounts were not really "anthropological" (or "ethnological") because they did not use critical methodology and comparisons between cultures—preferring mostly to describe them.

3. W.H.R. Rivers in his opening address claimed that changes in human societies were a direct consequence of the mixture of peoples and cultures. Here Rivers referred to the works of German ethnologists (Fritz Gräbner and Bernard Ankermann, both of whom presented their groundbreaking papers in Berlin in 1905, in support of the Leo Frobenius' theory of "cultural circles"), who were establishing a diffusionist model for the development of cultures. This model would provide a crucial tool for Rivers' monumental *History of Melanesian Society,* because as Melanesian cultures were "complex" (as they included a mixture of elements from a variety of different cultures), their histories could not be studied using evolutionary theories.

   Rivers also had a frequently overlooked influence on functionalism, as his first student in Cambridge was Radcliffe-Brown, while Malinowski took to the field the edition of *Notes and Queries* prepared by him.

4. Non-members of the American Anthropological Association are required to pay the "processing fee" if they want to submit to the journals like *American Anthropologist, American Ethnologist,* or *Cultural Anthropology,* for example. This fee of around 30 USD can be quite steep for someone living in a developing country, where it can form a substantial part of one's monthly salary.

5. This seems to be so different from the situation in the late nineteenth century—for example, Tylor's *magnum opus, Primitive Culture,* was soon after its original publication in 1871 translated into Russian and German, and the editions in French and Polish soon followed.

6. Several papers were presented at the September 2004 meeting of the EASA in Vienna, at the workshop "Other Anthropologies," convened by Bošković and Eriksen.

7. The idea of anthropology as a "handmaiden of colonialism" is a greatly exaggerated and essentialized image of only *a number* of traditions and *some* anthropologists—it can easily be contrasted with early anthropologists like Rivers or Haddon (who were socialists and who despised colonialism), for example, as well as some of the key liberation figures of African postcolonial resistance, like Z.K. Matthews in South Africa, or Jomo Kenyatta in Kenya (see Ntarangwi in this volume).

8. The source is the "Index Translationum," see <http://databases.unesco.org/xtrans/stat/xTransStat.a?VL1=C&top=50&lg=0>.

9. As such, it provides an interesting response to a question raised by Peter Pels, "what does a Parisian anthropology look like from Brazil?" (2003: 144, 148).

REFERENCES

Archetti, Eduardo P. 2003. "O 'gaucho,' o tango, primitivismo e poder na formação da identidade nacional Argentina." *Mana* 9, 1: 9–29.

Asad, Talal. 1982. "A Comment on the Idea of Non-Western Anthropology." In Fahim 1982: 284–7.

Augé, Marc. 1989. "Les lieux de mémoire du point de vue de l'"ethnologue." *Gradhiva* 6: 3–12.

Bošković, Aleksandar, and Ilana van Wyk. 2005. "Troubles with Identity: South African Anthropology, 1921–2004." *Etnografičeskoe obozrenie* 2/2005: 96–101.

Brumana, Fernando Giobellina. 2002. "Entre Tintín y Tartarín: la mission Dacar-Yibuti En el origen de la etnografia francesa." *Revista de Antropologia* 45, 2: 311–59.

Brumen, Borut. 2000. *Sv. Peter in njegovi časi.* [St. Peter and its Time.] Ljubljana: c/f.

Cardoso de Oliveira, Roberto. 2000. "Peripheral Anthropologies 'versus' Central Anthropologies." *Journal of Latin American Anthropology* 4, 2/5, 1: 10–30.

Detienne, Marcel. 2002. "Murderous Identity: Anthropology, History, and the Art of Constructing Comparables." *Common Knowledge* 8, 1: 178–87.

Diamond, Stanley. 2004. "Anthropology in Question." *Dialectical Anthropology* 28: 11–32.

Eriksen, Thomas Hylland. 2005. *Engaging Anthropology.* Oxford: Berg.

Fahim, Hussein, Katherine Helmer, et. al. 1980. "Indigenous Anthropology in Non-Western Countries: A Further Elaboration." *Current Anthropology* 21, 5: 644–63.

Fahim, Hussein, ed. 1982. *Indigenous Anthropology in Non-Western Countries.* Durham: Carolina Academic Press.

Gellner, Ernest, ed. 1980. *Soviet and Western Anthropology.* London: Routledge.

Hannerz, Ulf, and Tomas Gerholm, eds. 1982. *The Shaping of National Anthropologies.* Special issue of *Ethnos* (Stockholm) 47, 1–2.

Krotz, Esteban. 1997. "Anthropologies of the South: Their Rise, their Silencing and their Characteristics." *Critique of Anthropology* 17, 3: 237–51.

Latour, Bruno. 2004. "Whose Cosmos, which Cosmopolitics? Comments on the Peace Terms of Ulrich Beck." *Common Knowledge* 10, 3: 450–62.

Lévi-Strauss, Claude. 1987. [1960.] "Les trois sources de la réflexion ethnologique." *Gradhiva* 2: 37–41.

Madan, T.N. 1982. "Anthropology as the Mutual Interpretation of Cultures: Indian Perspectives." In Fahim 1982: 4–18.

Mingming, Wang. 2002. "The Third Eye: Towards a Critique of the 'Nativist Anthropology.'" *Critique of Anthropology* 22, 2: 149–74.

Narayan, Kirin. 1993. "How Native is a 'Native' Anthropologist?" *American Anthropologist* 95, 3: 671–86.

Pels, Peter. 2003. "Editorial/Éditorial." *Social Anthropology* 11, 2: 143–51.

Quinlan, Tim. 2000. "Anthropologies of the South: The Practice of Anthropology." *Critique of Anthropology* 20, 2: 125–36.

Restrepo, Eduardo, and Arturo Escobar. 2005. "Other Anthropologies and Anthropology Otherwise." *Critique of Anthropology* 25, 2: 99–129.

Ribeiro, Gustavo Lins, and Arturo Escobar, eds. 2006. *World Anthropologies: Disciplinary Transformations in Systems of Power.* Oxford: Berg.

Tishkov, Valery. 1992. "The Crisis in Soviet Ethnography." *Current Anthropology* 33, 4: 371–94.

Vermeulen, Han F., and Arturo Alvarez Roldán, eds. 1995. *Fieldwork and Footnotes: Studies in the History of European Anthropology.* London: Routledge.

Chapter 1

Russian Anthropology: Old Traditions and New Tendencies

Anatoly M. Kuznetsov

INTRODUCTION

The interest in Russian (Soviet) ethnography and its affiliated disciplines was present in the West for a number of decades. There were publications in the US, the UK, and other countries (Gellner 1980; Clay 1995; Eidlitz 1985; Rethmann 1999; Skalník 1988). The articles by Russian authors in English began to appear more frequently. All of this gives one a possibility of understanding current conditions of ethnology and anthropology in Russia (Elfimov 1997; Slezkine 1991, 1996; Tishkov 1992). However, due to its lengthy development, the territorial extent, and the sheer quantity of scholars involved, Russian ethnology (or Soviet ethnography) is still an enormous topic to be covered by a single author. The situation was additionally complicated and the understanding impeded by the language barrier on both sides. In this essay, I address the questions not substantially covered by my predecessors.

One of the peculiarities of social anthropology in Russia is that it was publicly acknowledged quite late, despite the long history of its development. Nowadays, when Russian specialists are free to take part in international conferences and discuss anthropological issues with their foreign colleagues, we can see the different approaches in examining these issues. On the one hand, a particular position of Russian (Soviet) ethnologists (or ethnographers) could be simply traced to the dictate of the communist ideology twenty years ago. After the period of "Khruschev's thaw" in 1956, Soviet scientists had the opportunity to access foreign literature. Visits of foreign colleagues to the USSR also became a practice. However, the acquaintance with the conditions and the problems of the West—European and American socio-cultural anthropology—was only possible in the USSR through criticism from Marxist positions (Averkieva 1979; Bromley 1979; Grigulevich 1976; *Puti Razvitiya Zarubezhnoj Ethnologii* 1983). Such a simplified explanation is no longer effective. Many Russian scientists continued to keep the ideas of Soviet ethnography and ethnos conception even after *perestroika,* the period when ethnography relieved of its ideological dictate (Akademik U.V. Bromlej i Otechestvennaya Etnographiya 1960–1990s, 2003). In this case, we should look at other reasons that contribute to the tendency of the great majority of Russian specialists of accepting certain ideas, while refuting others. The first step in explaining this is understanding it—meaning both the knowledge of modern conditions and the history of the discipline.

FORMATION AND INSTITUTIONALIZATION OF RUSSIAN ANTHROPOLOGY

The start of materials collection in Russia dates back to the period of Peter the Great's reorganization in the eighteenth century. In 1714, the first museum, Kunstkamera, was established in St. Petersburg. The different collections, including the ethnographic ones, were concentrated there. The decisive event was the establishment of the Academy of Sciences in 1725. This event initiated complex studies of Povolzhe, Siberia, the North of the Far East of Russia, and then of Middle Asia within the bounds of geographic (Oriental) expeditions. During these expeditions, different ethnographic materials were collected and described by V.N. Tatischev (1744), S.P. Krasheninnikov (1756), G. Georgy (1776–1780), and others. Extensive ethnographic collections were presented by the participants of the great Far Eastern expeditions and around the world seaside expeditions, undertaken between 1725 and 1849 (V. Bering, U.V. Lisianski, I.F. Krusenshtern, V.M. Golovin, and others).

The Oriental scholarly tradition was established on the basis of the research in early nineteenth century Russia. In accordance with this tradition, the primary task of the Oriental studies was "to study the culture in the broadest sense of the word." These studies resulted in the opening of a special Asian Museum in St. Petersburg. Also, as the new data was collected, the conditions were ripe for the emergence of anthropology.

The Ethnographic Museum separated from the Kunstkamera in 1836 and became one of the first ethnographic institutions in Russia. The next stage of the development of Russian ethnography was the establishment of the Russian Geographic Society in 1845. The Ethnographic Bureau of this Society implemented its research programs and published the Ethnographic collections of articles (1853–1864). With the ongoing investigations of Central and Eastern Asia, the famous expedition of Nikolai Mikluho-Maklai to New Guinea was organized by the Geographic Society during the 1870s. The Geographic Society departments in different parts of the country, including Siberia (East Siberian in Irkutsk and Troitsko-Savskoe in Kiyahta), and the Far East (CisAmurian in Khabarovsk, South Ussurian in Nikolsk-Ussuriiski) thus made many contributions to the development of ethnography, archeology and physical anthropology. It was not accidental that future Russian ethnology (anthropology) studies proved to be influenced by geography and Oriental studies.

The appearance of the separate subdisciplines traditionally included in anthropology was not simultaneous. At first in the 1840s, physical anthropology as a separate discipline emerged at the Russian Academy of Science. The biologist Karl Ber, who came to Russia from Königsberg (Prussia) in 1834, played an important role in its formation. He was also instrumental in the formation of the anthropological cabinet in 1842 in St. Petersburg.

Archeology was established in the 1840s. Its beginning was based on the amateur digs of classical ancient relics in the South of the country (the end of the eighteenth and beginning of the nineteenth century). The Society for History and Archeology was founded in Odessa in 1839. One of the first centers for systematic research was the Archeological Numismatic Society, based in 1846 in St. Petersburg. A young aristocrat, Count Alexi Uvarov, became the Head of this Society. He played a great but contradictory role in the history of Russian archeology. The Imperial Archeological Commission, established in 1859, was another institution devoted to archeological research. In 1864, the Moscow Archeological Society emerged through Uvarov's initiative. In 1866, the Archeological Numismatic Society was reorganized and became the Russian Archeological Society. Count Uvarov was also the initiator of the establishment of the Moscow Museum of History in 1883.

Ethnographic societies established in the 1840s also influenced Russian science. In 1864, the Moscow Society of Amateurs of Natural Science, Anthropology and Ethnography was established by Moscow University. They began to publish the Society's News and then the Works of this department. The All Russia Ethnographic Exhibition in 1867 was the one of the first prominent activities of the Society. After this exhibition, its collections were moved to the Moscow Public Museum and set the basis for the Dashkovski Museum. In 1879, this Society organized an Anthropological exhibition with ethnographic and archeological displays. The Society of Archeology, History and Ethnography was established at the Kasanski University in 1878. In the spirit of that period, the Ethnographic Museum in Petersburg was reorganized in 1879 into the Museum of Anthropology and Ethnography. The Russian Museum that included the Department of Ethnography was established in 1897 in Petersburg. Its task was to study the ethnography of the Russian population.

As the new science of ethnography was being formalized, the question of specialized ethnographic training arose. Vsevolod Miller, Nicolai and Vera Harusina in 1885 received the permission of the Ministry of National Education to give lectures on ethnography in Russian Universities. This discipline was also included in the program of anthropology, initated by Dmitri Anuchin at the Faculty of Geography of Moscow University in 1884. Edward Petry did the same at Petersburg University. The problem of the lack of textbooks was taken up by N.N. Haruzin, who prepared the first publications of them early in the twentieth century. A review of the foreign and Russian ethnography position of this period was written, and the problems of ethnography were examined, in this textbook. N.N. Kharuzin directed his attention to the evolutionary theory of Tylor and considered discovering the law of human development to be the main task of ethnography. The first part of this textbook dealt with problems of general and material culture, the second with family and marriage, the third with property and primitive society, and the fourth with old beliefs. The next important event was the foundation of the first specialized journal, *Etnografičeskoe obozrenie, The Ethnographic Review,* in 1889 (Kerimova 2003).

There was no state support for ethnographic research at this stage, and so it also developed through private initiative. An example of this is the work of the Ethnographic Bureau in Petersburg, established by the Prince V. N. Tenishev in 1897. This great landowner and businessman wanted to write a major work about Russian social life, because of the broad revolutionary movement that had developed throughout the country. For this purpose, he organized intensive research of Russian peasants. At first, he wanted to act via the Society of Amateurs of the Moscow University, but then he decided to work for himself. The results of the research about peasants living in the central part of Russia (published in Smolensk in 1897) contained the following sections: physical and natural features of the peasants, local conditions of peasants' living, holidays, community ownership, and specific features of the peasants from different regions—the principles of functionalism (Nachinin 1955).

The political exiles of the nineteenth century also played a great role in the formation of Russian ethnography, as well as in archeology. They collected complete and sometimes unique information about the aboriginal populations of Siberia and the Far East. Some of the former exiles—including Vladimir Bogoraz, Vladimir Iohilson, Bronislav Pilsudski, and Lev Shternberg—became famous Russian ethnographers.

Gradually, the practical needs of the state, caused by the multiethnic character of the country, forced the government to extend the quantity of the institutes connected with ethnographic research. In the case of history, archeology, linguistics, and ethnography, the prominent role was played by the Russian Committee for Studying Central and Eastern Asia, established at the Academy of Science in 1903. The Commission for Aboriginal Population Structure of Russia and Neighboring Countries, led by Sergey Oldenburg, the academician and secretary of the Academy of Sciences, was founded only in 1917. In the beginning of the twentieth century, Russian ethnography (as well as physical anthropology and archeology) passed through the formative period and became well institutionalized in the scientific and academic associations. It also acquired a certain influence within society. In 1913, Vladimir Arseniev, the famous writer and researcher of the Far East of Russia, established the Ethnography Amateur Study group in Khabarovsk. Only a year later, based on this study group, the Department of Archeology, History, and Ethnography was formed at the Priamurski Section of the Russian Geographic Society.

The problems of ethnography and related sciences initiated a discussion in 1916. The obvious tendency to join ethnography to other scientific disciplines—like geography, archeology, and physical anthropology—and to form a new and more general discipline, was established during this discussion. The question was raised as to what name this new synthetic discipline should have. Finally, the debate ended with the idea of creating the new complex science, ethnology. Russian ethnology was formed with the input of natural sciences (geography, biology) and was based on the evolutionary theory.

THE OCTOBER REVOLUTION AND THE EMERGENCE
OF SOVIET ETHNOLOGY

By the October Revolution of 1917, ethnology had been developing on the basis of an earlier tradition. A remarkable feature of formerly Russian and Soviet ethnology was the direction of this science toward complex studies of local varieties of cultures. The methods of ethnological research were applied to the past, so paleoethnology also developed. The transformation of science from ethnography to ethnology was strengthened with the reorganization of the existing and newly emerging scientific centers. At the same time, the total reorganization of the Universities and search for the new institutional and substantial (revolutionary) forms of teaching and scientific work led to the instability of many of the chairs, faculties, and institutes which appeared at that time. Another attempt to determine ethnography as a part of anthropology dated from the period of the Civil War. The famous Russian scientist Dmitri Anuchin, who studied at Sorbonne, developed a concept of anthropology as a unity of ethnography, archeology, and physical anthropology. He managed to establish the Chair of Anthropology within the Natural Studies Department of the Moscow State University in 1919. In 1922, this chair was reorganized into the Institute of Anthropology, named in honor of Anuchin after his death in 1923. However, other Russian specialists did not provide support for the idea of general anthropology and took the concept of ethnology as the universal science. It is significant to notice that there were no principal differences of views on origin, objects, and problems of this science between the anthropologists and the ethnologists.

The leading role in the formation and development of ethnology as well as Russian science in general at this stage belonged to specialists in Petersburg (and Leningrad thereafter). The ethnographic department was formed at the newly established Institute of Geography within Petrograd University in 1918. In the mid-1920s, the Institute of Ethnology was established in Leningrad, with Lev Shternberg as the head. In 1928, the Ethnographic Scientific Research Institute was formed on the basis of the Department of Ethnology at the State Leningrad University. As a result of the progressive policy toward the developing of the northern areas of the country during the 1930s, the Institute for Northern People's Studies was also established. In 1924, the Board of Languages and Northern Caucasus Ethnic Cultures Studies was established within the Academy of Sciences, along with the Museum of Anthropology and Ethnography, and the Commission for Indigenous Structure Studies. The journal of the professional association, *Ethnography,* began to be published in 1926 in Leningrad.

Moscow was another important center. A very significant factor for that period was that besides the Anuchin Institute of Anthropology, the Ethno-Linguistic Department at the Faculty of Social Science Studies was established in 1922 on the basis of the former Faculty of History and Philology. The Chair of Ethnology was established at this facility in 1923. Then followed the new reorganization, causing the formation of the Faculty of Ethnology within the Social Sciences Faculty. The departments of history and material culture, ethnography, literature, and fine arts were included.

The dean and the famous ethnologist, P.Ph. Preobrazhenski said, the primary purposes for this faculty were: "to form professional ethnographers and ethnologists, researchers of the USSR people culture; to form scientists-theorists combining particular specialty with broad humanitarian minds; to prepare practical cultural and political instructors for national minorities." The changes applied to the museums as well. In 1923, the Central Museum for People Studies (based on the Rumiyantsev Museum) was established in Moscow. It was one of the most important ethnological institutions (Markov, Pimenov, Solovey 1999; Solovey 2001).

The Civil War led to the opening of new universities in Irkutsk (1918) and in Vladivostok (1920). The main role in organizing these universities belonged to the ethnographers from Petersburg who were in Siberia and the Far East because of the war. Sergey Shirokogoroff, who led the second expedition to Manchuria and the Far East, played an active role in Vladivostok. Alexandr and Ludmila Mervart were also in Vladivostok in 1918. They took an active part in creating the private Faculty of History and Philology in 1918 and opening of the State Far Eastern University. The Chair of Ethnography and Geography of the Far East and the Chair of Peoples' Studies were formed at Vladivostok University.

By the late 1920s, Russian ethnology resembled Western European and American sociocultural anthropology. It was based on the idea of combining ethnography, archeology, and physical anthropology, and these disciplines set the necessary terms for ethnologists to know ethnic languages. The long expeditions were considered to be the main method of collecting the information. However, by the end of 1920s, the situation in the country and the science had changed significantly, interrupting Russian ethnological traditions by force. The Communist Party began to work towards the socialist reconstruction of all areas of the country's life—including science and university education. The struggle to reconstruct ethnology started after discussions of the correlation between Marxism and ethnology (1926–1929). These continued during the All Russian Archeological Ethnographic meetings in the early 1930s. The result was the conclusion that Marxism was incompatible with ethnology. Only ethnography, extracted from the "bourgeois" ethnology for the needs of Marxist science, was useful, but it was supposed to be transformed into the subdiscipline of universal history (Slezkine 1991).

The primary methods of scientific reconstruction were applying Marxist theory instead of the "outdated bourgeois" concepts. On the other hand, university teaching staff and researchers were replaced by specialists who received their education during the Soviet period and had "proper" (mostly working class) social origins. M.N. Pokrovski, the leader of the Soviet historical Marxists of this period, appealed "to take science away from scientists and take it to 400 students of the working faculty who will graduate from university in 1929" (Perchenok 1995). In 1929, many of the historians and other scholars were being arrested, Russian ethnology was being transformed into Soviet ethnography.

The most prominent Marxist theorists represented the *Stadialist School* of Nikolai Marr, Vladimir Aptekar, and Sergei Bikovski, as well as party promoted worker Nikolai Motorin (Slezkine 1996). The historian Motorin, who had been promoted to solve the ethnographical problems, at first led the Museum of Anthropology and Ethnography in 1930. He formulated the object of ethnography from the standpoint of the formation theory, according to which there was only one science—history. The history was conceived in accordance with party leaders and ideologists conceptions as "the most class-aware and political science." The Faculty of Ethnology at Moscow State University was reorganized and closed in 1931. The Faculty of Ethnology at Leningrad State University was closed in 1932. Teaching ethnology and ethnography at the Soviet universities ceased for several years. Ethnography existed only within the system of the Academy of Sciences and Museums. This destruction interrupted the development of the previous scientific traditions, especially the ones developed by scientists who emigrated abroad (Mogiliyanski, Iohilson, Lopatin, Shirokogoroff, and others). But on the whole, Soviet ethnography began to develop on other institutionalized and conceptualized bases.

The activity of academic institutes and universities was put into the spotlight in 1929. The conclusion was that the work of the Museum of Anthropology and the Commission for Indigenous Population of Russia and Neighboring Countries' Studies was considered to be identical. In order to improve the situation, the decision was reached to establish the Central Institute for the World Peoples Studies at the Academy of Science of the USSR. But political events changed the original plan; on 1 February 1930, they opened the Institute for USSR Peoples Studies instead of the Commission. Marr was the head of this institute and Motorin was his deputy. In accordance with the basic organizing principle of the Soviet State, i.e., only one coordinating center in the head of each sphere of industry and culture, the ethnological offices were reorganized again. At the public meeting at Academy of Science of the USSR (2 February 1932), it was decided to consolidate the Museum of Anthropology and Ethnography and the Institute for USSR Peoples Studies into the Institute of Anthropology and Ethnography. Motorin was also head of this new Institute.

Being the leading ethnological center in the USSR, the Institute resumed the publication of the works of the Institute of Anthropology and Ethnography at Academy of Science of the USSR, as well as the journal

Soviet Ethnography (since 1931). The new institute also emphasized the development of archeology, and in April 1935, the institute was renamed the Institute of Anthropology, Ethnography, and Archeology. From then on, the Institute published a special collection of articles on Soviet archeology. In accordance with the new ideology, the following scientific research groups were approved in the institute: primitive communism (led by Matorin), clan order decay and class formation origin (led by Bikovski), race theory and criticism (Bikovski), primitive household and technique history (Ravdonikas), and primitive social structure history (Koshkin). However, the head Leningrad theorists and ethnography leaders (V.B. Aptekar, S.N. Bikovski, Matorin, Y.P. Koshkin, and others) were accused of anti-Soviet activity, and were arrested and executed after 1935. Afterwards, the Institute was headed by Meshaninov, Marr's closest associate. This academic institute was soon exposed to new reorganizations. At first, the reason was Bogoraz's death in 1937. Then, the Presidium of the Academy of Science of the USSR decided to reorganize this institute in June. It was joined with the Peter the Great Museum of Anthropology and Ethnography and named the Institute of Ethnography of the Academy of Science of the USSR. V.V. Struve, historian and Orientalist, was appointed director of the new institute. Because of his views, physical anthropology and archeology were removed from the institute for a short period of time, as well as some of the divisions that had existed at the Museum of Anthropology and Ethnography. These events marked the end of this discipline's developing process. The final transformation of Russian ethnology into Soviet ethnography led to the renewal of the Department of Ethnography at the Leningrad State University in 1938, but at the faculty of philology. After new reforms in 1944, the Department of Ethnography at Leningrad University was transferred to the Faculty of Oriental Studies. The Department of Ethnography and Physical Anthropology was established within the Faculty of History in 1968 (Its 1974; Reshetov 2003).

The most difficult situation with the abolishment of ethnology was at the Moscow University. At first, the Faculty of Ethnology was divided into the Faculty of History and Ethnology, and the Faculty of Material Culture in 1929/1930. Later, these faculties were consolidated again within the Institute of Social Studies, where there was no place for ethnography. The arrests of Preobrazhenski, former Dean of the Faculty of Ethnology, and some other ethnologists in 1930s had destructive consequences. It caused, as Zolotarev noticed, "the stuff being dispersed and fatal 'extinction' of ethnography in Moscow" (1934). Gradual reconstruction of ethnography at the Moscow University started in 1934. Ethnography and archeology were organized at the Institute of Anthropology (physical). In 1939, following the initiative of Sergey Tolstov, the Department of Ethnography was reestablished

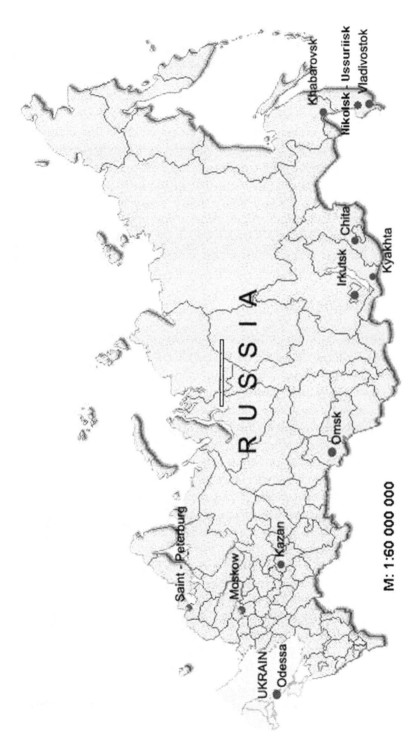

Map 1: Map of Russia, with places mentioned in this chapter. Image by author.

at the Faculty of History. The result of these transformations was the separation between ethnography on the one hand, and physical anthropology and
archeology on the other. Ethnography was placed within the exaggerated
historical science.

The new developing period of ethnography in the USSR was connected
with the period of the Great Patriotic War (1941–1945). Moscow was transformed into the united center of ethnographic science. The Presidium of the
Academy of Science of the USSR was transferred from Leningrad to Moscow
in 1934. The Institute of Ethnography was the next to transfer to Moscow.
Most of the research officers were evacuated from Leningrad in 1942. Tolstov became the head and was given the right to organize the Moscow group
of the Institute of Ethnography. This division was organized in 1943. After
the end of the Great Patriotic War, the Moscow division became the leading
Institute of Ethnography at the Academy of Science.

POSTWAR TENDENCIES

The institutional forming of the Soviet ethnography had come to the end.
Under the conditions of partial and sometimes full isolation from international scientists, the opposition of two different social and political systems,
and then the Cold War, the basic aims and positions of this science changed.
Soviet ethnography was not conceived as the synthetic discipline with its
own theory. Its status was the subsidiary to history that was based on Marx
and Lenin's philosophy of historical materialism. That is why historicism
(the tendency to consider analyzing events in its developing) and methodology and macro-level problems orientation (nation, social, and economic
formation, etc.) are nonetheless among the most prominent features of Soviet ethnography. Another feature of this discipline was the critical attitude
to everything that "bourgeois" science provided, coupled with the rejection
of the concept of social and cultural anthropology. In contrast to foreign
anthropologists' works, Russian ethnographers began to realize their own
"global" projects—like the series on "Peoples of the world" published during
the 1950s.

Between the 1940s and the 1960s, there was a period of further realiza-
tions and growth of the new direction of scientific development. Departments and sub-faculties of ethnography were established within universities
and research centers of the republics of the USSR, complex institutes for
language, literature, and historical studies (that included ethnographic sections) were established in the capitals of autonomous republics, and new science centers, including ethnography departments at the institutes of history,

were founded first in Novosibirsk, and later in Vladivostok and Sverdlovsk (Ekaterinbourg). The numerical growth of ethnographic departments and the growth of the number of ethnographers throughout the country was impressive. But post-graduate studies were possible only in the leading capital centers of the USSR. The Specialized Councils, which provided opportunities for doctoral degrees, were also inaugurated there. These organizations, as well as the only conceptual (Marxist) foundation, provided and kept the highest level of homogeneity in Soviet ethnography. The dominated status of the USSR in the social sphere and its attempt to intensify its position among the Third World countries was realized in the practice of the education policy. The students from Third World countries were actively interested in education based on privilege. Foreign and Soviet students were released from paying a fee and received state scholarships. These programs included ethnographic specialties at the leading universities of the country. Students from Albania, East Germany, Vietnam, Spain, China, Mongolia, Peru, Romania, Czechoslovakia, Ecuador, Yugoslavia, and many other countries studied at the Department of Ethnography of the Moscow State University. This list could be more impressive if the data were available from Leningrad. For example, the well-known anthropologist Peter Skalník graduated from Leningrad University.

Between the 1960s to the 1980s, Soviet ethnography surpassed the political limits of the USSR and transformed into a global phenomenon which had influence on ethnography of at least some East European countries and some so-called Third World countries. However, it also had to pay for this numerical growth. At first, it was the loss of the previous connection with physical anthropology and archeology. Then the gap between the university departments of ethnography and ethnographic divisions at the Academy of Science and their activities, became more prevalent. New tendencies in the development of this discipline had not played a significant role. However, at the beginning of *perestroika* in 1985, they led to the destruction of the fundamental structure of the Soviet ethnography.

The changes in political life in the USSR caused a dictatorship of the official Marxist ideology and the collapse of previous organizational structures of science; as a result of *perestroika,* the movement for new reorganization began. First of all, the reorganization was expressed in the changing of names. The appropriate ethnological bodies appeared instead of departments, institutes, and chairs of ethnography. The Institute of Ethnography in Moscow was renamed the Institute of Ethnology and Anthropology in 1992. The central journal, *Soviet Ethnography,* was renamed *Ethnographic Review,* etc. Moreover, a number of institutes at the Leningrad Science Center, which were the offshoots of the Moscow central institutes, reclaimed their independence. A former Leningrad department at the Institute of Ethnography at the Academy of Science of the USSR was transformed into the Peter the Great Museum of Anthropology and Ethnography again, and the Leningrad department of the Institute of Archeology at the Academy of Science became the Institute of History of Material Culture. At the same time, the latest disciplines, including social anthropology, were generally recognized at last. This specialization (social anthropology) appeared only in 1995 in the list of the Russian Ministry of Education. It is not accidental that there are still very limited numbers of published works on social and cultural anthropology in Russian.

Public acknowledgement of social anthropology in a country which had strong traditions in ethnographic/ethnological and Oriental studies led to some contradictory consequences. Sociologists and philosophers like Vladimir Dobren'kov and Urii Resnik took the initiative to introduce social anthropology as a separate discipline in Russia. This is the reason why the state educational standards of social anthropology do not differ enough from sociological standards. It is probably due to the peculiar logic that everything considered "social" can be covered by sociology. It is significant that very few Russian ethnographers/ethnologists are ready to identify themselves with social anthropology. The leading figure among them is Valeriy Tishkov. Most of the ethnographers/ethnologists think these two areas of knowledge are principally homogeneous (Bromley 1979; Golovnev 2000). The situation of a correlation between a traditional discipline and a new discipline in Russia can be demonstrated by an example of textbooks with anthropological contents written by Svetlana Lurie and Yan Chesnov, published as *Historical Ethnology* (Lurie 1997) and *Lectures on Historical Ethnology* (Chesnov 1998). Later, Lurie partly changed her position, publishing the new textbook as *Psychological Anthropology* (Lurie 2003).

Scholars from areas as diverse as history, Oriental, and African studies tend to see themselves as social anthropologists. At present, we can establish a fact that a particular school of political anthropology had been formed in Russia. The problems of "political genesis" were studied within this new tradition (Kradin 2004), and L.E. Kubbel was one of its initiators (Kubbel 1988). The group of specialists within this school from Moscow (D.U. Bondarenko, A.V. Korotaev) and from Vladivostok (N.N. Kradin) prepared a number of conferences on the origin and features of early states. The great success of a new discipline is marked by the activity of the Moscow School of Historical Anthropology, formed at the Institute of Universal History at the Academy of Science. Aron Gurevich, Leo Batkin and Yuri Bessmertni were among the initators of this school, which developed following the traditions of the French *Annales* school. Due to Tishkov's efforts, legal anthropology has also been developing. However, all of these disciplines remain largely isolated from each other, and many other fields of research within contemporary social and cultural anthropology abroad have not yet reached Russia.

At the same time, social scientists, whose work had been very useful through Marx's and Lenin's philosophy and related disciplines (like science communism), have turned to this discipline which is new and little known in Russia. They consider social anthropology as a theoretical (speculative) science in the tradition of philosophical anthropology of the philosopher Immanuel Kant. Good examples are the textbooks of sociologist Albert Kravchenko and philosopher Vladimir Sharonov (Kravchenko 2003; Sharonov 1995). The introduction of Kravchenko's book relates to problems of theory and method in anthropology. The authors pay much attention to the problem of anthropogenesis and sociogenesis, based on information downloaded from the Internet. The final part is devoted to a model of social structure organization. But for all that, the problems of culture and its variations, as well as a number of other anthropological issues, have not been examined enough in this book. The problems of freedom and the meaning of human life are mainly discussed in Sharonov's textbook. Quick acknowledgement and the development of the civilized method emphasized the problems of cultural research, which were caused by the radical shift of the USSR from the philosophy of Marx and Lenin to other theoretical bases. This explains why the science of culture ("culturology"), as a new educational and scientific discipline, had been established earlier than social anthropology and occupied part of the issues usually researched by anthropologists. The coexistence of ethnology, the science of culture ("culturology"), and social anthropology since the 1990s reflects both the changes within Russian science and the attempts of Russian social anthropology to determine its connection to other disciplines. There is no connection with archeology and physical anthropology. The language programs for anthropology students in accordance with the State educational standard do not differ from other disciplines. Hence, the fact is that Russian social anthropology is not homogeneous and some of its variants remain outside the main tradition of anthropological science. The difficulties of the development of the new discipline are reflected by the fact that institutes and faculties of social anthropology had, by 2003, been opened only at eight universities (in Moscow, St. Petersburg, Omsk, Vladivostok, Irkutsk, and Chita).

The formation of the "great" anthropological tradition in Russia, which occasionally includes socio-cultural anthropology, ethnology, Oriental studies, African studies, historical anthropology, and now social anthropology also gives rise to an important question: *what is social anthropology?* We see the necessity of this question because the Russian variant of anthropology is considered closer to sociology and philosophy than to other sciences. In order to find the answer and understand it, we need to refer to the ideas and theories that have been developing in Russian ethnography and ethnology, Soviet ethnography, and Russian social anthropology.

FORMATION AND DEVELOPMENT OF THE THEORETICAL BASIS OF RUSSIAN ETHNOLOGY–SOVIET ETHNOGRAPHY

At its first stage of development, Russian ethnography theoretically depended completely on basic directions and schools of foreign science. While ethnography kept its position as a mainly university discipline between Russian scientists of the second part of nineteenth century until the beginning of twentieth, evolutionary studies remained the most influential. However, other foreign developments, primarily anthropogeography and diffusionism, also made it to Russia. The developing of practical field researches increased criticism of the evolutionist theory, first of all because of the data being used. One of the most ardent critics of evolutionism was A.P. Maksimov, ethnographer of Slavic ethnic groups. The ideas of the "culture and personality" school of Franz Boas had definite resonance among Russian scientists— mainly in Moscow. Sergey Tolstov, who became the director of the Institute of Ethnography at the Academy of Science, had been under this influence for a long time. Nikolai Trubetskoi, one of the famous Eurasians, suggested the idea of the independent importance of all the cultures—contradicting evolutionism (Trubetskoi 2003). Nevertheless, most Russian ethnographers, including Bogoraz, Anuchin, and Shternberg, remained real evolutionists.

   In the course of the discussion about an object of ethnography which took place at the department of ethnography within the Imperial Russian geographic society in 1916, N.M. Mogilianski announced that the object of ethnography was not mankind and its culture, but *ethnos* (Mogilanski 1916). It was the first claim for the creation of the original theory of *ethnos*. Sergey Shirokogoroff, during his visit to Vladivostok 1918–1922, worked out the absolute variant of the theory of ethnos as ethnic groups (Shirokogoroff 1923). But, as a result of emigrating to China in 1922, and then of being listed as involved in counterrevolutionary activity in the Far East of Russia in 1918– 1921, his works were not available in the USSR. Nikolai Trubetskoi, one of the famous Eurasians, suggested the idea of the independent importance of all the cultures—contradicting evolutionism (Trubetskoi 2003).

   Revolutionary transformations in Russia sharply brought to the fore the transformation of the sciences on the basis of Marxism, as it became both the State ideology and the primary scientific universal theory. The application of Marxism to science happened in several stages and had contradictory features. The demands of the time brought the practical realization of Marr's theory—which influenced the social sciences, including ethnology. The famous linguist, Orientalist and archeologist Nikolai Marr (1865–1934), accepted the social revolution (the position of working class) and suggested revolutionary "new studies of language." The idea of *stadialism* was formed on the basis of these studies and then extended to other social sciences, including ethnography and archeology. According to Alpatov (1991, 1993), this theory was based on the concept of separate languages appearing independently. Further development was conceived through the alteration of speed at the same stages, characteristics of which were determined by the social and economic conditions of a society. According to Marr, with "new quality sources of material life, techniques and social structure," new thinking and new ideology of language construction and its technique also appeared. As a result of this, languages progressed through revolutionary changes, which modified their contents and structure. The linguistic base of the theory of *stadialism* is also demonstrated in the interpretation of language as "a driving force in the area of additional category of society." Marr supported the class origin of language and thinking. It was no accident that one of the most important results of the Russian revolution was expected to be the formation of an absolutely new language. The initial condition of plurality of different languages, as claimed by the theory of *stadialism*, changed during several periods, as characterized by the reduction in the quantity of different languages. A single universal language was supposed to be formed in the future (Slezkine 1996).

Culture, conceived as a class universal, also played its role:

> Ethnic cultures (…) do not exist, there are no tribal cultures of different origins, but only one human culture in certain stages of development (…) the culture itself has only one origin and its variations are derived from a single creative process at different stages of its development. Do the variants exist? Of course yes, but these variants have not mystic-national, but real-class features (Marr 1933: 236).

Despite critics pointing out that this theory was based on fantastic ideas never tested, *stadialism* played a great role in Russia from the 1930s until 1950. As Olga Freidenberg wrote: "Marr was our thoughts, our social and scientific life, our biography. We worked for him without thinking about him, and he lived for us without knowing it" (Freidenberg 1988). As Alpatov mentioned, the influence of *stadialism* was mainly conditioned by its mythological content. But the main idea was that the basic points of this concept fully corresponded to the revolutionary discourse and expectations of the country being transformed. Another attractive feature of the theory was the sharp distinction from "Western bourgeois" theories, developed at the end of nineteenth century to the beginning of twentieth century (diffusionism, structuralism, etc.). *Stadialism* was most successful in archeology, as it contradicted the view of the authors who based their theories on the ideas of migration. It was not accidental that the future leader of Soviet ethnography, Tolstov, reported: "any deviation from Marr leads to racism, fascism" (Ivanova 2003: 48). As opposed to foreign theories, *stadialism* became the original theory. The works of stadialists-archeologists such as A.P. Kruglov and G.V. Podgaetski greatly influenced Gordon Childe during his visits to the USSR since 1935 (Klejn 1993). The theory was developed in a few institutes established by Marr, including the State Academy of Material Culture History, established in Petersburg in 1919. The department of the Academy also opened in Moscow and was led by ethnographer Bogdanov.

Another tendency of applying Marxism to ethnography/ethnology was reflected in the works of pre-revolutionary scientists. They tried to combine basic ideas of Marxism with the ideas of traditional ethnographical/anthropological schools. Bogoraz, in his *The Expansion of Culture on Earth,* tried to write the basic ethnogeography through anthropogeography. Preobrazhenski tried to find synthesis of Marxism and the school of culture and history. Russian ethnologists were interested in not only the new theory of Marxism, but also in new foreign theories. Development of numerous local societies in the USSR and the establishment of institutes like the State Museum of the Central Industrial Area demonstrated the interest of Moscow scholars in the ideas of Boas. The problems of cultural areas and diffusions in the case of the Central Russia ideas were disscussed in meetings in Moscow in 1926 and 1929. In these meetings, evolutionary theory was criticized by Bogdanov and Zelenin (Alymov and Reshetov 2003: 230–32).

Russian ethnology of the 1920s shows the formation of the new anthropological school. It could have included some ideas of Marxism as well as basic concepts of foreign social/cultural anthropology. The Marxist line, the school of research in *ethnos,* synthetic West-Russian tendencies, and other schools could have been established in the Soviet ethnology. However, political changes prevented this from occurring.

In the struggle to approve the principles of Marxism, different organizations and unions took the initiative to organize a series of discussions on the problems of Marxism and ethnology. The discussion took place at the social sector of the Society of Historians-Marxists in 1927. In 1928, V.B. Aptekar gave a report on "Marxism and ethnology." He demonstrated the problem of the undeveloped basic categories of ethnology, primarily of "culture," and pointed to Marxist "anomalies" in the works of earlier scholars.

Having stated the value of ethnology and the attempts to combine it with Marxism, he concluded they were incompatible—meaning that ethnology had to be abolished. P.I. Kushner and V.K. Nikolski disagreed. They accepted the need to transform ethnology to ethnography, which would result in the collection of the information about "retrograde peoples." Bogoraz's attempt to combine Marxism with anthropogeography was criticized at the first All Union Conference of Historians-Marxists. At the same time, Tolstov suggested understanding ethnography as one of the historical disciplines, united in the method of historical materialism and having " the object of [the] study [of] culture, by way of accumulated efforts of humanity" (Solovey 1998, 2001).

The fate of ethnology was finally settled at the Meeting of Ethnologists in Moscow and Leningrad in April 1929. Now that the previous discussions had been criticized and cruel appraisals had been given, even Preobrazhenski in his "Ethnology and its method" considered ethnology as a historical one. In his next report on "Marxism and ethnology," Aptekar stated that "ethnology is the bourgeois substitute of social sciences." In the documents signed at the Meeting, ethnology received the official name of ethnography. Moreover, the very existence of ethnology as an independent theoretical science was denied. Studying social formations and their concrete variants was to be the primary task of the social sciences, including ethnography (Reshetov 2003; Solovey 2001; Slezkine 1991).

Transformation of the "bourgeois" ethnology into Soviet ethnography on the principles of *stadialism* was legitimated. This was accomplished through "organized" conclusions, as a result of which some scientists lost their jobs (Nikolski, Tokarev). The destiny of the newly established ethnography was not clear. However, in the early 1930s, party statements and letters written by Stalin demonstrated to scientists that only the party authorities made decisions in science. Because of these interferences, ethnography was inadvertently preserved.

The institutional and conceptual transformations that took place and marked the appearance of Soviet ethnography were based on very specific causes. There was active interference by the authorities, who attempted to turn the theory and structure of the science socialist, while at the same time, conflicts within the scientific association also occurred behind the scenes. These conflicts happened because of the emergence of a new generation of scientists. They were educated during the post-revolutionary period and wanted to be placed in basic positions in science. The position of ethnography and its orientation for solving the tasks of social organization were confirmed in 1932 at the special section of the first All Union Geographical Congress and the All-Russian Meeting of Archeology and Ethnography.

Repression was the first tactic taken by the authorities. The Academy of Science and the universities throughout the country were also targeted. The ethnographers P. Preobrazhenski, B. Zukov, A. Haruzin, and others were victims of this repression. After Marr died in 1934, his close associates Aptekar, Bikovski, and Motorin were arrested and executed. The annihilation of not only scholars who belonged to the "old school" like Preobrazhenski and Haruzin, but also Aptekar and Bikovski who were the *stadialists*-Marxists, and former functionary Matorin, shows that this repression was based on different grounds. Scientists and theorists who struggled for Marxism without emphasizing party organization (like Aptekar and Bikovski) were also prosecuted. Some ethnologists were arrested because of a personal rivalry.

The repression was a devastating blow to ethnography and other sciences in the USSR. At the same time, when many famous scientists stopped their activities, there was the situation not only of suppression without any semblance of freedom, but there was also the fear of suggesting new ideas. It was not accidental that V.A. Shnirel'man noticed: "in some periods, the theoretical researches in our country resembled the work of a sapper" (1992: 11). Soviet ethnography then turned from theoretical discussion to the developing of the primary and secondary tasks. Constant political influence caused the practice of using quotations (without detailed explanation) from the works of Marx, Engels, Lenin, Stalin, and Marr. Following the discussion of June 1950, *stadialism* was abandoned. Since that time, as Ivanova mentioned, Tolstov publicly said: "We were wrong, only Tokarev was right" (Ivanova 2003: 49). The theoretical basis for ethnography became Stalin's studies of the nation and his statement of culture that had national form and social content—as well as the philosophy of Marx and Lenin. In *Marxism and the National Question,* Stalin described the nation as the following: "It is the steady union of language, territory, social life and turn of mind demonstrated in the area of culture having been formed historically." As soon as the ideology of Stalin was denounced in 1956, his works were deleted from the scholarly bibliographies, although his ideas continued to be used. Soviet ethnography remained a part of historical science, following the basic points of Engels' *The Origin of the Family, Private Property and the State,* and a number of units from Marx's *Capital.* The problem was finding the facts to justify basic statements of the classics of Marxism. The historicism of ethnography was mainly seen in the research on issues concerning history of primitive society.

With further political liberalization in the 1960s and 1970s, ethnographers felt more confident and began to discuss topics like the basis of some of Morgan's statements, used by Engels. The conceptual empty space devoted to national problems needed to be filled. This task was left to Yulian Bromley, whotook over as head of the Institute of Ethnography at the Academy of Science after Tolstov in 1966. The new director was more interested in sociology, and as a result, ethno-sociological research developed at the Institute. Another innovation was the establishment of the theoretical section of the History of Primitive Society. However, the main result of Bromley's activities was the reanimation of the *ethnos* theory (Bromley 1973, 1983). Following the debates of the 1920s, this theory was replaced by *stadialist* concepts. Stalin's theory of nation and philosophical statements of historical materialism were substituted for it later. However, a need arose for a unique theoretical base for Soviet ethnography.

Bromley formulated his version of the theory on the basis of Shirokogoroff's ideas and then added some basic ideas from Marx's and Stalin's theory of social formations. As a result, he had to consider this initial category *ethnos* through both micro- and macro-level approaches. According to the first: "ethnos (in the narrow meaning of the word) in the most general form can be defined as a historically formed community of people possessing common, relatively stable specific features of culture, as well as being aware of their unity and difference from other similar communities." (Bromley, 1973: 37; 1983: 57–58). Shirokogoroff defined *ethnos* as "a group of people speaking the same language, recognising a common origin, who has a system of customs and a mode of life preserved and sanctioned by tradition and differing from other similar groups" (Shirokogoroff 1923: 13). The macro-level meaning was seen as a more complicated phenomenon—an ethno-sociological organism (ESO). "Such kinds of formation along with ethnic (cultural first of all) usually have territorial, economic, social and political community (it is so called maximal variant). But its basic components are the ethnic factors on the one hand and socio-economic factors on the other." (Bromley 1973: 40; 1983: 62–63).

Just like Shirokogoroff, Bromley saw *ethnos* as a developing phenomenon (dynamic system), but he compared it to certain social formations, and not to the stages of *ethnos* development: "belonging to one or another formation formed its (ethno-social) body, particular character. This fact is mainly underlying in general for our literature of the last period accentuating such historical-stage types of ethno-social communities as tribal, nationality, bourgeois and social nation." (Bromley 1983: 63). Categories like the ethno-social organism gave the possibility for combining this theory with categories like productive force and industrial relations (Bromley 1983: 224ff). The new version of this theory played the role of the theoretical base for Soviet ethnography until the 1980s. It seemed to have taken the ideas of Shirokogoroff, who was not a Marxist (*ethnos*), as well as of Marx, Engels (production method), Stalin (five basic formations), and Brezhnev (Soviet people as the new historical community). In this sense, Bromley's theory of *ethnos* marked the end of the period of development of Soviet ethnography.

At the same time, another theory of *ethnos* was developed by Lev Gumilev in the late 1960s. He resuscitated the idea of ethnology as a geographical science, based on the fact that man is a part of nature and each phenomenon of ethnogenesis happened to take place in a certain landscape. Therefore, *ethnos* was considered by Gumilev as a natural phenomenon and a stage in the process of ethnogenesis (Gumilev 2001: 177, 255). Not being Marxist, this theory was prohibited for a long time, but it is a vivid example of the potential of Russian ethnology without ideological constraints.

CONCLUSION

The changes of the theoretical bases of ethnography started at the end of *Perestroika* and when the official (dogmatic) Marxism lost its powerful position in the USSR. A series of works criticizing the Soviet period were published in the early 1990s (Basilov 1992; Markov 1992; Snirel'man 1992). The most radical theory on the theoretical foundations of Soviet ethnography (Bromley's theory of *ethnos*) was by Valery Tishkov. He tried to consider Russian anthropology as being on the course of a "great tradition," with the principles of methodological individualism, constructive approach, and theory of ethnicity.

> Ethnology and anthropology have its own clear subject—to study peoples and cultures, their interactions, to analyze the most difficult social phenomenon—ethnic features, as well as its own distinctive method—field research based on personal investigation and analyzing techniques for cultural phenomenon. (Tishkov 1992: 4)

Tishkov appealed for the turn from historical observations to contemporary studies (2003a). However, the attempts of the director of the Institute of Ethnology and Anthropology at the Russian Academy of Science to reconsider foundations of ethnology caused the negative reaction of many scientists from this Institute. One of them, V.I. Kozlov, commented on Tishkkov: "his argumentation, with its speculative character, is sometimes so harsh, and conclusions so radical, that it probably caused more fear than thinking which, as I understood, the author appealed for" (Kozlov 1992: 3). It is no less significant that the book of collected articles in honor of Bromley was published in 2003; most of Moscow's ethnologists and a few philosophers' devotion to his variant of *ethnos* theory was clearly demonstrated by this (*Academic Y. V. Bromley i Otechesvennaya Ethnographiya 1960–1990s*, 2003).

The history of Russian ethnology shows that this discipline used to be connected with certain basic theories that were supposed to provide it with a sense of self sufficiency. This sense was clearly explained by Kozlov: "I often had to socialize with American scientists from the prestige universities, as well as from the average ones, and I must say that their 'doctors' and 'professors' are scientifically inferior to ours" (1992: 5). I would refrain from stating the superiority of Russian ethnology to foreign anthropology. These appraisals reflect the existence of real differences among the fundamentals of different scholarly traditions. During its development, Soviet ethnography/ Russian ethnology formed its own view of the subject, of the object of research, and of the legitimization of knowledge that was achieved. It was expressed into the orientation for various types of evolutionism with *Marrism* and other versions of Marxism. Another special feature of Russian science is that it was focused upon the problems of nation and *ethnos*—rather than on ethnicity or ethnic identity. Because of its complex character, our ethnography was always in need of firm theoretical foundations. In order to be accepted internationally, this tradition needs to be introduced to a wider international audience. This can be one of the tasks of the recently emerged Russian social anthropology. As Tishkov wrote in 2000:

> The subject of anthropological research in Russia has undergone important changes. The crisis that Russian anthropology has suffered from in the late 1980s until the early 1990s has been successfully overcome in many of its subdisciplines, but it still much to be done remains in terms of theoretical reevaluation of the Russian anthropological tradition.

So, what is to be said about the current situation of anthropology in Russia? On the one hand, we can see an extended point of view that this science has the same features as ethnology. In this case the question is, can we consider anthropology as a separate discipline? On the other hand, the situation when scholars can identify themselves as anthropologists and not as ethnologists returns them to the problem of the subject and goals of their activity. Today, when social (cultural) anthropology in Russia coexists with ethnology, sociology, history (including archaeology and ethnography), culturology, and Oriental studies, the scope of its research could be extended into the area of ethnic and cultural interconnections, as well as among different (national) scientific traditions.

REFERENCES

Alpatov, V.M. 1991. *Istoriya Odnogo Mifa*. Moscow.
——. 1993. "Marr, Marrism i Stalinism." *Philosofskie Issledovaniya* 4: 271–88.

Alymov, S. S., and Reshetov A.M. 2003. *Boris Alekseevich Kuftin: Izlomy Zhiznennogo Puti. Repressirovannye Ethnography.* Moscow.

Averkieva, U.P. 1979. *Istoriya Teoreticheskoj Mysli v Amerikanskoj Etnografii.* Moscow.

Bethmann, Petra. 1997. Chto Delat'? Ethnography in the Post-Soviet Cultural Contexts. *American Anthropologist* 99, 4: 770–4.

Bromlej, U.V. 1973. *Ethnos i Etnografiya.* Moscow.

——. 1979. "O Predmete Kul'turnoj-Sotsial'noj Antropologii I Etnografiiv Traktovke Anglo-Amerikanskih I Sovetskih Uchenyh (opyt sravnitel'nogo analiza)." In *Etnografiya za Rubezhom,* pp. 7–22. Moscow.

——. 1983. *Ocherki Teorii Ethnosa.* Moscow.

Chesnov, Ya. V. 1998. *Istoricheskaya Ethnologia.* M. Gardarica.

Clay, C.B. 1995. "Russian Ethnographers in the Service of Empire, 1856–1862." *Slavic Review* 54, 1: 45–61.

Eidlitz, K. 1985. *The Revolution in the North: Soviet Ethnography and National Policy.* Stockholm.

Elfimov, Alexei. 1997. The State of Discipline in Russia, Inetrviews with Russian Anthropologists. *American Anthropologist* 99, 4: 775–85.

Freidenberg, O.M. 1988. *Vospominaniya o N. Ya. Marre.* Moscow: Vostok-Zapad.

Gellner, Ernest (ed.) 1980. *Soviet and Western Anthropology.* London.

Georgi, G. 1776–1780. *Opisanie Vseh v Rossiiskom Gosudarstve Obitautshih Narodov, Takzhe ih Zhiteiskih Obryadov, Ver, Obyknovenij, Zhilish, Odezhd i Prochih Dostopamyatnostej,* 4 vols, Sankt-Peterburg.

Golovnev, A.V. 2000. "Ethnographiya i Ethnologiya v Gumanitarnom Obrazovanii." In *Istoricheskaya Nauka i Istoricheskoe Obrazovanie na Rubezhe XX-XX1 stoletij.* Ekaterinburg.

Grigulevich, I.R. 1976. "Sotsial'naya Antropologiya: Est' li u nee Budutshee?" In *Kontseptsii Zarubezhnoj Etnologii. Kriticheskie Etudy.* Moscow.

Gumilev, L.N. 2001. *Ethnogenez i Biosphera Zemli.* Moscow.

Its, R.F. 1974. *Vvedenie v Etnographiu.* Leningrad.

Ivanova, Yu. V. 2003. "Iz Istorii Instituta Ethnographii (ochen lichnye vospominania)." *Etnografičeskoe Obozrenie,* 5: 43–53.

Kerimova, M.M. 2003. "Semja Etnographov Kharuzinyh i ih Epistolarnoe Nasledie." *Etnografičeskoe Obozrenie* 4: 90–106.

Klejn, L.S. 1993. *Phenomen Sovetskoj Arheologii.* Leningrad.

Kozlov, S.Y a., ed. 2003. *Akademik U.V. Bromlej i Otechestvennaya Etnographiya 1960–1990-s.* Moscow.

Kozlov, V.I. 1992. "Mezhdy Ethnographiej, Ethnologiej i Zhizn'u." *Etnografičeskoe Obozrenie* 3: 3–15.

Kradin, N.N. 2004. *Politicheskaya Antropologiya.* Moscow.

Krasheninnikov, S.P. 1756. *Opisanie Zemli Kanchatki.* Sankt-Peterburg.

Kravchenko, A.I. 2003. *Sotsial'naya Antropologiya.* Moscow.

Kubbel, L.E. 1988. *Ocherki Potestarno-Politicheskoj Etnographii.* Moscow.

Lurie, S.V. 1997. *Istoricheskaya Etnologiya.* Moscow.

——. 2003. *Psihologicheskaya Antropologiya.* Moscow.

Marr, N.Ya. 1933. *Izbrannye Raboty.* Vol. 1. Moscow-Leningrad.

Markov G.E., and Solovej T.D. 1990. "Etnogradichrskoe Obrazovanie v Moskovskom Gosudarstvennom Universitete (k 50-letiu kafedry etnografii istiricheskogo fakul'tebe MGU)." *Sovetskaya Etnografiya* 6.

Markov G.E., Pimenov V.V., and T. D. Solovey 1999. "60-letie Kafedry Ethnographii (Ethnologii) Istoricheskogo Facul'teta MGU," *Etnografičeskoe Obozrenie* 6.

Mogilyanskij, N.M. 1916. "Predmet i Zadachi Etnografi," *Zhivaya Starina,* 1.

Nachinin V. 1955. "Materialy «Ethnographicheskogo Buro» knyazya V.N. Tenisheva v Nauchnom Arhive Gosudarstvennogo Muzeya Ethnographii Narodov SSSR," *Sovetskaya Etnografiya* 1.

——. 1983. *Puti Razvitiya Zarubezhnoj Etnologii.* Moscow.

Perchenok, F.F. 1995. "Delo 'Akademii nauk' i 'Velikij Perelom' v Sovetskoj Nauke." In *Tragicheskir Sud'by: Repressirovannye Uchenye Akademii Nauk SSSR,* pp. 201–35. Moscow.

Reshetov, A.M.. 2003. "Institut Antropologii I Ethnographii - Institut Ethnographii AN SSSR 1933-1943 gg.." *Etnografičeskoe Obozrenie* 5: 24–42.

Skalník, Peter. 1988. "Union soviétique–Afrique du Sud: les 'théories' de l'etnos." *Cahiers d'Etudes Africaines* 38, 2: 157–76.

Sharonov, V.V. 1997. *Osnovy Sotsial'noj Antropologii.* Sankt-Peterburg.

Shirokogoroff, S. M. 1923. *Ethnos. Issledovanie Osnovnyh Printsipov Izucheniya Etnicheskih i Ethnographicheskih Yavlenij.* Shanghai.

Shnirel'man', V.A. 1992. "Nauka v Usloviyah Totalitarizma." *Etnografičeskoe Obozrenie* 5: 7–18.

——. 1993. "Zloklucheniya Odnoj Nauki. Etnogeneticheskie Issledovaniya i Stalinskaya Natsional'naya Politika." *Etnografičeskoe Obozrenie* 3: 52–68.

Slezkine ,Y. 1991. "The Fall of Soviet Ethnography, 1928-1938." *Current Anthropology* 32, 4: 476–84.

——. 1996. "Ia. Marr and the National Origins of Soviet Ethnogenesis." *Slavic Review* 56, 4: 826–9.

Solovey, T.D. 1998. "Ot 'Burzhuaznoj' Etnologii k 'Sovetskoj' Etnografii." In *Istoriya Otechestvennoj etnologii pervoj treti XX v.,* pp. 112–36. Moscow.

——. 2001. "'A radical turn' in Our Domestic Ethnography (Discussion on the Object of Ethnological Science: Late 1920's–Early 1930's)." *Etnografičeskoe Obozrenie* 3: 101–21.

Tatischev, V.N. 1744. *Vvedenie k Istoricheskomu i Geograficheskomu Opisaniu Velikorossijskoj Imperii.* Sankt-Peterburg.

Tishkov, Valery A. 1992. "The Crisis in Soviet Ethnography." *Current Anthropology* 33: 371–82.

——. 2000. "Anthropologiya Rossijskih Transformatsij." *Etnografičeskoe Obozrenie* 1: 3–19.

——. 2003a. "Rossijskaya Anthropologiya: Status Distsipliny, Sostoyanie Teorii i Rezul'taty Issledovanij," *Etnografičeskoe Obozrenie* 5: 3–23.

——. 2003b. *Rekviem po Ethnosu. Issledovaniya po Sotsial'no-Kul'turnoj Anthropologii.* Moscow.

Trubetskoj, N. 2003. "Evropa i Chelovechestvo." In *Klassika Geopolitiki.* Moscow.

Zolotarev, A. 1934. Ethnographia v Moskve. *Sovetskaya Ethnographia* 4: 118–9.

Chapter 2

Anthropology in the Netherlands: Past, Present, and Future

Han F. Vermeulen

INTRODUCTION

Anthropology in the Netherlands is a rich field of socio-cultural studies that has been practiced in the Netherlands and its overseas colonies from the 1770s and was institutionalized from the 1830s onward.[1] It is the result of a complex interaction between scholarly interests in peoples at a distance, several centuries of colonialism and international trade, as well as political decisions on the structuring of higher education and research in the Netherlands and its former colonies.[2] To a large extent, this historical background has shaped the way research is currently organized and funded.

Seen from a Dutch colonial perspective, stretching over 350 years of trade and colonizing in the East and West Indies (van Goor 1994; de Jong 1998), and covering 400 years of trade relations with China and Japan (Blussé 1989; Blussé et al. 2000), and 300 years in South Africa (Ross 1999, 2001), anthropology was relatively late in arriving on the scholarly scene. Its institutionalization took place during the nineteenth century, in line with developments in other European countries and in the USA. But this was preceded by another period, a process of conceptualization taking place in the eighteenth century (Vermeulen 1995, 1996). From 1740, ethnography developed in Siberia, Russia, and Germany. From 1770, ethnography, physical anthropology, and folklore studies (*volkskunde*) were actively pursued in European scholarly discourse—relating not only to the world beyond Europe, but also to Europe itself (Vermeulen 1999, 2002a, 2006).

From the 1770s, anthropology was pursued in the Netherlands and the Netherlands Indies, but its institutionalization began in the 1830s. This was a slow process, partly due to the fact that the study passed through two basic types, namely general anthropology (ethnology), usually of a comparative kind, and regional anthropology (ethnography), predominantly of Indonesia but also of Surinam and the Netherlands Antilles (later of other parts of the world). Since regional anthropology (ethnography) was embedded in the military and colonial civil service training programs from 1836, general anthropology (ethnology) was not easily established. The first university chair in the ethnography of Indonesia was founded at Leiden in 1877, but a chair in general (comparative) ethnology was only founded in Amsterdam in 1907, and in Leiden as late as 1922.

This particular development of Dutch anthropology has led to a dual identity that continues to the present day. In the early nineteenth century, there was a basic distinction between ethnology (general anthropology) and ethnography (regional anthropology); in the late nineteenth and early twentieth centuries between ethnology and Indology (the civil service training programs); and after World War II, between cultural anthropology and non-western sociology. The latter distinction, introduced in 1952, has increasingly come under discussion.

In this essay I focus on cultural anthropology, prior to 1953 called ethnology, and on non-western sociology, seen in the broader context of anthropological studies in the Netherlands. By 1955, the field consisted of ethnology (*volkenkunde*), folklore studies (*volkskunde*), and physical anthropology, all three functioning as separate studies (van Bork-Feltkamp 1938, 1948, 1955). Up until then, ethnology had been a subject in the degree programs of geography at the universities of Amsterdam and Utrecht, in the degree programs of "Indology" and "East Indies Law" at the universities of Leiden and Utrecht, and in a master's program of *ethnologie* (general anthropology) provided at the University of Leiden since 1929. In 1953, the degree program in ethnology was renamed "cultural anthropology" (CA), conforming to American usage (although some preferred the term "social anthropology"). In 1952, a new degree program developed from the Indology and Indies Law programs, which received the name "non-western sociology" (NWS) and, from 1983, became known as the "sociology of non-western societies" (SNWS).

From the 1950s, the dual character of Dutch socio-cultural anthropology persisted in the development of cultural anthropology (CA) and of non-western sociology (NWS) in conjunction with and opposed to each other, often in the same department. Although the latter subject is clearly different from social anthropology as understood in the British tradition, I translate the complexities of Dutch terminology and praxis by referring to both fields as socio-cultural anthropology, thus as including cultural anthropology (CA) and development sociology (OS). Together these studies correspond to what in the UK is seen as social anthropology and development studies. As Wim Wertheim later recalled, non-western sociology was set up to correct anthropology's bias of "primitive isolates" and serve as a "temporary panacea" to amend sociology's ethnocentric bias by including the study of non-western societies (Wertheim 2002).

In the following, I outline the historical development of socio-cultural anthropology in the Netherlands and deal with its various chairs and traditions. I then discuss the present state of anthropology in the Netherlands, and conclude with some critical remarks on its future.

THE HISTORY OF ANTHROPOLOGY IN THE NETHERLANDS

Anthropology in the Netherlands developed in the wake of Oriental studies,[3] and in close interaction with linguistics, history, geography, in particular human (or social) geography, customary law (*adatrecht*),[4] and sociology. Relations with folklore studies (*volkskunde*),[5] physical anthropology,[6] and prehistoric archaeology have been weak and, even today, are virtually nonexistent. These disciplines are considered independent, as is sociology, in particular since the establishment of a Faculty of Social Sciences at Dutch universities in 1963. Prior to this date, the subject of anthropology was taught either in the Faculty of Arts (as *ethnologie*) or in the Faculty of Medicine (as *anthropologie*); these studies were, after World War II, designated with the terms "cultural anthropology" and "physical anthropology," respectively. Sociology originated in the Faculty of Law from the 1870s; in Amsterdam sociology and social geography merged into a subject named *sociographie* (from 1913).

From the beginning, anthropology in the Netherlands has had a strong overseas orientation. It focused on the study of the East Indies (Indonesia), although interests were not confined to this region. Dutch studies of other regions of the world, including the West Indies, Africa, the Americas, and Australia have been published, but it would be difficult to speak of any tradition of research in these areas before decolonization. Reports on the peoples of Indonesia were written ever since the first Dutch voyage to the Indonesian archipelago (1595–97). The Dutch East India Company (VOC), founded in 1602, may in retrospect be called the first multinational company in the world (Akveld and Jacobs 2002). As a trading company, however, the VOC did not allow its employees to publish anything likely to damage its commercial interests. In spite of a VOC ban on publications, a number of authors managed to write now famous books: Rogerius (1651) and Baldaeus (1672) on South Asia, Dapper (1668) and Bosman (1701) on Africa, Rumphius (1687) and Valentijn (1724–26) on Southeast Asia, especially Eastern Indonesia. Yet, as a result of this setback, systematic ethnography developed slowly and ethnographic details remained hidden in voluminous "histories" and travel accounts.

The Batavian Society of Arts and Sciences (KBG), founded in 1778, was the first learned society in Asia. The KBG made an interesting start by putting ethnography on the agenda. Adopting ideas first formulated in the German Enlightenment, founding members such as W. van Hogendorp and J.C.M. Radermacher produced topographic and ethnographic descriptions of the Indonesian islands that were published in the society's treatises (*Verhandelingen van het KBG*, 1779–86). However, British historians such as Marsden, Raffles, and Crawfurd made a breakthrough during the late eighteenth and early nineteenth century. As a consequence, the origins of Dutch socio-cultural anthropology (*ethnologie*) are usually traced no further than the second half of the nineteenth century, with G.A. Wilken as a figurehead.[7]

The history of Dutch physical anthropology clearly dates back to the eighteenth century. Descriptions of foreign races and of the differences between men and apes were published by Dutch physicians such as Bontius, Vosmaer, and Camper. Dutch scholars became renowned for presenting anatomical details of primates never seen, but described by Buffon (Dougherty 1995, 1996). The work of Petrus Camper on the "facial angle" among humans and on the Orang Outang (1770, 1778) was of international importance (Meijer 1999, 2004). The Dutch Protestant minister J.F. Martinet made a local contribution to physical anthropology by measuring the growth of boys in Amsterdam in a mixed-longitudinal study during 1770–76, reported on in his *Catechism of Nature* (1777–79) (Roede 2002).

In the 1780s, historians such as E.M. Engelberts (1784–99) and Martinus Stuart (1780–88, 1802–6) also began to pay attention to ethnographic details. Martinet published a nine volume history of the world (1780–88) in which he attempted to reconcile data on the plurality of nations, manners and morals with the Biblical chronology (Ensel 1994, 2002). Isaac Titsingh dealt with Japan (1787), John Gabriël Stedman wrote on Surinam (1796), while Jacob Haafner published on South India and Ceylon in a critical manner, opposing the VOC mentality (de Moor and van der Velde 1992–97).

The abolition of the VOC in 1798 marked the beginning of a new period when trade made the way for state formation (Ellen 1976; Hüsken et al. 1984). After the creation of the Kingdom of the Netherlands in 1813, the Dutch colonies regained their importance. In 1830, R.P. van de Kasteele, director of the Royal Cabinet of Curiosities in The Hague, made a plea for a general *ethnologie* (*volkenkunde*), which he contrasted with regional *ethnogra-*

phie. Ethnography came to the fore in the context of a renewed interest in the colonies during the 1830s. It is telling that when in 1836 a first chair was created for training colonial officers at the Royal Military Academy (KMA) in Breda, its subject was the geography and ethnography (*land- en volkenkunde*) of the Malay Archipelago. In the Netherlands East Indies, however, strict censorship again ruled from 1830 to 1870, hindering the development of ethnography.

In Leiden, an ethnographic museum was founded as a Japanese Museum in 1837. Its founder was Ph.F.B. von Siebold, a German physician who had worked for the Dutch in Deshima, Japan, where he had collected widely. This marked the beginning of the National Museum of Ethnology (RMV), one of the oldest ethnographic museums in the world (van Wengen 2002).

From 1843, training courses for colonial civil servants (*Indologie*) included ethnography as a subject. These courses were first given at an intermediate level at administrative schools in Surakarta (Central Java, 1832–43), Delft (1843–1900) and Leiden (1864–91). They were later promoted to an academic level by inclusion of its courses in the curriculum of the universities at Leiden (1902–56) and Utrecht (1925–55). In Batavia (now Jakarta), courses were also given in Indonesian languages, history, geography, Islam, colonial and customary law, as well as in ethnography (*volkenkunde*). In general, however, the training of colonial civil servants was offered in the Netherlands, rather than in the colonies. The courses for a law degree (*Indisch recht*, or East Indies Law) were provided at the universities, both in the Netherlands (as of 1877) and in the Netherlands East Indies (as of 1924).[8]

Due to the fact that ethnography had become part of the colonial civil servant training programs at an early stage, general anthropology had difficulty establishing itself as an independent subject. A first university chair in ethnology was founded at Leiden University in 1877 and rates as one of the earliest (structural) chairs in socio-cultural anthropology in the world.[9] However, the Leiden chair was established as a chair in regional anthropology, entitled "Geography and Ethnography of the Netherlands East Indies" (*Land- en Volkenkunde van Nederlandsch Oost-Indië*). The foundation professor was P.J. Veth, who held the Leiden chair from 1877 to 1885 (van der Velde 2000, 2002, 2006).

The institution of this chair represented an important step forward since ethnography had earlier almost exclusively been part of the training programs for colonial civil servants and colonial legal servants. Veth's successor, G.A. Wilken, built a bridge to general anthropology by turning anthropology into a comparative evolutionist study of Indonesia.

Chairs in general anthropology were established from the early twentieth century onward. In 1907, a chair in *volkenkunde* (ethnology) was established at the University of Amsterdam, and S.R. Steinmetz, who had studied in Leiden, was appointed as chair head. In contrast to Leiden and Utrecht, those entering the curriculum in Amsterdam were mainly students in geography, a situation that continued until after World War II. For these students, Steinmetz designed a separate branch of studies that he called *sociographie* (Heeren 1993; 1998; Heinemeijer 1998). He also developed a comparative kind of ethnology, which was evolutionist and sociological in nature (Köbben 1992; Heinemeijer 2002). In 1913, a chair in general anthropology (actually combining ethnology and physical anthropology) was instituted at Utrecht University, which was held by J.H.F. Kohlbrugge until 1935. In 1917, a second (supernumerary) chair (*bijzondere leerstoel*) was founded in Amsterdam, endowed by the Colonial Institute and occupied by J.C. van Eerde until 1935. At Leiden, a second (supernumerary) chair in general anthropology came into being in 1922. J.P.B. de Josselin de Jong was appointed to this position, which he held until his appointment to the main (regional) chair at Leiden in 1935. In Utrecht, H.Th. Fischer was appointed supernumerary professor of ethnology in 1936, becoming ordinarius in 1945 until his retirement in 1970.

In this way, during the first half of the twentieth century, three centers evolved in which ethnology was pursued: in Leiden and Utrecht for students of Indology and Indies Law, in Amsterdam and Utrecht for students of geography.[10] In all three centers supplementary chairs were established to allow for new developments. In Amsterdam, there was a chair in "colonial ethnology" (occupied by Van Eerde, who was succeeded by B.J.O. Schrieke in 1936), in Leiden in general ethnology or *"algemeene volkenkunde"* (de Josselin de Jong), and in Utrecht in ethnology (*volkenkunde*) as such (Fischer). This signalled a second phase in the liberation of ethnography from being merely a subject in the colonial degree programs.

An important but often overlooked center existed in Batavia (now Jakarta), where a chair in sociology and ethnology was established in the Faculty of Law as early as 1924. B.J.O. Schrieke held this chair from 1924 to 1929; he was succeeded by F.D. Holleman (1929 to 1935) and B. ter Haar (1935 to 1938). All three taught ethnology and sociology in conjunction with their main subject, customary law (*adatrecht*). Later, the chair (now for ethnology only) was transferred to the newly established Faculty of Arts at Batavia and occupied by J.Ph. Duyvendak (1938 to 1942), G.J. Held (1946 to 1955) and E.M.A.A.J. Allard (1956 to 1958).

After the independence of Indonesia in 1949, ethnology was renamed "cultural anthropology" (1953), while the subjects "Indology" and "Indies Law" were transformed into "non-western sociology" (*sociologie der niet-westerse volken,* or *sociologia gentium non occidentalium*) in 1952. This transformation

took place during the first years of decolonization in an effort to remove colonial topics from the curriculum. Consequently, the name non-western was
chosen as an alternative for the older term Oriental studies, which excluded
the Americas, Africa, and Oceania.[11] From then on this new discipline, described earlier as applied anthropology,[12] but today generally labelled as
"development sociology," was practiced in close connection but also strong
competition with cultural anthropology. Departments combining both subjects were established from the mid 1950s onward. This implied a fundamental change insofar as anthropology, formerly one of the subjects in the
geography curriculum and in the Indology and Indies Law programs, was
now on a par with non-western sociology, a transformed version of Indology
and Indies Law.

Anthropology was not only pursued at the universities and in the colonial civil service schools, but also (and before World War II primarily) in
ethnographic museums, learned societies, and in specialized research institutes. Ethnographic museums were established at Batavia/Jakarta (1836),
Leiden (1837/1859), Amsterdam (1838/1910/1926), Delft (1864), Rotterdam
(1885), Kampen (1900–1923), The Hague (1904), Breda (1905, 1923–56,
1970–93), Arnhem (1912), and, more recently, at Enkhuizen (1947), Berg en
Dal (1954/1958), Nijmegen (1960/1972–2005), Groningen (1968/1978–2003),
and Cadier en Keer (1980).

Chairs in ethnology (cultural anthropology) were founded in Leiden
(1877 and 1966), Amsterdam (1907 and 1962), Utrecht (1913 and 1960), Batavia (1924 and 1938), and, after World War II, at Wageningen Agricultural
University (1946), the Catholic University of Nijmegen (1948), the University
of Groningen (1955), and the Free University of Amsterdam (1956).

Chairs in non-western sociology were instituted at the University of Amsterdam (1946 and 1987), Utrecht (1955), Leiden (1950 and 1956), Wageningen (1955), Nijmegen (1958 and 1973), the Free University of Amsterdam
(1962), and the Economic University of Rotterdam (1964), now the Erasmus
University.

Institutions with anthropological interests are: the Royal Institute of Linguistics, Geography, and Ethnography of the Netherlands Indies (KITLV),
now the Institute of Southeast Asian and Caribbean Studies, founded at Delft
in 1851, moved to The Hague a few years later and to Leiden in 1967 (Kuitenbrouwer 2001); the Royal Netherlands Geographical Society (KNAG),
founded at Amsterdam in 1873 (Wentholt 2003); the Royal Tropical Institute (KIT), established as the Colonial Institute at Amsterdam in 1910, com-
plemented by a Tropical Museum in 1926; the Institute for Social Research
of the Dutch People (ISONEVO), founded at Amsterdam in 1940, renamed
the Netherlands' Universities Institute for the Coordination of Research in

Social Sciences (SISWO) in 1960, now focusing on Social Policy Research; the African Studies Centre (ASC), founded at Leiden in 1958; the Centre for Latin American Research and Documentation (CEDLA), founded at Amsterdam in 1964, which became an inter-university institute in 1971.

The Netherlands Anthropological Society (NAV) was established at Amsterdam in 1898, and in practice included physical anthropology, ethnology (*volkenkunde*), folklore studies (*volkskunde*), and prehistoric archaeology. The Netherlands Sociological Society (NSV) was established in 1936. Dutch cultural anthropologists and non-western sociologists participated in professional associations such as NSAV (1971 to 1993) and NVMC (1993 to 2004).[13]

POSTWAR DEVELOPMENTS

After 1945, the traditional faculty system in the Netherlands slowly eroded, to be replaced by a new system in the 1960s. In the new faculties of Social Sciences, established in 1963,[14] cultural anthropology was developed in separate sub-faculties (later departments) together with non-western sociology. I shall briefly describe these centers by their central chairs.

At the University of Amsterdam (UvA), W.F. Wertheim succeeded Schrieke on a full chair in the modern history and sociology of Indonesia (1946 to 1972), later reformulated as non-western sociology. This chair came alongside the chair in ethnology, which was held by J.J. Fahrenfort, as a successor to Steinmetz (1935 to 1955). Fahrenfort was succeeded by A.J.F. Köbben, who held the chair in cultural anthropology from 1955 until 1976. He was succeeded by J. Fabian, who taught general and African anthropology (1980 to 1999). Fabian's successor is N. Besnier, a specialist in Polynesian anthropology and linguistics (from 2005). A second chair in cultural anthropology was first held by J. Pouwer (1962 to 1966), then by J. Boissevain (1966 to 1993), and now by J. Verrips (from 1995). A personal chair in social and cultural anthropology of Europe was created for A. Blok (1986 to 2000). Wertheim's successor was O.D. van den Muijzenberg (1975 to 2004). A second chair in non-western sociology was held by J.C. Breman, who served as professor of comparative sociology from 1987 to 2001.[15] M. Rutten succeeded both Breman and van den Muijzenberg as professor of comparative sociology of Asia in 2003. In Amsterdam, three distinct traditions developed: Asia studies around the chair of Wertheim, van den Muijzenberg, and Breman; European studies around the chair of Boissevain and Blok (van Ginkel, Strating, and Verrips 2002); and, general anthropology around the chair of Köbben and Fabian. The Amsterdam Department was the first to prescribe the

study of anthropology and non-western sociology for each degree program.
The Department, at first called Antropologisch-Sociologisch Centrum (ASC,
from 1966), has now merged with western sociology in a joint Department of
Sociology and Anthropology (SOCA). The Amsterdam Department has several supernumerary professorships, including chairs in medical anthropology held by J.D.M. van der Geest, in health and health care by A.P. Hardon,
and in museum anthropology and material culture at the KIT, first held by
H. Nooy-Palm (from 1968 to 1983), now by S. Legêne. The Institute for Development Research Amsterdam (InDRA), with a strong gender input, was
directed by J.Th. Schrijvers from 1989 to 2002; it now forms part of AMIDSt
and is led by I.S.A. Baud (from 2004). Amsterdam also has a research center
"Religion and Society," directed by P.J. van der Veer from 1992 to 2004, now
integrated in SOCA. Amsterdam's main specializations have been the social
study of South and Southeast Asia, and the anthropology of Europe and the
Mediterranean (Euromed).

At the University of Leiden (UL), an Institute (now Department) of Cultural Anthropology and Sociology of Non-Western Peoples (now Development Sociology) was founded in 1955–56.[16] Its founder was G.W. Locher, a
pupil of J.P.B. de Josselin de Jong, who held a new chair in cultural anthropology and sociology of Southeast Asia from 1954 to 1956, and in general
cultural anthropology and sociology of non-western peoples (1956 to 1973).
Occupying the main chair, reformulated as a chair in cultural anthropology, in particular of Southeast Asia and Oceania, J.P.B. de Josselin de Jong
was succeeded by his nephew P.E. de Josselin de Jong, who held this chair
for thirty years (1957 to 1987). The latter taught both general anthropology
and the anthropology of Southeast Asia, renewing the tradition of structural
anthropology and fieldwork in a comparative context introduced by his predecessor in the 1920s and 1930s. Successors for the anthropology and sociology of Indonesia are R. Schefold (1989 to 2003) and P. Speyer (as of 2003). A
second anthropological chair, in the anthropology and sociology of Africa,
was established in the early 1960s and held by K.A. Busia (1960 to 1962), J.F.
Holleman (1963 to 1969), J.H.M. Beattie (1971 to 1975), A.J. Kuper (1976 to
1985), and P.L. Geschiere (1988 to 2002). The present incumbent is P. Pels
(as of 2003). A second (extraordinary) chair in applied non-western sociology was occupied by R.A.J. van Lier (1950 to 1980), but abolished in 1985
due to budget cuts. A pupil of Van Lier from Wageningen, B.F. Galjart, succeeded G.W. Locher in 1974; this chair was also discontinued, when Galjart
retired in 1998. As a result, Galjart's assistant P. Silva left in 2004, to accept
a chair in the Faculty of Arts for the study of modern Latin America.

A third field in Leiden since 1966 has been that of M&T: methods and
techniques of social research. Chairs were held by J.D. Speckmann in quan-

tative methods and techniques (1966 to 1999) and by A.A. Gerbrands for ethnography and ethnocinematographic filmmaking (1966 to 1983). The influence of this group on the quality and structure of the Leiden degree programs CA and SNWS was significant, especially through its supervision of the compulsory fieldwork periods abroad of three or more months. M&T is still important, even when after the retirement of Gerbrands and Speckmann, both chairs were discontinued due to budget cuts. An innovative research center has been VENO (women and development), later renamed VENA (women and autonomy), directed by E. Postel-Coster and J.Th. Schrijvers. Conducting policy research and action research from 1976, this center was successful in generating a great deal of research, some action oriented, and in putting women and gender issues on the development agenda. H.J.M. Claessen held a chair in political anthropology (1984 to 1994), specializing in the evolution of early states; he also taught general anthropology, filling the gap left by P.E. de Josselin de Jong's retirement in 1987.

The Leiden Department now has five supernumerary professors, including a chair in the position of women in changing societies held by E. Postel-Coster from 1986 to 1990 and by C.I. Risseeuw as of 1992; a chair in material culture of Africa held by R.M.A. Bedaux from 1997; a chair in medical anthropology and ethnobotanical knowledge systems and development, held by L.J. Slikkerveer as of 1999; and a chair in urban anthropology held by P.J.M. Nas from 2003. J.G. Oosten held two chairs, one (supernumerary) in religious anthropology at Utrecht (1998 to 2003); the other in oral traditions at Leiden (from 1997). Leiden's main specializations are the anthropology and sociology of modern Indonesia and the anthropology and sociology of Africa south of the Sahara. Its strong points have been structural anthropology; M&T, including visual anthropology, and development sociology.[17]

Utrecht University (UU) has had an Institute of Ethnology from 1914 onward and it is thus the oldest anthropological department in the Netherlands. Utrecht has never had an ethnographic museum such as those that exist in Leiden and Amsterdam. Alongside the chair in anthropology held by H.Th. Fischer (1936 to 1970), a chair in non-western sociology was established for J. Prins in 1955, but it was discontinued after his retirement in 1972. Fischer was succeeded by H.U.E. Thoden van Velzen (1971 to 1991). A third chair was established, held by J. van Baal (1960 to 1975) and by H. Hoetink (1977 to 1992). A. de Ruijter held a chair in social anthropology from 1984 to 2003, when he switched to the Utrecht School of Governance (USBO) as professor of comparative studies of the multicultural society (also serving as professor of social sciences and dean of the Faculty of Social Sciences at Tilburg since 2000). In 1993, two full professors were appointed,

A.C.G.M. Robben for anthropology and comparative sociology of Latin America, D.N.A.M. Kruijt for development issues, plus one parttime professor, G.J. Oostindie, for the anthropology and comparative sociology of the Caribbean. There was also an extraordinary chair in the anthropology of Brazil held by G.A. Banck (1987 to 2002), and there is a supernumerary chair in the anthropology and ethnohistory of the Indian peoples of Latin America held by R.A.M. van Zantwijk (1987 to 1997) and A. Ouweneel (1998 to 2003). Utrecht's main specializations are Latin America and the Caribbean. The (national) Centre for Resource Studies for Human Development (CERES), was founded at Utrecht in 1992 (see below).[18] Social anthropological studies are also conducted by F. Bovenkerk, professor of criminology since 1993 at Utrecht University.

At Wageningen Agricultural University (WAU), a readership in ethnology existed before World War II. It was first held by T.J. Bezemer (1909 to 1939) and was occupied by F.H. van Naerssen from 1946, but discontinued after the latter's departure for Sydney in 1957. A chair in empirical sociology and sociography of non-western regions was created for R.A.J. van Lier, who remained in this function from 1955 to 1980 (while keeping his part-time position as professor of applied non-western sociology in Leiden). This chair was reformulated as sociology of rural development and occupied by N. Long from 198 1to 2002. The present incumbent is L. Visser, who studied in Leiden and who is intent on building creative relationships between gamma and beta scientists.[19] Another Leiden graduate, A. Niehof, also holds a chair in Wageningen, teaching sociology of consumers and households. F. von Benda-Beckmann has been professor of law in developing countries from 1981 to 2000. Wageningen's main specialization is in tropical studies and development sociology.

At Nijmegen (RU, formerly KUN), an extraordinary chair in ethnology was established in 1948 and occupied by B.A.G. Vroklage. His premature death in 1951 resulted in a professorship for R.J. Mohr (1952 to 1970). A chair in non-western sociology was created in 1958 and occupied by Elisabeth Allard, the first woman to hold a chair in anthropology in the Netherlands. Readers included L.F. Triebels (1963 to 1980, professor from 1980 to 1986), A.A. Trouwborst (1964 to 1971, professor of social anthropology from 1971 to 1989) and G. van den Steenhoven (1963 to 1972, professor of customary law from 1972 to 1981). Allard retired in 1969 and was succeeded by G.J. Huizer as a professor with a different brief (1973 to 1998) and L.J. de Haan (1999 to 2004). Huizer became the director of the Third World Centre (DWC), established in 1973, which on its 25th anniversary was transformed into the Centre for International Development Issues (CIDIN). A. Blok succeeded Mohr as professor of cultural anthropology in 1973 (to return to

Amsterdam in 1986). A chair in economic anthropology was occupied by W.G. Wolters (1985 to 2005). F.A.M. Hüsken succeeded both Trouwborst and Blok on a joint chair in cultural and social anthropology (as of 1990). W.H.M. Jansen holds a chair in gender studies (from 1992). A.P. Borsboom was professor of anthropology of Oceania and Australia from 1998 to 2007 (Meurkens 1998; 2002). H.G.G.M. Driessen holds a supernumerary chair at the Faculty of Arts (as of 2002); H.J.M. Venbrux a part-time chair in the anthropology of religion (as of 2006). Nijmegen had an ethnological museum, which was founded in 1960, but it was closed down in 2005. It has CIDIN, now directed by R. Ruben, who also succeeded both Wolters and de Haan as professor of development studies in 2006, and a Centre for Pacific and Asian Studies (CPAS), established in 1991 and directed by Borsboom. Nijmegen's specializations are the anthropology of Oceania and the Pacific, economic anthropology, and development studies.

In Groningen (RUG), A.H.J. Prins was presented with a brief in comparative ethnology in 1951. This was changed to a readership in cultural anthropology in 1955 and a full professorship in 1972, held by Prins until 1984. The Ethnological Museum "Gerardus van der Leeuw" was founded in 1978 (and closed in 2004). The Department of Anthropology flourished but Prins was not replaced, and the department was closed down in 1985–89, due to severe budget cuts in the Netherlands (terminating Sociology at Leiden in 1987 and Dentistry at Utrecht). However, the University of Groningen now has a Centre for Development Studies (CDS) and anthropology is still being taught in the faculties of Law and Theology.[20] D.A. Papousek is reader in anthropology in the Faculty of Arts and director of the Centre for Mexican Studies. Groningen's main specialization was (and partly still is) in Arctic studies.

At the Free University (VU), Amsterdam, a chair in cultural anthropology was created in 1956 and held by L. Onvlee (1956 to 1966), H.G. Schulte Nordholt (1967 to 1978), and J. Tennekes (1978 to 2001). A chair in nonwestern sociology was founded in 1962 and occupied by J.W. Schoorl (1962 to 1988) and P. Kloos (1988 to 2000); its current incumbent is D.J. Winslow, from Canada, who has served as professor of social anthropology since 2000. A chair in religious anthropology was held by J. Blauw (from 1962), J.M. Schoffeleers (from 1975), and A.F. Droogers (1989 to 2004). A chair in nonwestern history was occupied by J. Thijs (from 1965) and H. Sutherland (1975 to 2001) (Selier 2002). G.J. Abbink holds a supernumerary chair in processes of ethnic identity formation in Africa at the VU since 2000 (succeeding W. van Binsbergen in this position). Droogers has been partly replaced by B. Meyer since 2004. The Department of Social and Cultural Anthropology of the VU has a special interest in Human Security. In 2004, two new professors were appointed in this Department: Maurice Bloch, from London, and Thomas Hylland Eriksen, from Oslo.

The VU also has a Department of Culture, Organization and Management (COM), specializing in corporate culture, organizational management, and cultural interventions. Set up in 1989 by J. Tennekes and A. Willemier Westra, this department has been very successful in attracting new students, particularly after the implementation of the new Bachelor/Master model (BaMa) in September 2002. W.C.J. Koot served as a professor at COM (1994 to 2003) and was succeeded by H. Dahles (from 2003) and M.B. Veenswijk (as of 2004).

The Institute of Social Studies (ISS), founded in The Hague in 1952, has a strong interest in development studies and promotes an interdisciplinary approach. H.Th. Chabot served there as professor of social studies from 1955 to 1970. Several professors teach development studies at the ISS. The Erasmus University of Rotterdam (EUR) had a chair in comparative sociology including development sociology, held by J.C. Breman from 1976 to 1987. Rotterdam has a chair in non-western history, occupied by P.L. Geschiere from 1985 to 1988 and by A. van Stipriaan until 2004. K. von Benda-Beckmann has been professor of legal anthropology from 1998 to 2006. W. van Binsbergen holds a supernumerary chair in intercultural philosophy at Rotterdam since 1999. Tilburg University (UvT) has a Department of Intercultural Communication in the Faculty of Arts, where W.A.R. Shadid (from Leiden) has held a chair in intercultural communication from 1994. At Tilburg, A. de Ruijter is setting up a Faculty of Social Sciences, beginning in 2000. R.S. Gowricharn holds a chair in social cohesion and multicultural society in transnational perspective since 2001.

These are only broad outlines of the postwar development of anthropology and non-western sociology in the Netherlands. The chairs mentioned functioned as centers of gravity for a small, sometimes expanding, circle of lecturers, researchers, and student-assistants working on the subjects mentioned. Most of the chair holders have been men, but since the 1990s, about a dozen female anthropologists have been appointed to professorships.[21]

In the 1950s and 1960s, most former colonies obtained a new status as independent nations. These were decades of adaptation in which departments of cultural anthropology and non-western sociology were established at most Dutch universities. During the 1970s, student numbers increased and the subject firmly established itself within Dutch academia. The final quarter of the twentieth century saw a flourishing of studies with a variety of innovations in both fields: visual anthropology (Leiden, UvA); gender studies at all universities (especially in Leiden); the anthropology of Europe and the Mediterranean (UvA, Nijmegen); the anthropology of Oceania (Nijmegen, Leiden); Latin American studies (Leiden, Utrecht); ethnic and migrant studies (Utrecht, UvA, Tilburg); medical anthropology (Leiden, UvA); urban anthropology (VU, Leiden); economic anthropology (Nijmegen, Leiden); political anthropology (VU, Leiden); and religious anthropology (VU, Leiden). At almost all universities and at the ISS (The Hague), development studies came to the fore.

From 1974, shrinking state budgets for education led to tightening conditions in the universities, budget cuts and a reorganization of departments. A new audit culture, with management tools for planning and controlling academic production, was imported from the USA. To face this challenge, from 1975 onward, a national committee compiled several disciplinal plans for cooperation between departments and for a division of specializations; these efforts served well to protect the interests of the subject until the mid 1990s (Claessen and Schoorl 2002). But these disciplinal plans could not prevent the six anthropology departments from being severely downsized during the 1980s, while a seventh at Groningen University was closed in 1989.[22]

PRESENT DUTCH ANTHROPOLOGY AND DUTCH SOCIETY

The Netherlands now has fourteen universities, six of which have an anthropology department, namely Leiden (UL), Amsterdam (UvA and VU), Utrecht (UU), Nijmegen (RU), and the rural sociology department at Wageningen (WAU). Anthropology is strong in Leiden, Amsterdam, both at the VU and the UvA, in Utrecht, and in Nijmegen. Development studies play a role in Amsterdam (UvA), Nijmegen, Leiden, Utrecht, Amsterdam VU, and especially at the ISS in The Hague and in Wageningen.

Despite the long and varied course of its history, and rising student numbers, prospects for sufficient state funding for Dutch anthropology and development studies are not good. In spite of improving economic conditions, especially during the late 1990s, investments in anthropology remain poor. Budgetary constraints are met by focusing resources in broad multidisciplinary research schemes. The VU is now probably the most prominent university for anthropology in the Netherlands. As a confessional university, it has sufficient funds to invest in new, young, and foreign professors in the department of social and cultural anthropology. While the VU invests in new professors and departments, other universities, depending on the national budget, have endured economy measures for 30 years. In Leiden, socio-cultural anthropology has become smaller and smaller (from forty-five staff members, including eight full professors in 1979, to fifteen staff members, including two full and five supernumerary professors in 2006); nevertheless, its teaching programme attracts many students (114 in 2004–05, 106 in 2005–6) and in 2004 was chosen by Dutch students as the best of all anthropology programmes in the Netherlands for the third time in succession.[23]

During the 1980s, the terminology shifted again and most non-western sociologists now prefer to be called anthropologists. Earlier, non-western sociologists had been confident about an improvement of socio-economic conditions in the Third World; from the mid 1980s, increased scepticism about the effectiveness of development cooperation in Asia and Africa led to the abandonment of the modernization theory. Debates on development were no longer dominated by non-western sociologists, but by economists. In addition, Dutch development aid was linked to bilateral trade at the level of the Ministry. Moreover, from the 1970s, anthropologists moved into areas earlier dealt with by non-western sociologists. This reflected general concerns about development issues, growing inequality, especially of women in the South, and about environmental problems (Postel-Coster and van Santen 2002). The earlier Dutch interest in applied anthropology was now seen as a contribution to development studies in general.

The anthropologists André Köbben, Peter Kloos, and Frank Bovenkerk, and the non-western sociologists Wim Wertheim, Jan Breman, and Paul Hoebink have probably been the most outspoken in public debate. Kloos was the author of a well-known handbook on cultural anthropology (six editions; Kloos 1972; 1984; see also Kooiman et al. 2002). Together with Henri Claessen, Kloos was one of the greatest popularizers of anthropology in the Netherlands (Kloos and Claessen 1975; 1981; 1991).[24] At present, four anthropologists are members of the Royal Dutch Academy of Sciences (KNAW) in Amsterdam, namely André Köbben, Bonno Thoden van Velzen, Peter Geschiere, and Peter van der Veer; of these only the last is still active (the other three are considered to be "retired members"). Köbben (born in 1925) is the *éminence grise* of Dutch anthropology and probably the best known of all living anthropologists in the Netherlands; he is certainly the most prolific. Köbben was influential through his work on minorities and migrants, both as the former director of the Centre for the Study of Social Conflicts and Tensions (COMT) in Leiden (1976 to 1990) and as a former chairman of the advisory committee on cultural minorities in the Netherlands (ACOM).[25]

Despite its long history, anthropology is not a well-known subject in the Netherlands. To most Dutch citizens its existence will be unfamiliar; the proverbial man-in-the-street does not know what anthropology is, let alone understand the subject. Although part of anthropology's terminology has entered Dutch vocabulary, the term *antropologie* itself has to be explained; the earlier name *volkenkunde* is still better known, especially through the older names of the ethnographic museums. The main reasons for this lack of familiarity are threefold: anthropology is not taught in high schools, most Dutch anthropologists conduct work outside Europe, and there are few anthropologists who appear in the Dutch media.

While in the 1970s and 1980s anthropologists regularly took part in public debates, this is not often the case now. Development cooperation and the Third World are no longer appealing issues for Dutch television or the press. Dutch newspapers pay a fair amount of attention to anthropological subjects, but display a preference for exotic items. The anthropologist-essayist Gerrit Jan Zwier partly fills this need. Some newspaper reporters such as Sjoerd de Jong and Dirk Vlasblom graduated in anthropology and report on subjects that are related to anthropology, but neither of them is ever introduced as an anthropologist. Sjaak van der Geest, a medical anthropologist from Amsterdam, reviews anthropological books for the Dutch newspaper *de Volkskrant*, but his occupation is never mentioned.

The label anthropology does not seem to have much significance in the Dutch media. Anthropologists are either seen as people who measure skulls, or as scholars taking an interest in people far away. Development workers are often seen as overpaid consultants. The problem seems to be that editors of news programs and newspapers know what anthropology is, having learned about it at university, but assume that the Dutch public does not know much about it. Another reason why Dutch anthropologists and non-western sociologists seldom write for newspapers is that, from 1989, there has been a new system for evaluating publications in which Dutch language publications, especially those in popular media, no longer receive much credit. In the context of the sought after internationalization of Dutch academia, English language publications are valued more highly.

As a consequence, anthropology does not play a dominant role in Dutch society at large. Its role is limited to the academic sectors of Dutch society, to the universities, research institutes, and ethnographic museums. Anthropologists and development sociologists do play a more direct role in development aid organizations, such as NGO's, advisory institutions, ministries, and international organizations, but this work is less visible to the general public.

CONCLUDING REMARKS

Anthropology is a historically well-established study of culture and society that has developed in the Netherlands and its overseas colonies since the 1770s. Its institutionalization took place from the 1830s onward. In the colonial period, regional anthropology developed as the ethnographic study of Indonesia, Surinam, and the Antilles. During the 1920s and 1930s, general anthropology was formulated as comparative ethnology in Leiden, Amsterdam and Utrecht. From the 1950s, non-western social sciences, including development studies, prospered in the Netherlands. Since 1963, cultural anthropology and non-western sociology were seen as belonging to the social sciences and these studies were predominantly pursued in tropical regions of Asia, Latin America, and Africa. The anthropology of Europe and the Mediterranean developed from the late 1960s onward, followed by gender studies and minority and conflict studies in the 1970s and 1980s. Immigrant studies and Islam studies have come to the fore since the 1990s. Since 2001, the integration of cultural or religious minorities and the study of multiculturalism have been high on the research agenda.

Dutch anthropological research has focused predominantly on the non-western world. As a result, Dutch anthropology is mostly regionally organized. Studies on Asia, Africa, and Latin America make up the large majority. Research in Australia and the Pacific, Japan and the Arctic has been conducted as well. From the 1960s, the anthropology of Europe was set up by Boissevain, Blok, Verrips, and others in Amsterdam and Nijmegen. Minorities and migration have been studied by Köbben, Shadid, Bovenkerk, Penninx, de Ruijter, and others in Leiden, Amsterdam, Utrecht, and Tilburg. Despite these recent innovations, the predominant orientation remains overseas. As a consequence, philosophers and sociologists, rather than anthropologists, dominate current debates on multiculturalism in Europe.

Of central concern in this context is the persistence of a perceived opposition between Here and There, Us and Them, We and The Other. The colonial idea that the West is in the West and that the Non-West is not in the West can no longer be taken for granted. The fundamental contribution of the historical sociology promoted by Wim Wertheim was to show that these worlds are interconnected and interdependent.

The influence of Dutch socio-cultural anthropology on Dutch society is largely indirect. Its impact on policy is more substantial, especially on international development through gender research, empowerment, and development studies. Applied anthropology has been and still is a strong component of Dutch anthropology and non-western sociology. Many former students are working in the field of international development cooperation, both abroad and at home. Development cooperation is one of the main tasks of the Dutch Ministry of Foreign Affairs. The Netherlands spends four billion euros a year on tackling global poverty. However, most Dutch anthropologists conduct research overseas. As a consequence, they have more experience in studying the world beyond Europe than in studying multiculturalism at home. Since the 1970s and especially the 1990s, this situation has been partly remedied by research conducted on cultural and religious minorities in the Netherlands and in Europe at large (Vermeulen and Penninx 2000; Lucassen and de Ruijter 2002; Vermeulen and Slijper 2003).

Topics of special interest are gender studies, medical anthropology and reproductive health, minorities and migrant studies, multiculturalism, and development studies. Less fundable are such fields as museum anthropology, visual anthropology, history of anthropology, and general anthropology–despite continuous interest in these subjects.

Dutch anthropology is a rich field of studies of culture and society in the world beyond Europe and in Europe, with hundreds of participants, today and for the past two centuries. It has a long history and great potential for the future. Dutch anthropology is well equipped to study cultural diversity, multicultural behaviour, and group dynamics in contemporary societies in the western and the non-western world–both in the North and in the South. The need for anthropologists will probably increase, both in teaching and research. The current situation is stable, but there are many challenges. One is the dual character of Dutch socio-cultural anthropology, which for the past fifty years has expressed itself in the fundamental research of fieldwork-based anthropology and the applied research of development-oriented sociology. These sides are highly competitive in situations of under-funding. Since 1974, the Netherlands has been reducing funds for higher education and research in anthropology. As a percentage of its gross national product, the Dutch pay 1.76 percent for research, lower than European Union countries generally (1.92 percent) and much lower than the USA (2.67).[26] Dutch policy makers do not yet seem to sufficiently acknowledge the societal and scholarly importance of anthropology and continue to economize on education and research. The study of transnational and multicultural society is not yet taken seriously enough. This is only one of the challenges for Dutch anthropologists and development sociologists.

NOTES

1. Many smaller studies exist on the history of anthropology in the Netherlands, most of them in Dutch. Most of these are listed in Vermeulen and Kommers eds. *Tales from Academia: History of Anthropology in The Netherlands,* 2 parts, (Nijmegen/Saarbrücken 2002). This book presents 37 studies on aspects of the history of this field of studies from 1770 to 2000, written in English. The present article

reworks themes from the introduction to this book and summarizes chapters dealing with the history of anthropology departments, ethnographic museums, and anthropological specializations in the Netherlands. I am grateful to Jan Abbink, Jan van Bremen, Hans Claessen, Arie de Groot, Frans Hüsken, Roy Jordaan, André Köbben, Otto van den Muijzenberg, Peter Nas, Anke Niehof, Peter Pels, Els Postel-Coster, Jan Pouwer, Rob de Ridder, Carla Risseeuw, Ton Robben, Henk van Rinsum, Stuart Robson, Arie de Ruijter, Loes Schenk-Sandbergen, Pim Schoorl, Joke Schrijvers, Wasif Shadid, Jojada Verrips, Leontine Visser, Jaap Timmer, and Albert Trouwborst for comments on and suggestions for this article. An earlier version of this essay has appeared in Russian translation in *Etnograficheskoe Obozrenie* no. 2-2005: 75–95.

2. For earlier overviews, see van Eerde (1923); Schrieke (1948); Bovenkerk et al. (1978); Hovens and Triebels (1988).

3. The relation between anthropology and Oriental studies remained strong until about 1960, see Drewes (1957); Uhlenbeck (1957); de Josselin de Jong (1960).

4. Adat law (*adatrecht*) was transformed into the anthropology of law during the 1960s and 1970s. On the history of legal anthropology in the Netherlands, see Franz von Benda-Beckmann and Keebet von Benda-Beckmann (2002); Burns (2004).

5. Chairs in folklore studies (*volkskunde*) existed at several Dutch universities, now only at the universities of Amsterdam and Groningen. On the history of Dutch *volkskunde,* see Dekker (2000, 2002). G.W.J. Rooijakkers holds a chair for Dutch Ethnology (*Nederlandse etnologie*) at the University of Amsterdam since 2000.

6. Chairs in physical anthropology existed at the Universities of Leiden, Groningen, Utrecht, and Amsterdam, but most of them were abolished during the 1970s and 1980s. On physical anthropology, see Roede (2002); van Duuren (2007). G.J.R. Maat was appointed professor of anatomy and physical anthropology at the University of Leiden in 2003.

7. Biographies of sixteen Dutch anthropologists appeared in Winters (1991), including H.F.C. ten Kate, J.H.F. Kohlbrugge, L. Serrurier, Ph.F. von Siebold, P.J. Veth (written by P.Th.F.M. Hovens); Jan van Baal, Johannes Jacobus Fahrenfort, Henri Théodore Fischer, Gerrit Jan Held, Jan Petrus Benjamin de Josselin de Jong, Freerk Christiaans Kamma, Albertus Christiaan Kruyt, Willem Huibert Rassers, Sebald Rudolph Steinmetz, Bernardus Andreus Gregorius Vroklage S.V.D., George Alexander Wilken (written by J.J. de Wolf and S.R. Jaarsma).

8. On colonial civil service training courses, see Warmenhoven (1977); de Josselin de Jong and Vermeulen (1989); Fasseur (1993). Fasseur discusses the history of the Indology courses, but neglects the part played by anthropology in these courses; aspects of this relationship have been covered in de Josselin de Jong and Vermeulen (1989: 282–286, 294–295, 311–312).

9. Comparable chairs were established in Oxford, New York and Berlin. E.B. Tylor was Reader in Anthropology at Oxford from 1884, being promoted to professor in 1896. Franz Boas was Professor of Anthropology in New York from

1899. Adolf Bastian was associated with the University of Berlin from 1869 and extraordinary Professor of Ethnology during 1871–75, but this was not a structural chair and he had no direct successors.

10. On geography in Amsterdam, see Knippenberg and van Schendelen (2002); on geography in Utrecht, see de Pater et al. (1999).

11. On the origins of non-western sociology, see Kloos (1988, 1989); Vermeulen (2002b: 111–112).

12. On applied anthropology and non-western sociology, see Held (1953); Schoorl (1974); Jongmans (1976); de la Rive Box and Papousek (1981); Hüsken et al. 1984; Kloos (1990-1991).

13. For a history of organized anthropology in the Netherlands, see de Wolf (1998). Dutch anthropologists and development sociologists are now organized in ABV (Antropologische Beroepsvereniging CA/SNWS) and LOVA (Netherlands Association of Gender and Anthropology, founded in 1979). Some participate in the Nedworc Association, an organization of independent consultants working in the fields of development cooperation, international cooperation, and relief and rehabilitation, founded in 1986.

14. At the University of Amsterdam a Faculty of Political and Social Studies (PSF) was established as early as 1948; see Gevers (1998).

15. On cultural anthropology and non-western sociology at the University of Amsterdam, see the chapters by André Köbben, Wim Wertheim, Jan Breman, Loes Schenk-Sandbergen, and Peter Pels in *Tales from Academia* (2002). Interviews with seven retired anthropology professors from the University of Amsterdam and the Free University Amsterdam were published in the special issue "Dutch Masters" of *Etnofoor* 18(2), 2005.

16. On cultural anthropology and non-western sociology at the University of Leiden, see the chapters by Reimar Schefold, Han Vermeulen, and Coen Holtzappel in *Tales from Academia* (2002).

17. On the history of visual anthropology in the Netherlands, see Nijland (2002). On visual ethnography, see Postma and Crawford (2006).

18. On cultural anthropology at Utrecht, see Jan de Wolf (2002; 2005).

19. On rural sociology at Wageningen, see Jan den Ouden (2002).

20. On cultural anthropology at Groningen, see Papousek (1988); Papousek and Kuiper (2002). On the museum at Groningen, see Arnoldus-Schröder (1998; 2002).

21. On feminist anthropology and gender studies in the Netherlands, see Postel-Coster and van Santen (2002).

22. On anthropological studies during the 1980s, see Kloos (1991). On the demise of cultural anthropology at Groningen, see Papousek and Kuiper (2002).

23. *Elsevier,* October 2004: 19, 89. On the situation in Leiden, see Vermeulen (2002b).

24. Kloos and Claessen edited three widely distributed volumes (1975; 1981; 1991) that helped to make Dutch socio-cultural anthropology better known abroad.

25. Köbben's current interest is in the anthropology of science (see Köbben 2003).

26. For these percentages, see Maarten Huygen, "De Nederlandse wetenschap wordt tot slaaf gemaakt van de politiek," *NRC Handelsblad,* 2 June 2007.

REFERENCES

Akveld, Leo, and Els M. Jacobs, eds. 2002. *De kleurrijke wereld van de VOC.* Bussum/ Amsterdam: Thoth with Rijksmuseum, Amsterdam.

Arnoldus-Schröder, Victorine, ed. 1998 *The Power of Joy/The Collection van Baaren.* Groningen: Volkenkundig Museum "Gerardus van der Leeuw."

Arnoldus-Schröder, Victorine. 2002. "Browsing at the Neighbours: History of the Ethnological Museum Gerardus van der Leeuw." In Han Vermeulen and Jean Kommers, eds. *Tales from Academia: History of Anthropology in The Netherlands,* part 2, pp. 979–94. Nijmegen/Saarbrücken.

Benda-Beckmann, Franz von, and Keebet von Benda-Beckmann. 2002. "Anthropology of Law and the Study of Folk Law in the Netherlands after 1950." In Vermeulen and Kommers, eds., *Tales from Academia,* part 2, pp. 695–731.

Blussé, Leonard. 1989 *Tribuut aan China: Vier eeuwen Nederlands-Chinese betrekkingen.* Amsterdam: Otto Cramwinckel.

Blussé, Leonard, Willem Remmelink, and Ivo Smits, eds. 2000. *Bewogen betrekkingen: 400 jaar Nederland-Japan.* [*Bridging the Divide, 1600–2000: 400 Years The Netherlands-Japan.* Leiden/ Hilversum; *Nichiran koryu 400 nen no rekishi to tenbo*]. Hilversum,/ Leiden: Teleac/NOT.

Bork-Feltkamp, Adèle J. van. 1938 *Anthropological Research in the Netherlands: Historical Survey at the Request of the Committee for the Physical-Anthropological Investigation of the Dutch Population.* Verhandelingen der Koninklijke Nederlandsche Akademie van Wetenschappen, Afdeeling Natuurkunde, tweede sectie, deel 37, no. 3. Amsterdam.

——. 1948. "Anthropology." In B.J.O. Schrieke, ed. *Report of the Scientific Work done in the Netherlands on behalf of the Dutch Overseas Territories during the period between approximately 1918 and 1943,* pp. 26–30. Amsterdam: Noord-Hollandsche Uitgevers-Maatschappij.

——. 1955. "The Netherlands and Belgium: An Anthropological Review for 1952–1954." In William L. Thomas, Jr., ed. *Yearbook of Anthropology,* pp. 541–61 . New York: Wenner-Gren Foundation for Anthropological Research.

Bovenkerk, Frank, H.J.M. Claessen, B. van Heerikhuizen, A.J.F. Köbben, and Nico Wilterdink, eds. 1978. *Toen en Thans: De sociale wetenschappen in de jaren dertig en nu.* Baarn: Ambo.

Burns, Peter. 2004. *The Leiden Legacy: Concepts of Law in Indonesia.* Leiden: KITLV Press.

Claessen, H.J.M., and J.W. Schoorl. 2002. "Protected by Paper; Or How Dutch Anthropology was Quite Effectively Protected for Nearly Thirty Years by a Series of Consecutive Memoranda." In Vermeulen and Kommers, eds. *Tales from Academia,* part 1, pp. 569–98.

Dekker, Ton. 2000. "Ideologie en volkscultuur ontkoppeld: Een geschiedenis van de Nederlandse volkskunde." In Ton Dekker, Herman Roodenburg, and Gerard Rooijakkers, eds., *Volkscultuur: een inleiding in de Nederlandse etnologie,* pp. 13–65. Nijmegen: SUN.

———. 2002. *De Nederlandse volkskunde: De verwetenschappelijking van een emotionele belang-stelling.* Amsterdam: Uitgeverij Aksant.

Dougherty, Frank W.P. 1995. "Missing Link, Chain of Being, Ape and Man in the Enlightenment: The Argument from the Naturalists." In Raymond Corbey and Bert Theunissen, eds., *Ape, Man, Apeman: Changing Views since 1600,* pp. 63–70. Leiden : Department of Prehistory.

———. 1996. *Gesammelte Aufsätze zu Themen der klassischen Periode der Naturgeschichte/Collected Essays on Themes from the Classical Period of Natural History.* Göttingen: Norbert Klatt Verlag.

Drewes, G.W.J. 1957 "Oriental Studies in the Netherlands: An Historical Survey." *Higher Education and Research in The Netherlands* 1, 4: 3–13.

Duuren, David van, et al. 2007 *Physical Anthropology Reconsidered: Human Remains at the Tropenmuseum.* Amsterdam: KIT Publishers.

Eerde, J.C. van. 1923. "A Review of Ethnological Investigations." In *The History and Present State of Scientific Research in the Dutch East Indies* part III, pp. 3–30. Amsterdam: De Bussy, Koninklijke Akademie van Wetenschappen, Internationale Circumpacifische Onderzoekcommissie (ICO-Commissie),

Ellen, Roy F. 1976. "The Development of Anthropology and Colonial Policy in the Netherlands: 1800–1960." *Journal of the History of the Behavioral Sciences* 12, 4: 303–24.

Ensel, Remco. 1994. "Tussen woestheid en beschaving: Martinus Stuart als zedekundige en verlicht etnoloog." *Antropologische Verkenningen* 13, 3: 36–52.

———. 2002. "The Death of James Cook as a Cultural Encounter Gone Astray: Morality and Ethnology in Dutch Enlightenment Writings." In Vermeulen and Kommers, eds. *Tales from Academia,* part 2, pp. 601–26.

Fasseur, Cees. 1993. *De Indologen: Ambtenaren voor de Oost 1825–1950.* Amsterdam: Bert Bakker.

Gevers, Anne, ed. 1998. *Uit de Zevende: Vijftig jaar politieke en sociaal-culturele wetenschappen aan de Universiteit van Amsterdam.* Amsterdam: Het Spinhuis.

Ginkel, Rob van, Alex Strating, and Jojada Verrips. 2002. "Trials and Tribulations of the Euromed Tribe: A History of Anthropology of Europe and the Mediterranean Area in Amsterdam." In Vermeulen and Kommers eds. *Tales from Academia,* part 1, pp. 341–63.

Goor, Jur van.1994. *De Nederlandse koloniën: Geschiedenis van de Nederlandse expansie, 1600–1975.* 's-Gravenhage: SDU.

Heeren, Henk J. 1993. *Van sociografie tot sociologie: De Amsterdamse sociografische school en haar betekenis voor de Nederlandse sociologie.* Utrecht: Faculteit der Sociale Wetenschappen.

———. 1998 *Sociografie studeren in Amsterdam: terugblik op de jaren 1940–1948.* Utrecht, privately printed.

Heinemeijer, Willem F. 1998. "H.D. de Vries Reilingh: De sociografie in de PSF" in Johan Goudsblom, Piet de Rooy and J. Wieten eds. *In de Zevende: De eerste lichting hoogleraren aan de politiek-sociale faculteit te Amsterdam,* pp. 152–166. Amsterdam: Het Spinhuis.

———. 2002. "A Short History of Anthropology at Amsterdam: Steinmetz and his Students." In Vermeulen and Kommers eds. *Tales from Academia,* part 1, pp. 227–43.

Held, Gerrit Jan. 1953. "Applied Anthropology in Government: The Netherlands." In A.L. Kroeber, ed., *Anthropology Today: An Encyclopedic Inventory*, pp. 866–879. Chicago: University of Chicago Press.

Hovens, Pieter, and Leo F. Triebels, eds. 1988. *Historische ontwikkelingen in de Neder-landse antropologie*, special issue *Antropologische Verkenningen* 7, 1–2.

Hüsken, Frans, Dirk Kruijt, and Philip Quarles van Ufford eds. 1984. *Trends en tradi-ties in de ontwikkelingssociologie.* Muiderberg: Dick Coutinho.

Jong, Joop de. 1998. *De waaier van het fortuin: De geschiedenis van de Nederlanders in Azië en de Indonesische archipel, 1595–1950.* 's-Gravenhage: SDU.

Jongmans, D.G. 1976. "Wat stelt Nederland voor op het terrein van de toegepaste antropologie?" In Peter Kloos ed. *Culturele antropologie: Portret van een wetenschap*, pp. 35–48. Meppel: Boom/Amsterdam: Intermediair.

Josselin de Jong, P.E. de. 1960. "Cultural Anthropology in The Netherlands." *Higher Education and Research in The Netherlands* 4, 4: 13–26.

Josselin de Jong, P.E. de, and H.F. Vermeulen. 1989. "Cultural Anthropology at Leiden University: From Encyclopedism to Structuralism." In W. Otterspeer, ed,. *Leiden Oriental Connections, 1850–1940*, pp. 280–316. Leiden: Brill.

Kloos, Peter. 1972. *Culturele antropologie: Een inleiding.* Assen: Van Gorcum.

———. 1984. *Antropologie als wetenschap.* Muiderberg: Dick Coutinho.

———. 1988. "Het ontstaan van een discipline: De sociologie der niet-westerse volken." *Antropologische Verkenningen* 7, 1–2: 123–46

———. 1989. "The Sociology of Non-Western Societies: The Origins of a Discipline." *The Netherlands' Journal of Social Sciences* 25, 1: 40–50.

———. 1990–91. "Development Research in the Netherlands: Origins and Character-istics." *Netherlands Review of Development Studies* 3: 133–43.

———. 1991. "Anthropology in the Netherlands: The 1980s and Beyond." In Peter Kloos and H.J.M. Claessen, eds., *Contemporary Anthropology in the Netherlands: The Use of Anthropological Ideas*, pp. 1–29. Amsterdam: VU Uitgeverij.

Kloos, Peter, ed. 1976. *Culturele antropologie: Portret van een wetenschap.* Meppel: Boom/Amsterdam: Intermediair.

Kloos, Peter, and H.J.M. Claessen, eds. 1975. *Current Anthropology in the Netherlands.* Rotterdam: Anthropological Branch of the Netherlands Sociological and An-tropological Society (Ministerie van Onderwijs en Wetenschappen). Appendix: Anthropological Institutions in the Netherlands, pp. 181-84.

———. 1981. *Current Issues in Anthropology: The Netherlands.* Rotterdam: Anthropological Branch of the Netherlands Sociological and Anthropological Society (Afdeling CA/SNWV, Nederlandse Sociologische en Antropologische Vereniging). Ap-pendix: Anthropological Institutions in the Netherlands, pp. 244–49.

———. 1991. *Contemporary Anthropology in the Netherlands: The Use of Anthropological Ideas.* Amsterdam Amsterdam: VU Uitgeverij.

Knippenberg, Hans, and Marijke van Schendelen, eds. 2002. *Alles heeft zijn plaats: 125 jaar geografie en planologie aan de Universiteit van Amsterdam, 1877–2002.* Am-sterdam: Aksant.

Köbben, André J.F. 1992. "Sebald Rudolf Steinmetz (1862–1940): Een hartstochtelijk geleerde" in J.C.H. Blom et al. eds. *Een brandpunt van geleerdheid in de hoofdstad: de Universiteit van Amsterdam rond 1900 in vijftien portretten*, pp. 313–40. Hilversum/ Amsterdam: Verloren/Amsterdam University Press.

———. 2002. "J.J. Fahrenfort (1885–1975): Schoolmaster and Scholar." In Vermeulen and Kommers, eds., *Tales from Academia*, part 1, pp. 245–65.

———. 2003. *Het gevecht met de Engel: Over verheffende en minder verheffende aspecten van het wetenschapsbedrijf.* Amsterdam: Mets & Schilt.

Kooiman, Dick, et al,. eds. 2002. *Conflict in a Globalising World: Studies in Honour of Peter Kloos.* Assen: Van Gorcum.

Kuitenbrouwer, Maarten. 2001. *Tussen oriëntalisme en wetenschap: Het Koninklijk Instituut voor Taal-, Land- en Volkenkunde in historisch verband, 1851–2001.* Leiden: KITLV Uitgeverij.

Lucassen, Jan, and Arie de Ruijter, eds. 2002. *Nederland multicultureel en pluriform? Een aantal conceptuele studies.* Amsterdam: Aksant.

Meurkens, Peter C.G. 1998. *Vragen omtrent de mensheid: Culturele antropologie in Nijmegen (1948–1998).* Aalten: Fagus.

———. 2002. "Between Nostalgia for the Past and Ethical Enthusiasm: Half a Century of Anthropology in Nijmegen, 1948–1998." In Vermeulen and Kommers, eds., *Tales from Academia*, part 1, pp. 493–513.

Meijer, Miriam Claude. 1999. *Race and Aesthetics in the Anthropology of Petrus Camper (1722–1789).* Amsterdam and Atlanta: Rodopi.

———. 2004. "The Century of the Orangutan." *XVIII New Perspectives on the Eighteenth Century* 1, 1: 62–78.

Moor, J.A. de, and Paul G.E.I.J. van der Velde, eds. 1992–97. *De werken van Jacob Haafner.* 3 vols. Zutphen: Walburg Pers.

Nijland, Dirk J. 2002. "A History of Ethnographic Film, Video and Multimedia in the Netherlands." In Vermeulen and Kommers, eds., *Tales from Academia*, part 2, pp. 893–935.

Ouden, Jan den. 2002. "Development Sociology and Anthropology at Wageningen University, 1898–2002." In Vermeulen and Kommers, eds., *Tales from Academia*, part 1, pp. 393–419.

Papousek, Dick A. 1988. "Terug naar af: Antropologie in Groningen." In P. Hovens and L.F. Triebels, eds., *Historische ontwikkelingen in de Nederlandse antropologie*, special issue of *Antropologische Verkenningen* 7, 1–2: 147–63.

Papousek, Dick A., and Yme Kuiper. 2002. "A Small Institute in a Wicked World: Cultural Anthropology at the University of Groningen, 1951–1989." In Vermeulen and Kommers, eds., *Tales from Academia*, part 1, pp. 515–46.

Pater, Ben de, with M.W. Heslinga, et al. 1999. *Een tempel der kaarten: Negentig jaar geografiebeoefening aan de Universiteit Utrecht.* Utrecht: Faculteit Ruimtelijke Wetenschappen.

Postel-Coster, Els, and José van Santen. 2002. "Feminist Anthropology in The Netherlands: Autonomy and Integration." In Vermeulen and Kommers, eds., *Tales from Academia*, part 2, pp. 867–92.

Postma, Metje, and Peter I. Crawford, eds. 2006. *Reflecting Visual Ethnography: Using the Camera in Anthropological Research.* Leiden and Højberg: CNWS Publications.

Rive Box, Louk de la, and Dick Papousek, eds. 1981. *Van theorie tot toepassing in de ontwikkelingssociologie: Sociologen en antropologen over ontwikkelingsproblemen.* Special issue *Mens en Maatschappij* 56.

Roede, Machteld. 2002. "A History of Physical Anthropology in The Netherlands." In Vermeulen and Kommers, eds., *Tales from Academia,* part 2, pp. 1033–94.

Ross, Robert. 1999 *A Concise History of South Africa.* Cambridge: Cambridge University Press.

——. 2001 *Zuid-Afrika: Een geschiedenis.* Amsterdam: De Arbeiderspers.

Selier, Frits. 2002. "The Search for Limitation: Aspects of Forty Years of CA/SNWS at the Free University, Amsterdam." In Vermeulen and Kommers, eds., *Tales from Academia,* part 1, pp. 547–67.

Schoorl, J.W. 1974. *Sociologie der modernizering: Een inleiding in de sociologie der niet-westerse volken.* Deventer: Van Loghum Slaterus.

Schrieke, B.J.O., ed. 1948. *Report of the Scientific Work done in the Nederlands on behalf of the Dutch Overseas Territories during the period between approximately 1918 and 1943.* Amsterdam: Noord-Hollandsche Uitgevers-Maatschappij.

Uhlenbeck, E.M. 1957. "Selected Bibliography of Oriental Studies." *Higher Education and Research in The Netherlands* 1, 4: 38–42.

Velde, Paul G.E.I.J. van der. 2000 *Een Indische liefde: P.J. Veth (1814–1895) en de inburgering van Nederlands-Indië.* Ph.D. thesis, University of Leiden. Amsterdam: Uitgeverij Balans.

——. 2002 "The Indonesia and Africa Specialist P.J. Veth (1814–1895): Founder of the First Chair of Anthropology in the Netherlands (1877)." In Vermeulen and Kommers, eds., *Tales from Academia,* part 2, pp. 647–72.

——. 2006 *A Lifelong Passion: P.J. Veth (1814–1895) and the Dutch East Indies.* Leiden: KITLV Press.

Vermeulen, Han, and Jean Kommers, eds. 2002. *Tales from Academia: History of Anthropology in The Netherlands.* 2 parts. Nijmegen: NICCOS/Saarbrücken: Verlag für Entwicklungspolitik.

Vermeulen, Han F. 1995. "Origins and Institutionalization of Ethnography and Ethnology in Europe and the USA, 1771–1845." In Han F. Vermeulen and Arturo Alvarez Roldán, eds., *Fieldwork and Footnotes: Studies in the History of European Anthropology,* pp. 39–59. London and New York: Routledge.

——. 1996. "Enlightenment Anthropology." In Alan Barnard and Jonathan Spencer, eds., *Encyclopedia of Social and Cultural Anthropology,* pp. 183–185. London and New York: Routledge.

——. 1999. "Anthropology in Colonial Contexts: The Second Kamchatka Expedition (1733–1743) and the Danish-German Arabia Expedition (1761–1767)." In Jan van Bremen and Akitoshi Shimizu, eds., *Anthropology and Colonialism in Asia and Oceania,* pp. 13–39. Richmond: Curzon Pres.

——. 2002a. "Ethnographie und Ethnologie in Mittel- und Osteuropa: Völker-Beschreibung und Völkerkunde in Russland, Deutschland und Österreich (1740–

1845)." In Erich Donnert, ed., *Europa in der Frühen Neuzeit: Festschrift für Günter Mühlpfordt,* Band 6, pp. 397–409. Cologne: Böhlau.

——. 2002b. "Contingency and Continuity: Anthropology and Other Non-Western Studies in Leiden, 1922–2002." In Vermeulen and Kommers, eds., *Tales from Academia,* part 1, pp. 95–182.

——. 2006. "The German Invention of *Völkerkunde*: Ethnological Discourse in Europe and Asia, 1740–1798." In Sara Eigen and Mark Larrimore, eds., *The German Invention of Race,* pp. 123–45. Albany, NY: State University of New York Press.

Vermeulen, Hans, and Rinus Penninx, eds. 2000. *Immigrant Integration: The Dutch Case.* Amsterdam: Het Spinhuis.

Vermeulen, Hans and Boris Slijper eds. 2003. *Multiculturalisme in Canada, Australië en de Verenigde Staten: Ideologie en beleid, 1950–2000.* Amsterdam: Aksant.

Warmenhoven, A.J.J. 1977. "De opleiding van Nederlandse bestuursambtenaren in Indonesië" in S.L. van der Wal ed. *Besturen overzee: herinneringen van oud-ambtenaren bij het binnenlands bestuur in Nederlandsch-Indië,* pp. 12–41. Franeker: T. Wever.

Wengen, Ger D. van. 2002. *"Wat is er te doen in Volkenkunde?" De bewogen geschiedenis van het Rijksmuseum voor Volkenkunde in Leiden.* Leiden: Rijksmuseum voor Volkenkunde.

Wentholt, Arnold, ed. 2003. *In kaart gebracht met kapmes en kompas: Met het Koninklijk Nederlands Aardrijkskundig Genootschap op expeditie tussen 1873 en 1960.* Utrecht: ABP Public Affairs in samenwerking met het Koninklijk Nederlands Aardrijkskundig Genootschap.

Wertheim, Wim F. 2002. "Globalization of the Social Sciences–Non-Western Sociology as a Temporary Panacea." In Vermeulen and Kommers, eds., *Tales from Academia,* part 1, pp. 267–96.

Winters, Christopher, ed. 1991. *International Dictionary of Anthropologists.* New York: Garland.

Wolf, Jan J. de. 1998. *Eigenheid en samenwerking: Honderd jaar antropologisch verenigingsleven in Nederland.* Leiden: KITLV Uitgeverij.

——. 2002. "Anthropology at Utrecht University" in Vermeulen and Kommers eds. *Tales from Academia,* part 1, pp. 421–42.

——. 2005. "Geschiedenis van de culturele antropologie [in Utrecht]." In Willem Koops, Henk van Rinsum, and Jan van Teunenbroek, eds., *De sociale wetenschappen in Utrecht: Een geschiedenis,* pp. 197–226. Hilversum: Verloren.

Chapter 3

Sociocultural Anthropology in Bulgaria: Desired and Contested

Magdalena Elchinova

INTRODUCTION

Anthropology as an academic discipline appeared in Bulgaria after the fall of the communist regime in November 1989, and was commonly regarded as a by-product of the democratization of Bulgarian society. I have discussed elsewhere the ideological reasons for the absence of anthropology during the era of state socialism and the development instead of folklore study and ethnography (Elchinova 2002; 2002a). Such a process may seem typical for the former communist countries in Europe, which had their own ways and traditions in the discipline (Skalník 2002). Anthropology had never been a part of the academic list of disciplines in less than a century and a half long history of Bulgarian scholarship. It lacked even the tradition, traced by singular prominent scholars, as were Gellner and Holy in the former Czechoslovakia, Gusti in Romania, or Malinowski in Poland. Nor had it the scarce but nevertheless existent experience of research in faraway cultures and societies of some scholars from the former Yugoslav republics—not to mention the Asian and Arctic studies in the former Soviet Union. My aim is not, however, to discuss here the historical background of the discipline in Bulgaria. I would rather try to tackle such questions as why anthropology emerged on the academic stage in Bulgaria in the 1990s, what kind of anthropology is it, and what changes has it undergone in its fifteen years of development, how are anthropological teaching and research organized, and what is the public image of anthropology in Bulgaria at present. In search for answers to these questions one needs to take into account such things as the institutionalization of the discipline, the academic programs and course syllabi, the research projects and publications, etc.

THE INSTITUTIONALIZATION OF ANTHROPOLOGY IN BULGARIA

Institutionalization is not among the core things that make a discipline. Nevertheless, it gives an idea about the position of the discipline in a certain society. It also provides legitimacy and could be very important for the social recognition of the discipline. The latter proved to be of vital significance for the development of anthropology and ethnology[1] in Bulgaria as newly established academic training. Among the legacies of the period of state socialism were the organization of academic and scholarly spheres on the basis of ideological evaluation of disciplines, centralized state administration of science and academic activity, compulsory unified standards for higher education and science, and the separation of teaching and research work. The last feature was most apparent in the double institutionalization of science—the Universities and the Bulgarian Academy of Sciences (BAS). The role introduced by the state standard register of academic disciplines still remains unchanged: it allows for the opening of faculties, departments, and research institutes, the elaboration of academic programs and syllabi, and the granting of scholarly degrees and valid diplomas. It was only in the summer of 2002 when the list of officially recognized academic fields and disciplines inherited from the socialist era was considerably transformed to include, among other new items, anthropology, situated in a joint academic field together with sociology and cultural studies.[2] Thus, until recently, the position of anthropology in the Bulgarian academic landscape was institutionally vulnerable and development of programs was seriously impeded. This explains why the first and, as yet, only department of anthropology in the country opened at a private university,[3] the New Bulgarian University (NBU), in 1993. Throughout the 1990s, sociocultural anthropology had an institutionally marginal position in Bulgaria—until 2002, even if having undergone fundamental anthropological training, students had to specialize in either ethnology, theory and history of culture, sociology, history, or folklore, as these subjects were officially in the register. The absence of anthropology from the official classification of academic disciplines was also among the reasons why the first programs to appear were in ethnology:[4] in 1992 at the Plovdiv University (PU), in 1995 at the South-West University in Blagoevgrad (SWU) and in 1996 at the Sofia University (SU). These programs vary in content between history and philology. Albeit the same title, they are based on different scholarly traditions (respectively, of ethnography and folklore). The first two lean on the achievements of the study of folklore and put the stress on language.[5] In line with this, they are incorporated into the departments of philology. Ethnology at SU is embedded in the Department of History, and is oriented towards historical science (the greater number of courses are similar to those taught in history) with a well-defined ethnographic profile.[6]

Only at NBU was anthropology proper introduced, with its development announced as a paramount priority. However, this university also had to comply with the state register. The solution was to combine anthropology with other disciplines officially recognized by the state. Until recently, there was a Bachelor's Program of Sociology and Social Anthropology (and students graduated as sociologists). In 2004/2005, a BA program in Anthropology was launched, with specializations in socio-cultural anthropology and sociology.

Changes also occurred at some of the institutes of the BAS to mark the (attempts at) institutionalization of anthropology and ethnology. Thus, for example, the *Bulgarian Folklore* journal of the Institute of Folklore began to use the subtitle "*Journal for Folklore Study, Ethnology and Anthropology.*" In 1995, the journal of the Ethnographic Institute with Museum changed its title from *Bulgarian Ethnography* into *Bulgarian Ethnology,* in keeping with the trend to modernize the discipline. These were the first journals with specialization in anthropology and ethnology. Already in 1999, the Department of Anthropology at NBU started publishing an annual series, entitled *Studies in Anthropology.* The aim of this series is to present the research of Bulgarian and foreign anthropologists, including graduate students, and to provide readings for lectures and seminars.[7]

THE QUEST FOR IDENTITY

For a newly emerging discipline, the question of creating an identity and negotiating the boundaries with cognate disciplines is very important. The short history of anthropology in Bulgaria is marked by a contradictory and often painful search for an identity of its own.

The previous section of my essay may have left the impression that anthropology and ethnology in Bulgaria were born in the 1990s in the cradle of folklore and ethnography. This is not exactly true,[8] as contemporary Bulgarian anthropologists come from more diverse backgrounds, including sociology, history, Thracian studies (*trakologiya*), philosophy, culture studies, etc. (for more details, see Elchinova 2002a: 25–28). It is well-known, however, that ethnography and folkloristics had been established and developed during the communist period in all the European countries of the former "Soviet bloc"—instead of anthropology and ethnology, which were condemned as ideologically improper disciplines. The Bulgarian specificity is perhaps the parallel and independent development of ethnography and folklore since the early 1970s. A decade later, these had already formed two separate and often rival fields of study (Elchinova 2002a).

The ideological connotations attributed to anthropology during the socialist period inevitably left their imprint, but in a reversed form, after the fall of communism. In general, the reasons for the rise of interest in anthropological study in Bulgaria are twofold: on the one hand, the sociopolitical changes after 1989, and, on the other, the specific developments in particular disciplines.

The emergence of anthropology in Bulgaria in the 1990s was rooted in the sociopolitical context, or the so-called period of transition. Moreover, quests and the topical issues of the discipline were changing in congruence with the shifts in the social conditions. Throughout the first decade of its existence, Bulgarian anthropology was deeply influenced by the rhetoric of transition and corresponded to the large-scale public strive for democratization. In line with the ideological interpretations of the word "anthropology," at the time it became a token sign of democratic reforms in the social sciences.[9] The key discourses in which the identity of present day anthropology in Bulgaria had been coined, were characterized by polarization and revalorization in all social spheres.

Polarization took form in the first place in the transition from the "Soviet" to the "Western" style of education. The two patterns were simplified and essentialized to the extent of neglect for the variety of national traditions and developments that lay behind them, and thus, became ideological opposites. The dominant discourses of polarity during the period were an expression of the large-scale process of transformation of public values and hierarchies. Reorganization of scholarship was affected by revalorization in both political and professional terms. Politically, it took the form of the departure from the "Soviet" pattern and ideology, and a shift to what was imagined to be coherent with the values of Western democracy. In the professional sphere, there was search for a more adequate name to denote the shifts in subject and method already taking place since the late 1980s. Scholars in different fields realized that over the last few years, they had been exploring new subjects, methods, and theories outside the traditional definitions of their fields of study. These changes were at times so substantial that their work could no longer be classified as belonging to one of the known disciplines. Moreover, such scholars were often criticized or not accepted by their fellow colleagues because they were not doing "proper" ethnography, folklore studies, history, etc. They had to create new titles to justify and classify their scholarly work (see for examples Elchinova 2002; Valtchinova 1997; Luleva 2002).

Whereas in sociopolitical terms the association of anthropology with "Western" scholarship has brought the discipline a democratic aura, in the professional sphere it fostered a heated debate about the nature of "true" anthropology. At first glance, that was a debate on the subject and method of anthropology and ethnology, but at the time it took the shape of a dispute about the dominant generalized pattern of anthropological and ethnological study. In the case of ethnology, there was a conflict about the "historical" or "philological" orientation of the discipline. In the case of anthropology, not directly derived from any formerly existing tradition of Bulgarian scholarship, it was rather an argument about whether there was anthropology in Bulgaria at all, and what proper anthropology should look like. Some of the sharpest issues of collision were: is fieldwork indispensable for true anthropological research; is someone who makes research "at home" and does not study faraway cultures and societies a real anthropologist; how shall we call our research—cultural or social anthropology (and after which greater tradition—British, French, American). Such discussions never reached solutions, for the simple reason that they were in fact debates about the priority of one or another anthropological tradition in the perceived unified "Western" anthropology. As futile as they may seem, these debates were conspicuous of the process of the seeking of new professional identities and they played their role at the initial stages of defining the frames of the discipline.

The quest for anthropology's own identity was an ambiguous and controversial process, often related to feelings of vulnerability and uncertainty. The vulnerability derived from the lack of a profound vision about the development of anthropology in the various Western countries, about its methodological, identity, and legitimacy quests and battles (Goddard, Llobera, and Shore 1994). Another source of identity sensitivity and crisis was the process of reassessment of Bulgaria's own scholarly traditions. The criteria for this reassessment were different, and not strictly scholarly. In the complicated and controversial process of reinventing traditions that has been taking place throughout the 1990s and until today, some went as far as to deny the existence of anything of value in the whole history of Bulgarian scholarship, or at least in its forty-five years of development under communism. The other side of the denial of what "we had" was the totally positive, often uncritical assessment of "what we could not have," that is, in relation to anthropology and achievements of the "Western" anthropological tradition. Many of the newly declared anthropologists in Bulgaria structured their professional identity in the frame of an imported model (e.g., British, French, or other), rather than on local and national scholarly traditions. The result was a blended, uncertain, and vulnerable identity, and a self-perception of being peripheral to anthropology in the West. The "little tradition" syndrome shaped the identity of Bulgarian anthropologists, reinforcing the idea of being able to do only specific kinds of anthropological research.

By using the past tense in my comments on the process of creating new identities, I am hinting at the assumption that these observations are characteristic of the earlier years of the development of anthropology in Bulgaria (the 1990s, the transition period). After 2000, some of the discussed trends are still to be observed; however, other topical issues have come to the fore. The dominant rhetoric of the last few years has become that of European integration (due to the growing involvement of the country in these processes). This has also brought about a change of focus in identity constructions, adding a flavor of belonging and integration to the greater European scholarly traditions. This generated a feeling of importance of the geographically and thematically restricted research carried out in Bulgaria, because in the new context of Europeanization it seemed to refer to a central issue for European anthropology concerning processes in Europe itself. The growing interest of the "West" for the countries of Central and Eastern Europe also increased the significance of research "at home." There is still the self-perception of being a "small" and "peripheral" anthropology; however, it is getting a clearer idea about its place and role on the international scene.

TEACHING AND RESEARCH

Both teaching and research pay very little attention to "primitive" and distant cultures. Anthropology in Bulgaria has a strong Euro-centric orientation, even Balkan-centric. Some call it the anthropology of the Balkans, others call it the anthropology of Southeastern Europe, and these denominations outline the scope of fieldwork and comparison in the studies of Bulgarian anthropologists. Yet, it is not correct to speak of a systematic anthropology of the Balkans or Southeastern Europe, not just because of limited fieldwork sites, but also because of limitations in subjects and methods of study. Thus, for example, teaching on the Balkans in Bulgaria focuses on symbolic geography, drawing back on historical literary sources, dating back to the fifteenth century, such as travelogues, diaries, etc. In such a paradigm, it is hard to distinguish between history and anthropology. At the same time, one can hardly find lecture courses or publications on comparative studies of Balkan kinship systems, or economic strategies on a local level, or gender in Balkan societies, etc. Altogether, a consistent comparative approach is the major deficiency of anthropological studies in Bulgaria.

University programs pay attention to historical anthropology and the processes of community formation and maintenance, with special reference to small scale rural communities. Attention is also paid to the study of complex societies, especially in relation to questions of power, polity, statehood and nationalism, and multiculturality. Economic anthropology is somewhat underdeveloped in the existing syllabi, but most basic anthropological issues, including myth, ritual, religion, marriage and kinship, ethnicity and nationhood, clothing and traditional cuisine, magic and medicine, etc., are duly represented.[10]

The BA program of Anthropology at the NBU seems more balanced in terms of subject matter and approach. Combining specializations in anthropology and sociology, it pays more attention to social organization and structures than to symbolic cultural forms in comparison to ethnology programs. It introduces major subject areas of anthropology (physical, political, economic, symbolic, visual, applied, etc., and combines lectures with practical training in different fieldwork methods). Perhaps the major gap is the unbalanced representation of the various cultural-geographical areas because of the lack of specialists on Asia, Africa, Australia, North and Latin America, and so on. This also implies insufficient training in the comparative study of cultures and societies.

All ethnology and anthropology programs at Bulgarian universities put a strong emphasis on fieldwork training. The scholars involved in these programs are of a different background, usually lacking specialized anthropological or ethnological training.

The lack of a full-rate academic training in sociocultural anthropology is perceived by the majority of the Bulgarian anthropologists as a professional vulnerability. At the same time, this has become a major goal of those involved in teaching anthropology and ethnology after the disciplines achieved institutional recognition.

It is difficult to briefly comment on the nature of ethnological and anthropological research in Bulgaria over the last fifteen years. The trends in research have been shaped under the impact of various factors, such as research traditions and developments in the disciplines that became related to anthropology; the preference for certain anthropological schools and conceptions; the influence of the ideas in present day international anthropology, etc. The shifting sociopolitical conditions also left their imprint on the development of anthropological studies, especially in the topics of investigation. For example, already at the beginning of the transition period, the prevailing financial sources of research became numerous international and local foundations, instead of the state-run funds. With their particular priorities, foundations quickly reshaped the sector of scholarly research. For instance, they put more emphasis on the study of ethnic and religious minorities in the country. Within a short span of time, this increased interest changed the content of ethnographic and folkloristic studies. It also influenced the work of many sociologists, philosophers, etc. Also, the topical issues of study have often changed with the shifts in the sociopolitical context. Thus, for example, whereas at the beginning of the transition, political rituals abundant at the time, were widely discussed, by the end of the 1990s issues such as migration, European and Atlantic integration came to the fore.

When speaking about the impact of the established anthropological traditions in Bulgaria, it is necessary to comment on the availability of specialized publications. Anthropological literature was to some extent already available in the country during the communist period. However, with a few exceptions (structuralism, semiotics, ethnography of speaking, etc.), the literature was more the knowledge and impact of individual scholars than of schools and traditions. This situation changed significantly in the 1990s. To meet the needs of university teaching for essential readings in anthropology, many translations of classical and modern works in anthropology were published, as well as a number of review articles and essays by Bulgarian authors.[11] However, an overall picture of the development of anthropology throughout the world is still lacking. Thus, for example, the development of world anthropology in the 1940s, 1950s, up to the late 1960s is, on a large scale, still *terra incognita* in Bulgaria. There is a somewhat clearer idea about the developments in the following decades.[12]

With such a perspective, it is interesting to mention the relationships with foreign anthropologists who do research in, and publish on, Bulgaria. In recent years, the involvement of Bulgarian anthropologists in joint international projects has gradually been growing. Although still on a limited scale, the international exchange of anthropology/ethnology students and professors has also grown. The number of representatives of the "great" anthropological traditions whose work is focused on Bulgaria is very small; by the time of writing of this chapter, there were just two monographs on the country written by Western anthropologists (Creed 1998; Kaneff 2004). Whereas the latter is recently published and its influence is still to be assessed, the former is a good example of the impact on the "outside" research of indigenous anthropologists. The book is scarcely referred to in local publications and seems to be not familiar among Bulgarian scholars and students, although the author continues his research in the country.[13]

If one tries to summarize the principal characteristics of anthropological research in Bulgaria, it is Europe oriented, very much engaged with ethnic groups and nationalist outbursts, and interested especially in the cultural "Others" at home. In a way, if its primary interests and research are located in Bulgaria, the Balkans, Southeast and Central Europe, and the Mediterranean, this type of anthropology could be described as regional and fairly restricted in scope. There are several reasons for this. The first is financial. The second is lack of expertise, which is related to the relatively limited geographical experience of the Bulgarian anthropologists—folklorists, ethnographers, sociologists—all used to carry out research within the home country or in other postcommunist countries. The third reason is related to the peripheral position Bulgarian anthropologists believe to have obtained. They still feel ill-equipped to offer the international community influential theory, but can provide valuable material through the study of local regions and topics. The latter reason has determined the character of anthropology in Bulgaria as more descriptive and based on fieldwork rather than theory.

Within an essay of this size, I am only able to map out some of the essential shifts in research subject and method that are to be observed in the short history of anthropology in Bulgaria.

One of the shifts concerns the viewpoint toward culture—from treating it as a heritage from the past or as a system of a-historically analyzed structures and patterns, the emphasis moved to a growing interest in current cultural processes and transformations regarded in their relation with the wider sociocultural context.

Another trend is the slow but visible shift in accent from culture and symbolic forms to social structures and phenomena; the view on culture has become more systemically contextualized in social realities. The latter is also related to the tendency from artifact oriented towards social actors oriented research.

Although field research remains confined within a national scope, since the 1990s (under the impact of the political conjuncture), there is an emphasis on the study of the culture and identity of various ethnic and religious groups (Roma, Turks, Muslim Bulgarians, *Gagauzes, Vlachs, Karakachans,* Jews, Armenians, etc.), as well as of the Bulgarians of the diaspora (Hungary, the Czech Republic, Slovakia, Poland, Serbia, USA, etc.) and their relationships with the autochthonous populations in the host countries.

The existing traditions (in ethnography, folklore study, sociology) of local community studies are sustained and elaborated towards a more systematic and indepth investigation of social structure and culture. Thus, for example, previously "neglected" or "forbidden" issues such as ethnic and religious diversity, religion, collectivization of land, social inequality or others are now attributed due attention in the community studies. Unfortunately, this well-developed research practice has not yet led to the publishing of significant community monographs.

Another tangible shift is from the study of rural communities and cultures to the study of urban communities and cultures. This was anticipated by the acquisition of adequate approaches of study of the diverse and often eclectic processes in urban culture.

To these I would also like to add the tendency for self-reflection and reassessment of the ideological restrictions and political management of social sciences during the communist era, as well as the discussions of the birth and growth of anthropology in the postcommunist European countries.

This overview of shifts in subject matter and method of anthropological research in Bulgaria is far from exhaustive. There is also a growing interest in and publications on topics like kinship, intermarriage, ethnic conflict and ethnic processes, religious diversity and cohabitation, "archeology" of the Bulgarian village under state socialism, migration and immigrant communities, consumerism, European integration and identification, economic progress and social pessimism.

The last point I would like to make is the move of anthropological research from compartmentalization to interdisciplinity. Anthropology in Bulgaria is not only emerging, but also merging with other disciplines. Coming from various backgrounds, for many years, the newly proclaimed anthropologists have found it difficult to leave the skirts of their "mother" disciplines and to start a productive dialogue with fellow anthropologists from other fields of study. As a result, Bulgarian anthropologists did not know each other's work very well and did not care about it very much, obsessed by the idea of "proving" their priority in the argument for "proper" anthropology. In the last few years, this has been progressively overcome and the current anthropological debate in Bulgaria has another, more constructive aspect, concerning the development of projects, discussions on method and theory, and publications. Successful interdisciplinary teams have already been formed. This move towards interdisciplinary research I consider among the most important trends in the discipline.

CONCLUSION

I will try to summarize the current goals and tasks facing Bulgarian anthropologists. One of them is the extension of fieldwork in terms of subject, method, and research areas. Another aspect is the involvement of a bigger number of students in research teams, as well as the provision of finance for long term fieldwork for doctoral students.

Another task is the elaboration in the curricula of underdeveloped and new subjects and areas of study. An imperative for those involved in teaching anthropology is to make the discipline more attractive for and corresponding to the interests of today's students.

A more practical and long term enterprise is to provide the necessary tools for the training of process specialists, textbooks, and training films, as well as wider academic exchange.

Inasmuch as higher education in Bulgaria is professionally oriented and anthropologists do not have a clear professional identity for the wider public, it is essential to build an adequate public image of the discipline. In the struggle to attract students to anthropology, it is very important to promote how anthropology graduates could apply their knowledge and qualifications in practice, how anthropology could be a profitable and socially important occupation, and to which social spheres anthropological expertise is relevant and indispensable.

NOTES

1. The two names received wider circulation among the Bulgarian public at about the same time and are often used as allonyms of the same field of study. However, there are certain differences between anthropology and ethnology in Bulgaria in terms of institutional status and perspective of study, some of which I will touch upon further in this text.
2. Limited changes in the register were made in 1997, when ethnology found a place in the register within the historical training.
3. Financially independent of the state, private universities are more flexible and can take the risk of not strictly following the state register.
4. Another reason for this was the elaborate tradition in Bulgaria of national-oriented studies and the total lack of studies of distant societies and cultures.
5. By 2004 the program at PU combines the training in ethnology with intense learning of English and French language and literature; the program at USU combined ethnology with training in Balkan and Slavic languages (Greek, Ukrainian, and Bulgarian).
6. See Valtchinova (1997) for a historical overview about the general orientation of folklore studies in Bulgaria toward language, and of ethnography/ethnology toward history.
7. Although some of the published articles cannot be described as strictly anthropological (due to the diverse background of the contributors), the series is the first specialized anthropological periodical in Bulgaria.
8. Although it would not be wrong to say that the greater number of people involved in anthropological research and teaching come from the fields of folklore studies and ethnography.
9. For many scholars, adopting the name *anthropology* meant that they had rejected the studies of Marxist ideology. That is why there was not much debate on

anthropology's proper method and subject during the 1990s (Elchinova 2002a: 28–34).

10. A representative illustration of university teaching of anthropology is the first "Bulgarian-made" textbook (Zhivkov 2000). As a whole, the author's approach is a mixture of methods, derived from the French ethnology and sociology, German philosophy and ethnology, and reconsidered Marxist views on culture and society. For more information about some of the ethnology programs see Ganeva-Raicheva (1999).

11. For a few examples see ABC (1992), ABC (1999), Stefanov and Ginev (1990, 1993), Krasteva (1999), Bochkov, Todorov (2002), Elchinova, Todorov (2003), Elchinova, Lazova (2004), Studies in Anthropology, vols 1–6 (2000–6), Nikolov, Daskalov (2000).

12. For example, it was only in the 1990s that Fredrik Barth's work of transactionalism (still not translated in Bulgarian) became well known in Bulgaria. The same situation occurs with most theories on ethnicity and nationalism. The works of Anthony Smith, Ernest Gellner, and Eric Hobsbawm are now widely translated and cited, while some ten years ago they were familiar only to individual scholars. Some classical works in anthropology, such as Durkheim's *Elementary Forms of Religious Life,* or Radcliffe-Brown's *Structure and Function in Primitive Society,* were translated for the first time into Bulgarian in the second half of the 1990s. The most influential contemporary developments and publications of anthropology remain unavailable. Works on religion attract much interest as a reaction to the communist taboo on the subject. Bulgarian universities still cannot afford subscriptions to the leading international journals in anthropology. Despite this rather bleak picture, tremendous progress in the knowledge and understanding of anthropology among the specialized public has been achieved in the last decade, and this is a token of the formation of a steady interest towards the discipline in Bulgaria.

13. Curiously, the Cyril and Methodius National Library in Sofia, the biggest library in the country, did not have a copy of this work by 2004.

REFERENCES

ABC na etnologiyata [ABC of ethnology], vol. 1, 1992; vol. 2. Sofia. 1999.

Antropologicheski izsledvaniya [Studies in Anthropology]. Vols 1–4. Sofia: New Bulgarian University. 1999–2003.

Bochkov, P., and O. Todorov, eds. 2001. *Lovtsi na umove. Lektsii po antropologiya* [Hunters of Minds. Lectures in Anthropology]. Sofia.

Creed, G. 1998. Domesticating Revolution: From Socialist Reform to Ambivalent Transmission in a Bulgarian Village. University Park, PA: Pennsylvania State University Press.

Elchinova, Magdalena. 2002a. *"In Statu Nascendi*: Anthropology in Bulgaria." In *A Post-communist Millenium: The Struggles for Sociocultural Anthropology in Central and Eastern Europe,* ed. P. Skalník, pp. 23–41. Prague: Set Out.

——. 2002b. "Bulgarian Ethnology and Folklore Study at the Present Time: Changing Paradigms and Perspectives." In *Europäische Ethnologien im neuen Millennium,* eds B. Emmrich and J. Moser, pp. 39–50. Dresden: Thelem.

Elchinova, Magdalena, and T. Lazova, eds. 2004. *Znachimi imena v antropologiyata* [Outstanding Names in Anthropology]. Sofia.

Elchinova, Magdalena, and O. Todorov, eds. 2003. *Lovtsi na umove - 2. Lektsii po antropologiya [Hunters of Minds - 2. Lectures in Anthropology].* Sofia.

Ganeva-Raicheva, V. 1997. "Pet godini universitetska etnologia" [Five Years of Academic Ethnology]. *B'lgarski folklor* 3–4: 144–51.

Goddard, Victoria A., Joseph R. Llobera, and Chris Shore. 1994. "Introduction." In *The Anthropology of Europe. Identities and Boundaries in Conflict,* eds V. A. Goddard, J. R. Llobera, and C. Shore. Oxford: Berg.

Ivanova, Radost. 2002. *Kultura na krizata–kriza v kulturata [A Culture of Crisis–Crisis in Culture].* Sofia.

Kaneff, Deema. 2004. *Who Owns the Past? The Politics of Time in a "Model" Bulgarian Village.* Oxford and New York: Berghahn.

Krasteva, A, ed. 1999. *Obshtnosti i identichnosti v Bulgaria [Communities and Identities in Bulgaria].* Sofia.

Luleva, A. 2002. "Die bulgarische Ethnologie – Forschungsschwerpunkte und Projekte." In *Europäische Ethnologien im neuen Millennium,* eds B. Emmrich and J. Moser, pp. 29–39, Dresden: Thelem.

Nikolov, B., and R. Daskalov, eds. 2000. *V payazhinata na smisala. Textove po simvolna antropologiya [In the Web of Meaning. Reader in Symbolic Anthropology].* Sofia.

Skalník, Peter, ed. 2002. *A Post-communist Millenium: The Struggles for Sociocultural Anthropology in Central and Eastern Europe.* Prague: Set Out.

Stefanov, I. and D. Ginev, eds. 1990-1993. *Idei v kulturologiyata [Ideas in Culture Studies].* 2 Vols, Sofia.

Zhivkov, T. Iv. 1994. *Etnichniyat sindrom [The Ethnic Syndrome].* Sofia.

——. 2000. *Uvod v etnologiata [Introduction to Ethnology].* Plovdiv.

Valtchinova, G. 1997. "How Large Are Issues of Small Ethnographies? Bulgarian Ethnology Facing New Europe." Unpublished manuscript.

Chapter 4

Refacing Mt. Kenya or Excavating the Rift Valley? Anthropology in Kenya and the Question of Tradition

Mwenda Ntarangwi

INTRODUCTION

The development and growth of anthropology in Kenya can be linked to the colonial project of the late nineteenth and early twentieth century. This relationship not only directed the line of inquiry (mostly a focus on "tribal" ways), but provided financial and administrative support necessary to meet the then needs of the colonial administration. However, anthropology as a taught subject in Kenya remained undeveloped until the mid 1980s—except for a handful of students trained in archaeology through the History Department at the University of Nairobi. Indeed, many who were trained in archaeology then studied under foreign or foreign-trained teachers. This does reflect the way the discipline developed in much of East Africa where archaeology was seen as an extension of the discipline of history and was thus taught within the history curriculum. It is no wonder that some of the oldest research centers in Kenya engaged in archeological work (the British Institute of Eastern Africa and the National Museums of Kenya) have continued to double up as research and resource centers for generating and enhancing historical knowledge.

In 1938, Jomo Kenyatta, who later became Kenya's first president, gave anthropology a local identity when he published one of the very first and seminal ethnographies—*Facing Mt. Kenya*—while studying under Bronislaw Malinowski in London. This was the first ethnography written "from a native's point of view." Thirty years later (and only fours years as an independent nation), Kenya's presence in the world of anthropology (paleontology) was boosted further by the discovery of human fossils by Louis and Mary Leakey along the Rift Valley. While these two examples point to two related yet often independent trajectories of anthropological work in Kenya—one an ethnography primarily in the realm of cultural anthropology and the other in the realm of archaeology—they both point to the question of what identity the practice of anthropology in Kenya has adopted over the years. What is clear is that it is neither a Kenyan anthropology, nor is it British, American, German, Danish, or Indian (where many Kenyan anthropologists have trained), despite certain strands of influence from such national anthropologies visible in Kenya. Kenya, like many other African countries, does not have an indigenous anthropological tradition, but may have varied practices shaped by each anthropologist's formal training in America or Europe. This is not because there has been no anthropological work in the country, but because of the general development of formal education in Kenya since its contact and connection to the West.

The majority of Kenyan anthropologists have been trained outside of the country under different anthropological traditions, and with this training comes different anthropological trajectories. These trajectories are capable of creating a national anthropological tradition that is a combination of various traditions that is mostly visible when we look at current curricular at the only two public universities in Kenya that offer graduate degrees in anthropology—Nairobi and Moi Universities. In most cases, anthropological training in America tends to favor a four-field approach that includes linguistic, physical, archaeology, and cultural anthropology (all often found in one department), while training in England tends to have archaeology and social anthropology as separate departments.[1] Both Moi and Nairobi Universities seem to have adopted both traditions, with archaeology and anthropology almost as separate departments at Nairobi (archaeology under the National Museums and anthropology at the Institute of African Studies), and as a single department at Moi (where archaeology is taught as a course among many in the anthropology program). As the oldest institution of higher education in Kenya, the University of Nairobi has also the oldest record of teaching anthropology (outside the realm of history), although the teaching only started in the mid 1980s following a presidential directive. It is thus clear that while anthropological inquiry and work has been going on in Kenya for over 100 years, formal training in anthropology is hardly two decades old.

ANTHROPOLOGY IN KENYA: A HISTORICAL PERSPECTIVE

Given that anthropology is itself a young discipline, only emerging formally as a discipline in the late nineteenth century, it should not come as a surprise that socio-cultural studies carried out in Kenya at the end of the nineteenth and beginning of twentieth centuries were not categorized as anthropological. Indeed, even in the current century, anthropological work is being carried out in multidisciplinary contexts where a distinct anthropological identity may be lacking. In the nineteenth and twentieth centuries, studies mostly by British and some German social scientists tended to dominate the anthropology terrain in Kenya as is evident in the publications of scholars like Bagge (1904), Brutzer (1902, 1905, 1910), Dundas (1910), Hobley (1903a, 1903b, 1905, 1906, 1908, 1910a, 1910b), Hollins (1905a, 1905b, 1909a, 1909b, 1910), Marquordt (1909), Merker (1903, 1904), and Northcorte (1907). Many of these scholars published articles or books on communities or ethnic groups that they identified as distinct—including the Luo, Maasai, Kikuyu, Nandi, Kamba, and Dorobo. They were a true reflection of the much acknowledged identity of anthropology as the study of the "other," or of small cohesive social groups. These communities written about by anthropologists in the past have continued to have a dominant presence in the socio-political terrain of modern day Kenya. Writing mostly between 1900 to 1915, these scholars published studies on customs of individual ethnic groups, most likely in response to two prevailing needs at the time—first, the desire by the colonial administration to learn as much as possible about native traditions for purposes of easier governance; and second, the rush by social scientists (anthropologists included) to record the customs and practices of African tribes before they disappeared following their encounter with the East and West through colonialism, Christian missionaries, and travel.

The latter was the guiding framework for anthropological work in Kenya under the British and has surprisingly had an interesting continuity in the post-independence era. Thus, many anthropological and related studies were meant to record native practices before they became extinct as well as aid in the smooth running of the colonial government.[2] Anthropological studies in Kenya in the period 1860–1920 would thus include specific geo-cultural areas divided up mainly along linguistic lines as noted by Schapera (1949). There was more to the colonial project than just recording the practices of native peoples—there were ideological effects that would endure past the actual colonial period.

Notably, colonialism inflicted a lasting scar on the culture and psyche of many Africans by degrading African cultures and societies. Besides the claims of Africa's lack of history and worldviews translatable into a philosophy, African religions were construed as heathen, where the practitioners were located at the lowest rank in human evolution, the primitive. This onslaught was successful in debasing Africans' self-image and self-confidence, which consequently led to a colonial domination over the human and natural resources in Africa. Intellectually, Africa and its people were dislodged from a reality of self-expression. Thus, as soon as they got a chance to articulate their own agenda and charter their destiny, Africans (especially intellectuals) sought first to reconstitute their societies from a colonial dislocation. Such dislocation included a reassessment of the role of socio-cultural studies in supporting the colonial agenda. Some saw anthropology as part of the larger colonial project and soon dissociated themselves from the discipline. Even those like Jomo Kenyatta who had benefitted from their training in anthropology soon found themselves in an ambivalent relationship with the discipline. For Kenyatta, dissociating with any colonial intellectual traditions through which anthropology thrived was desirable, yet its abilities to enhance a better understanding of the self was enticing because it encapsulated a destiny of an imagined political and ethnic community leading to self-rule. This imagined ethnic community was important for Kenyatta because it "enlarged the discursive arena within which (he and other Africans) renegotiated the core issues of political community and moral economy, or social obligation, in response to the impact of alien rule, Christianity, emergent capitalism, and standardized print vernaculars" (Berman and Lonsdale 1998:17).

It was an attempt to define an African identity and destiny that was keen on shoring both a reasserted African authenticity and an embraced modernity resulting from the colonial encounter. To do this Kenyatta had to turn to anthropology, especially the one espoused by Malinowski which advocated for the "native's point of view." Being Kikuyu, Kenyatta had the "native's view" and hence the authority to understand and write an ethnography on the Kikuyu. His work emerged at a time when the Kikuyu were under great economic, religious, and political pressure from missionaries and the colonial government. At this historical juncture, anthropology was a welcome ally.

Kenyatta's ethnography *Facing Mount Kenya* thus became an important tool, "a redemptive allegory of an idealized past that, by shaming a corrupted present, justified control over the future" (Berman and Lonsdale 1998: 29). Thus, although written primarily on the Kikuyu, *Facing Mount Kenya* became a treatise on a homogenous Kenyan polity, which while regaining a lost dignity of a people, reinvented the tribality that had been developed and emphasized by the colonial administration. That was to become yet another favored path to be taken by ethnographies in Kenya, with many anthropologists writing about isolated communities, especially those deemed "traditional." Upon ascending to important political leadership, Kenyatta abandoned this favored anthropological path to understand the emerging new nation he was to lead for fifteen years. He designed a philosophy of unity and nationalism where tribality was still sustained but not overtly encouraged. Anthropology thus lost any possible place in the public life of Kenyatta and never became part of the intellectual discourse of many scholars in the young nation.

While Kenyatta can be said to have participated in shaping some local approaches to cultural anthropology through ethnography, Louis Leakey helped shape the sub-disciplines of archaeology and physical anthropology in Kenya by giving it a more definitive and scholarly public presence. Born of British ancestry in Kabete, northwest of Nairobi, Louis Leakey maintained his Kenyan identity and often served the country in different roles. Fluent in Kikuyu, he often worked as a translator in the colonial courts, and acted as a translator in the 1952–53 trial of Jomo Kenyatta, then leader of the independence movement. Leakey had also worked as a curator at the then Coryndon Memorial Museum in Nairobi while leading archeological excursions in Olduvai Gorge in northern Tanzania. Archaeology in Kenya thus traces its development through the National Museum which was itself initiated in 1910 and continues to be the most critical locus of archeological work in Kenya today. The Museum was initiated by the Natural History Society in East Africa whose members (mostly colonial settlers and naturalists) needed a place to store a collection of various specimens.[3] By 1930 a new museum, Coryndon Museum, had been constructed to replace an older facility and became more than just a place to store collections; it was a site for continued archeological activity. Louis Leakey became quite involved in the activities of the Museum, including raising funds to expand its facilities in the 1940s.

Since 1936, when he married Mary, Louis Leakey continued to build his interest in archaeology through excavating fossils along the Rift Valley. Mary and Louis Leakey's efforts were rewarded in the 1950s, when their excavations yielded numerous primate fossils including *Australopithecus Boisei* (1959), *Homo Habilis* (the "Handy Man," 1964) and later *Kenyapithecus Africanus* (1967). Given that much of his archeological work was tied to the National Museum, Leakey was instrumental in the centrality of the National Museum as the engine of archeological research in Kenya. Today the museum, although connected to the University of Nairobi as an academic location for its archaeologists, has predominantly and independently become the home of archaeology. Its mandate to preserve and maintain important sites in Kenya has allowed the museum to secure sites such as Koobi Fora, Olorgesailie, and the Hyrax Hill for archaeological work by both local and foreign teams. Rutgers University in the USA, for instance, runs a regular archaeology program in conjunction with the National Museum.

Another of Leakey's important contributions to anthropology in Kenya is in the field of physical anthropology. In 1960, Louis established the Institute of Primate Research (IPR) with the aim of using monkeys as models to understand human evolution.[4] With the establishment of IPR, Kenya laid a firm foundation for its enduring history of biological anthropology to accompany archaeology and later, socio-cultural anthropology. IPR is an important research site in Kenya. Its scientists are engaged in biomedical research in response to the many health challenges facing Africa including the threat of HIV/AIDS. Louis Leakey died in London in 1969, two years after their last discovery, but his wife Mary continued his archaeological tradition. In 1978, the year that Kenyatta died, Mary found a trail of clear ancient hominid footprints of two adults and a child preserved and covered by volcanic ash in Laetoli, in northern Tanzania, west of Olduvai Gorge. All of these series of hominid remains continued to place archaeology squarely in Kenya with the National Museum assuming the role of the lead institution in such excursions.

THE TEACHING AND PRACTICE OF ANTHROPOLOGY IN POST-COLONIAL KENYA

Soon after independence, many African scholars and universities considered anthropology a colonial discipline with no relevance to the new independent states. Kenyatta, who had himself risen to political prominence through championing Kikuyu traditions (Kipkorir 1980), realized his interest in traditional African realities was incompatible with the goals of his new nation-state set for modernization. As Ogot says of Kenyatta and his contemporaries, "in the minds of many Kenyan leaders, modernization was also equated with Westernization (and) they could not modernize unless they altered or abandoned their traditional institutions, beliefs and values to suit the demands of development" (Ogot 1999: 114).

It seems that in this period anthropology had solely been associated with antiquity and thus was unable to respond and explain a Kenyan modernity. However, with the spectacular failures of the development projects of the 1970s and later in the 1980s, "the possibility that the so-called traditional societies could modernize without necessarily having to discard their institutions, beliefs and values became evident" (Ogot 1999: 114). It was clear that development as a modernization project had failed and this failure was mostly attributable to a lack of understanding of local worldviews and systems of knowing critical for cultural, economic, political, and ecological development. Development was propelled by economic institutions such as the World Bank and the International Monetary Fund, which rarely considered culture an important ingredient for enhancing socio-economic change. If anything, culture was often seen as a hindrance to development. Upon succeeding Kenyatta, however, Daniel Arap Moi soon placed culture at the center of socio-economic discourse and made attempts to reconceptualize "modernization" and "development" to take into account cultural dimensions (Ogot 1999: 115).

It was in Moi's government that anthropology slowly started to become acknowledged as an important mode of intervention in creating a national cultural *ethos*. Yet this had not just emerged from a vacuum. It was a culmination of small but consistent steps to Africanize some aspects of academic curricular at the university. In the earlier years, much of what we would consider anthropological knowledge was dominated by the nationalist problematic that emanated from a conscious response to the power of Western domination. In 1965, one year after independence, the then Nairobi University College (later named the University of Nairobi) established an Institute for Development Studies, which was divided into social science and cultural divisions. The former developed into the Institute of Development Studies, charged with research and generation of knowledge on matters related mostly to economic development from a multidisciplinary approach. The latter was charged with the task of developing resources to Africanize the content of cultural instruction within the university and throughout the country. When the University College became an independent national and public university in 1970, the Cultural Division of the Institute became the Institute of African Studies (IAS), with historian Bethwell Ogot as its first director. The IAS was expected to promote original research in the areas of "African archaeology, history, social anthropology, musicology, linguistics, oral literature, traditional arts, crafts and social systems" (Ogot 1999: 118). The IAS soon drew some of the top scholars in the country in the area of culture-related studies, including but not limited to, P.N. Kavyu and Washington Omondi (musicologists), H.S.K. Mwaniki and William R. Ochieng' (historians), and Okot p'Bitek and Taban lo Liyong (literary critics and creative writers). These scholars, together with many others from other departments in the University of Nairobi, contributed to manuscripts profiling cultural practices and histories of the majority of Kenyan ethnic groups under the "District Socio-Cultural Profiles" project. This project was formulated jointly by the Institute of African Studies and the Ministry of Economic Planning and Development" in 1981 (Ogot 1999: 119), the same year that the government created the Ministry of Culture and Social Services. The Ministry of Education introduced oral literature in the secondary school syllabus and made it compulsory, and thus entrenched cultural studies in the education system.

In 1982, President Moi commissioned a team to prepare a plan that would produce recommendations on the development and preservation of music and dance in the country. This led to a 214 page report presented in 1984 which recommended among other things, research, formal training, and public performance of music and dance across the different ethnic groups in the country (Ogot 1999). This was the first time anthropological knowledge was consciously sought to be used to shape the cultural *ethos* of the nation.[5] Most notable, however, was the interdisciplinary approach to anthropological knowledge that the government and the IAS preferred and which has continued to shape contemporary practices in anthropology. The following year (1985), the president asked the University of Nairobi to put together a curriculum to teach Kenya's many cultural practices and histories. Subsequently in 1986 the Institute of African Studies launched the first formal anthropology training program in the country. In this program were courses introducing students to the discipline of anthropology, medical, linguistic, economic, and ecological anthropology and material culture (Amuyunzu-Nyamongo, 2006). Many students have gone through the anthropology program at both Nairobi and Moi Universities, but only Moi has thus far produced a Ph.D.

Meanwhile, the practice and study of archaeology was quite underway in the department of history at the University of Nairobi, following a British tradition where archaeology was seen as part of history and thus taught and housed under the department of history. Archaeological work had been going on almost independently of any national policy on anthropological knowledge production. As mentioned earlier, the center of this work was the National Museums of Kenya. One can begin to see the practice of archaeology in Kenya by looking at the career of a prominent Kenyan archeologist such as Professor Simiyu Wandiba. Wandiba received his initial training in the department of history between 1970–73 writing his BA thesis on Bukusu forts.[6] It is after this training that in 1973 he had an opportunity to engage in the world of field archaeology by conducting surveys and excavations in Koobi Fora under the direction of Professor G.L. Isaac of the University of California, Berkeley, and thus marking another facet of archaeology in Kenya—institutional collaboration. Wandiba went on to earn a masters' degree in archaeology at the University of Nairobi's history department in 1976 and then joined the National Museums as a research fellow. In 1980 he earned a Ph.D. in archaeology from the University of Southampton, England, then returned to Kenya to head the division of archaeology at the Museum while also teaching archaeology on a part-time basis in the department of history at the University of Nairobi. Wandiba's career distinctly reflects not only the relationship between history and archaeology in Kenya but the visible presence of a British tradition that often sees archaeology as an extension of history. Indeed, Professor Wandiba is a member of the Historical Association of Kenya, the International Centre for Bantu Studies, and the World Archaeological Congress.

One emerging reality of anthropology in Kenya is thus its multidisciplinarity. It is not unusual to see someone trained in archaeology comfortably producing and engaging with information in the socio-cultural realm. Professor Wandiba, for instance, presented two papers in January and September of 1999 entitled "Petrological Investigation of Neolithic Pottery in Kenya," and "Polygyny and Child Care in Bondo District of Western Kenya," respectively. In a context where funds for research are scarce, where the demands of teaching lead one to cater to the different needs of the students, and where one's training has been in different schools and/or in different countries, one cannot afford to be so specialized in their discipline as to only teach or write about one area. Moreover, the public universities in Kenya are expanding to include what is locally referred to as the "Module II" curriculum, which caters to self-sponsored non-traditional students who often take courses in the evenings and over the weekends. In this new arrangement, instructors have had to stretch their course offerings beyond what would be considered their "traditional territories" to accommodate a more demanding, directly paying audience.

THE SHAPE OF THE ANTHROPOLOGY OF THE FUTURE IN KENYA

It seems plausible to state that anthropology will flourish rather than diminish in Kenya in the years to come. However, it will be unlike an anthropology that many are used to—the anthropology of thick descriptions emanating from months and years of fieldwork and participant observation. It will be the anthropology of short-term consultancies that not only dictate the duration, but also the direction of research. It is an anthropology borne out of an economically struggling community of scholars out for hire to anyone with a paycheck. Currently, interests are high in the fields of reproductive health and infectious diseases. Many anthropologists in Kenya are thus directly or indirectly engaged in some type of research project on health issues. The nagging problem of malaria and other tropical diseases as well as the emergent threat of HIV/AIDS, has also created a real need for anthropology in general, and medical anthropologists specifically, to navigate the delicate terrains of health, illness, and their related social manifestations. It is no wonder that the majority of anthropologists practicing in Kenya today are either medical anthropologists or anthropologists working on medical issues (see Appendix A). Many of them are able to work as anthropologists because of consultancies availed through international and national nongovernmental organizations working in the areas of health and disease control. Organizations such as the United States Agency for International Development, Family Health International, Engender Health, Path, Population Council, African Population and Health Research Center, African Medical Research Foundation, the World Health Organization, and the Ford Foundation, have all engaged the services of anthropologists in Kenya for various projects.

Anthropologists have become the much sought after "culture experts," who mostly work not on their own terms but under the stipulations and terms of reference produced by the funding agencies. Few, if any, have the luxury of spending many weeks in a community trying to figure out what would be the best approach to a socio-economic or cultural problem. Many of the consultancies are short and quick, with specific outcomes expected. The universities are responding to these development-oriented skills through their anthropology course offerings such as "Development Anthropology," Applied Anthropology," "Anthropology in Developing Countries," "Medical Anthropology," "Anthropology and Infectious Diseases," "Cultural Change and Development," and "Anthropology of Tourism." Moi University is already proposing a masters degree in medical anthropology besides its existing masters degree in anthropology.[7] This is not a major shift in the shape of anthropology in Kenya, as many anthropologists have in the past been engaged in development projects, working with foreign institutions and funding agencies to carry out research in marginalized groups such as pastoralists and women. As the demand increases for anthropological interventions in cultural matters pertaining to development, so too will the course offerings at the university reflect those demands. Many anthropologists in Kenya may not have the luxury of pursuing ethnography based on many months of research as would be desirable because of the reality of fledgling resources that have forced many to respond to development-oriented anthropology. This does not mean that anthropological research in the classic sense of thick descriptions is not being conducted in Kenya any more. It is happening, not by local anthropologists (that is, anthropologists living and working in Kenya), but by foreign anthropologists who continue to use Kenya as a viable research site. The key element in this dichotomy is funding for research and who is able to receive funding for research stretching a year or more.

CONCLUSIONS

It is quite instructive that despite having established much credibility as an African leader through his anthropological training and writing, Kenyatta seemingly and surprisingly abandoned the discipline after Kenyan independence, so much so that even though he was chancellor of the University of Nairobi and having the constituent teachers' College named after him, he never instigated the teaching of the discipline at the tertiary level. It is only in the mid 1980s when his predecessor, Daniel Arap Moi, asked the University of Nairobi and later Moi University (named after him) to consider introducing courses that would enable students to learn about their own and other related African cultures. It was in 1986 that the first group of anthropology students were enrolled at the University of Nairobi's Institute of African Studies to formally study anthropology, even though anthropological work had been going on in the country for decades prior to that formal enrollment. That anthropology is currently taught at the Institute of African Studies which comprises scholars from anthropology and other disciplines such as history and sociology, may say something about the discipline of anthropology in postcolonial Kenya. It says that the major identity it engulfed was one based on content rather than disciplinary tradition. Indeed, when the first batch of anthropology students joined the IAS in 1986, there were not enough anthropology teachers for the necessary courses and thus others with training in history and sociology were called in to fill the deficit.

NOTES

1. Examples of this dichotomy in the UK include the University of Cambridge, the University of Southampton, and the University of London, where some of Kenyan anthropologists have trained.
2. See also *Man*, No. 37 (1903: 72–73), for similar examples in Southern Africa.
3. <http://www.museums.or.ke>
4. Ibid.
5. I use the term anthropology here to refer to holistic approaches in understanding the human condition and which, in the context of Kenya has involved many social scientists not necessarily trained as anthropologists.

6. Information about Simiyu Wandiba is available at <http://www.uonbi.ac.ke/colleges/faculties/ias/wandiba.htm> accessed 12 September 2004.
7. Professor Joshua Akong'a, personal communication, 4 July 2004.

REFERENCES

Amuyunzu-Nyamongo, M. 2006. "Challenges and Prospects for Applied Anthropology in Kenya" in *African Anthropologies: History, Critique, and Practice*, ed. D. Mills, M. Babiker, and M. Ntarangwi. Dakar and London: CODESRIA and Zed Books.

Bagge, S. 1904. "The Circumcision Ceremony Among the Naivasha Masai." *Journal of the Royal Anthropological Institute* 34: 167–69.

Berman, B. J., and J. Lonsdale. 1998. "The Labors of Muigwithania: Jomo Kenyatta as Author, 1928–45." *Research in African Literatures* 29, 1: 16–42.

Brutzer, E. 1902. *Begegnungen mit Wakamba*. Leipzig: Evangelisch-Lutherische Mission.

——. 1905. *Der Geisterglaube bei den Kamba*. Leipzig: Evangelisch-Lutherische Mission.

——. 1910. "Tierfabeln der Kamba." *Archive Anthropology* 37: 23–42.

Dundas, K. R. 1910. "Notes on the Tribes Inhabiting the Baringo District, East African Protectorate." *Journal of the Royal Anthropological Institute* 40: 49–72.

Hobley, C. W. 1903a. "Notes Concerning the Eldorobo of Mau, British East Africa." *Man* 3, 17: 33–35.

——. 1903b. "Anthropological Studies in Kavirondo and Nandi," *Journal of the Royal Anthropological Institute* 33: 325–59.

——. 1906. "Kikuyu Medicines." *Man* 6, 54: 81–3.

——. 1908. "Notes on the Dorobo People and other Tribes." *Man* 8, 78: 119–20.

——. 1910a. *Ethnology of A-Kamba and other East African Tribes*. Cambridge: University Press.

——. 1910b. "Kikuyu Customs and Beliefs: *Thahu* and its Connection with Circumcision Rites." *Journal of the Royal Anthropological Institute* 40: 428–52.

Hollis, A.C. 1905a. *The Masai: Their Language and Folklore*. Oxford: Clarendon Press.

——. 1905b. "Masai Ear-ring of Stone." *Man* 5, 12: 22.

——. 1909a. "A Note on the Graves of the Wa-Nyika." *Man* 9, 8: 145.

——. 1909b. *The Nandi: Their Language and Folklore*. Oxford: Clarendon Press.

——. 1910. "A Note on the Masai System of Relationship and other Matters Connected therewith." *Journal of the Royal Anthropological Institute* 40: 473–82.

Kenyatta, Jomo, 1938. *Facing Mount Kenya*. London: Vintage.

Kipkorir, B.E. 1980. "Towards a Cultural Policy for Kenya: Some Views." *Institute of African Studies Seminar Paper* no. 131.

Marquordt, F. 1909. "Bericht Über die Kavirondo." *Zenj Ethnologie* 41: 753–57.

Merker, M. 1903. "Religion und Tradition der Masai," *Zenj Ethnologie* 35: 733–44.

——. 1904. *Die Masai: Ethnographische Monographie eines Ostafrikanischen Semitenvolkes*. Berlin: Dietrich Reimer.

Northcorte, C.A.S. 1907. "The Nilotic Kavirondo." *Journal of the Royal Anthropological Institute* 37: 58–66.

Ntarangwi, Mwenda. 2002. "Revitalizing Anthropology in East Africa: The Birth of EAAA." *The African Anthropologist* 9, 1: 60–65.

Ogot, B.E. 1999. *Building on the Indigenous: Selected Essays 1981–1998.* Kisumu: Anyange Press.

APPENDIX A: A selection of anthropologists resident in Kenya, their training and research interests*

Name	*Qualification*	*Research affiliation*
Abung'u, George	Ph.D.	Archaeology
Akong'a, Joshua	Ph.D.	Cultural Anthropology
Amuyunzu-Nyamongo, Mary	Ph.D.	Medical Anthropology
Birungi, Harriet	Ph.D.	Medical Anthropology
Brown, Judith	Ph.D.	Medical Anthropology
Egesah, Omar	Doctoral candidate	Medical Anthropology
Goldsmith, Paul	Ph.D.	Cultural Anthropology
Kareithi, Joram	Ph.D.	Cultural Anthropology
Kinunjia, Mzalendo	Ph.D.	Archaeology
Kituyi, Mukhisa	Ph.D.	Cultural Anthropology
Kong'ong'o, Maurice	Doctoral candidate	Medical Anthropology
Kyule, Mwanzia	Doctoral candidate	Archaeology
Lane, Paul	Ph.D.	Archaeology
London, Dennis	Ph.D.	Cultural Anthropology
Maithya, Harrison	Ph.D.	Medical Anthropology
Mbae, Ben	Doctoral candidate	Archaeology
Meegan, Mike	Ph.D.	Medical Anthropology
Muange, Vincent	Ph.D.	Medical Anthropology
Muia, Mulu	Doctoral candidate	Archaeology
Munene, Karega	Ph.D.	Archaeology
Munguti, Kaendi	Ph.D.	Medical Anthropology
Mwendwa, Fred	Ph.D.	Cultural Anthropology
Nangendo, Steve	Doctoral Candidate	Cultural Anthropology
Njeru, Enos	Ph.D.	Sociology
Nkwi, Paul	Ph.D.	Medical Anthropology
Nyamongo, Isaac	Ph.D.	Medical Anthropology
Ocholla-Ayayo, ABC	Ph.D.	Cultural Anthropology
Olenja, Joyce	Ph.D.	Medical Anthropology
Olunga, Owuor	Doctoral Candidate	Medical Anthropology
Ondicho, Tom	Doctoral Candidate	Cultural Anthropology
Onyancha, Edwin	Doctoral Candidate	Cultural Anthropology
Onyango-Ouma, Washington	Ph.D.	Medical Anthropology
Somjee, Sultan	Ph.D.	Cultural Anthropology
Were, Isaac	Doctoral candidate	Archaeology
Wandiba, Simiyu	Ph.D.	Archaeology

* This information is based on the author's estimates as of July 2004. Some of the anthropologists listed perform different roles in research and teaching, but heir research affiliation is based on where much of the research time and publications are channeled. There are a few other anthropologists with masters degrees and working in Kenya, but they have been omitted.

Chapter 5

Anthropology in Turkey: Impressions for an Overview

Zerrin G. Tandoğan

INTRODUCTION

This overview on Turkish social/cultural anthropology[1] is confined to the current status of the discipline, along with a brief political and historical background. Thus, it is by no means an exhaustive study aiming to cover all anthropologists and their work in and on Turkey. However, it can provide an insight for those who are not closely acquainted with the topic. Taking the venture of representation, I have to state that this essay is written from my perspective and it can neither claim a totally neutral position—nor deny the selectivity in perception. I will incorporate the views and assessments of the third generation Turkish anthropologists in the academy, relying on the recent discussions and debates in related literature. In addition to my personal and professional experiences in the field since the mid 1980s,[2] I asked some academics on the current status of anthropology in Turkey via email, telephone, and in informal interviews. When put together, the following collage came into view.

INSTITUTIONAL CONTEXT

The origins of anthropology in Turkey as an institutionalized research activity dates back to 1925, shortly after the establishment of the Turkish Republic in 1923. Magnarella and Turkdogan (1976: 265) state that:

Social anthropology in Turkey initially developed within the atmosphere of nationalistic purpose. The Anthropology Institute (*Antropoloji Enstitüsü*) also known as the Center for Anthropological Research in Turkey (*Türkiye Antropoloji Tetkikat Merkezi*), was established in 1925 in the Faculty of Medicine of Istanbul University. Most of its research dealt with physical anthropological topics, though it did publish some folkloric studies by George Dumezil (1928), who was Professor of the History of Religions at Istanbul University from 1925 to 1931, and a socio-statistical study of suicide in Istanbul by Max Bonnafous (1928), who taught sociology at Istanbul University at about the same time. The first real social anthropological work to emanate from the Institute was Kemal Gungor's *Ethno-anthropological Study of the South Anatolian Yuruks* (1940–41).

From a historical perspective, a developed rural sociology overlaps with anthropology in Turkey. Until the 1960s anthropological research was dominated by rural sociology in the form of both ethnographic and monographic village studies conducted by the pioneers of Turkish sociology Niyazi Berkes, Behice Boran, and İbrahim Yasa, Nermin Erdentuğ—the first female anthropologist, and by Mümtaz Turhan, a psychologist, between 1940 and 1960 (Magnarella et al, 1976; Erdentuğ et al. 2000/2). The interest in the study of folklore in Turkey dates back to the second half of the nineteenth century. According to Başgöz (1998), the first scientific study was connected with the establishment in the early 1920s of the Turkology Institute at Istanbul University by Fuad Köprülü. These studies were instituted in 1947, when the Chair of Folklore was founded by Pertev Naili Boratav, once an assistant of Fuad Köprülü, at Ankara University. Shortly thereafter, in 1948, Boratav was forced to leave due to the political pressures of the day and the department was closed down. The rebirth of the department as an independent one was not until 1980. Thus, there was an inactive period in folklore studies between 1950 and 1980 (Birkalan 2000/4; Başgöz 1998; Timuroğlu 1995).

After the 1960s, Turkey was dramatically affected by two coup d'etats (in 1971 and 1980). The impact of these obstructions on the social sciences and for the social scientists in the country requires particular scrutiny, one which lies beyond the scope of this essay. However, it is important to note that during this period, along with the establishment of the Higher Education Council in 1981, higher education had been restructured and directed towards a rigorously centralized system. This move, combined with the restrictive and oppressive character of the period, gave rise to an academic brain drain from the universities. In the post-1980 period, there was a radical shift toward privatization/neoliberalization of the economy and the society by all means. Özbudun (1993: 206) states that, "(W)ith the transition back to democratic politics in 1983, there has been a sudden surge of interest in liberal values and an increasing emphasis on civil society institutions." After the privatization of the higher education sector, the first private university, Bilkent University, was established in Ankara in 1984. However, it was in 1997 when the first anthropology department was instituted at the private Yeditepe University in Istanbul. As of today, out of fifty-three state universities, six offer training in anthropology, one in folklore, and there is one anthropology department out of the twenty-four private universities in Turkey.[3] Anthropologists who are employed in anthropology or in other social science departments have weak organizational ties. Erdentuğ and Magneralla (2000/2: 63) refer to the fact that: "Turkey's first Anthropology Association was not created until 1992. It has held meetings with either a single speaker or a panel of speakers two or three times a year since then. It also puts out a news bulletin to facilitate communication among members. According to its organizer, Nephan Saran, in 1997 this Istanbul-based association had 125 members, most of them being females." The same association organized the First National Anthropology Congress in 1999, and the Second National Anthropology Congress in June 2004 in Istanbul (see <http://www.antropoloji.gen.tr/>).

CURRENT STATUS OF THE DISCIPLINE

Anthropology as an academic discipline in Turkey at present displays an eclectic and fragmented character. It is difficult to observe cohesiveness or dominance of any anthropological tradition. However, it may be possible to distinguish some tenors in the field, such as the optimist and pessimist views on the current status of the discipline. Some Turkish anthropologists are optimistic by referring to the quantity and the quality of the anthropological studies in Turkey, while others are pessimistic due to the small underdeveloped structure of the field and the weak organizational ties of its members. A further pattern could be found between the Western and Turkish trained anthropologists, in the context of their epistemological and methodological orientations; while the former is practicing nonpositivist fieldwork, the latter is more involved with a positivist, survey type of research. Another observation is related with "colonized minds," that is, anthropologists who are in favor of their own knowledge production and the degree of authenticity in the studies as opposed to the extensive usage of "imported knowledge." In addition to these tenors, some of the Turkish anthropologists appear to conceive anthropology beyond its disciplinary boundaries, that is "anthropology as a worldview," as opposed to disciplinary chauvinism. In this context, worldview may refer to a particular understanding of the other, with reference to a non-positivist approach including an emphatic and interpersonal dimension between humans (Sirman 2002; Aydin 1998).

Though the views and perceptions of the "insiders" within Turkish anthropology might help us to assess the current status of the discipline, their
anthropological work (see bibliographies in Güvenç 1971; Erdentuğ 1985;
Erdentuğ et al. 2000/2) and their contribution to the discipline still remains
to be studied. Here, I will confine myself to the current discussions and controversial issues within the discipline. There are several very comprehensive
studies of the literature on the history and development of the discipline in
Turkey. There is a very comprehensive study on the development of anthropology in Turkey from the nineteenth century to 1972–73 written by Paul J.
Magnarella and Orhan Türkdoğan (1976), the other is a bio-bibliographic
documentary study of the past and present of social anthropology in the
Turkish universities written by Aygen Erdentuğ and Paul J. Magnarella
(2000/2). There are also other works such as bibliography of anthropology in
Turkey from 1935 to 1983 by Aygen Erdentuğ (1985), a short bibliography of
ethnological and anthropological studies written by Bozkurt Güvenç (1971),
and a study of the pioneers of anthropology in Turkey by Aygen Erdentuğ
(1998), as well as numerous periodicals such as: *Folklor/Edebiyat* (Folklore/
Culture), *Türk Kültürü* (Turkish Culture), and *Antropoloji* (Anthropology). A
number of observations about the current status of anthropology in Turkey
may be extracted from these studies:

(1) First, there is no consensus on the current status of the discipline
    in the country. Aydın (1998) presents an optimistic view regarding
    anthropological studies in Turkey, by referring to various studies on
    identity, ethnic or community monographs, the tradition of *Volk-
    skunde,* the anthropology of rituals, the anthropology of religion,
    political anthropology, kinship studies, social change, village and
    shantytown monographs, and study of local traditions, as well as
    general and theoretical books on anthropology in addition to hun-
    dreds of articles and theses written on these topics with which he
    opposes Eksigil's (1998) comment about a lack of anthropology in
    Turkey. Whereas, Sirman[4] does not find the already existing studies
    sufficient enough to talk about anthropology in Turkey.

(2) The low impact of anthropology in Turkish public life and in the
    making of social policies is a widely shared observation among the
    third generation anthropologists like Atay (2000), Aydın (2000/1)
    Özmen, (2000/1), and Gürsoy (1998). According to these anthro-
    pologists, anthropology and anthropologists in Turkey hardly ever
    take part in the local public debates and in mass media; it is a si-
    lent discipline. Thus, there is no dissemination of anthropological
    knowledge and views in the society. Discussions and debates seem

to stay within the literature and academic milieu. Besides, Atay (2000/1) argues that anthropology in Turkey faces a serious institutionalization problem and there is lack of information as to "what is anthropology?" for a vast amount of people in the society.

(3) The role of an official ideology over social sciences in general and on the studies of anthropologists is a subject of controversy. In this context, there are further ideological conflicts and debates among academics, due to their various perceptions of the relation between academic freedom and the state. It is a hot topic and critically elaborated by the anthropologists in the relevant literature (Aydın 2000/2; Gürsoy 2000/2; Özmen, 2000/2). Regarding this subject, it should be noted that at the time of the two military interventions, anthropologists, like all other social scientists, were viewed with a suspicion by the military authorities. Furthermore, in 1971, the Anthropology Research Area within the Sociology Department, and, in 1980, the Anthropology Department at Hacettepe University, were almost closed.

(4) Another dispute that takes place in the literature among the anthropologists and the social scientists in Turkey is on the notion of "imported science." Cigdem Kagitcibasi (1986) points at the extensive usage of Western concepts in the Turkish social sciences, a view that is widely acknowledged by many social scientists. Higher education has always been criticized by some academics (Kıray 1986; Öncü 1986; Kağıtcıbası 1986) with reference to the type of education dominant and common at the universities. It has been argued that heavy reliance on imported knowledge and foreign concepts in anthropology leads to a confusion by ignoring their academic and historical contexts within the Anglo-American and European anthropological traditions (Güvenç 1971: 98). In other words, anthropology at home requires "decolonized minds" and context specific production of knowledge from a cross-cultural perspective. According to Nalbantoğlu (2003: 29), in the academic world that is surrounded by global circumstances, there is the reproduction of imported cultural products. The hegemony of Western discourses on social sciences could be also associated with the lack of its own knowledge production in the periphery. Hannerz (1998: 167) observes the same in Swedish anthropology, "(F)ar from being brainwashed by the perspectives of foreign scholars, Swedish anthropologists may have some difficulty in pinning down and problematizing the peculiarities of their own compatriots."

(5) There is agreement among the native and foreign researchers that Turkish sociology and anthropology have been dominated all through their establishment by a positivist methodology, thus, using questionnaires and interviews instead of participant observation and long term field work. It is difficult to confine positivism exclusively to a research methodology; rather, it is viewed as an ideology (Belge 2004). The identification of positivism with the modernization and Westernization project of Turkey has been discussed extensively by the academics (Magneralla et al. 1976; Özdalga 1990; Aydın 1998; Erdentuğ 2001). The reflection of this ideology on the social sciences still remains to be overcome since it is difficult to talk about a paradigmatic shift toward a more qualitative research. Particularly in anthropology, the dominance of this paradigm leads to a confrontation between academics during academic promotions. An anthropologist who favors the positivist methodology may easily reject a candidate for doing reflexive anthropology.

(6) Anthropologists trained in the British and US traditions and employed at Turkish universities may constitute another category in the field. Nükhet Sirman, a British trained social anthropologist, writing extensively on feminism, the status of women, nationalism, and gender in Turkey, and currently working in the Sociology Department at Bogazici University, evaluates the present status of the discipline as follows:

> (A)ctually, there is a development of a new anthropology as far as my observations are concerned. Some of my students, for example are doing research in Syria and Egypt. There is an effort on doing new studies in the field of urban anthropology and there are approaches merging sociology and anthropology that are mostly feminist. In my opinion, it is still difficult to talk about anthropology in Turkey since the present studies are not adequate in that respect.[4]

There are not many Western trained Turkish anthropologists; however, the British trained anthropologists outnumber those trained in the US (see Erdentuğ et al. 2000/2). The British connection could partly be related to Paul Stirling,[5] who influenced the growth of the discipline and supervised a group of Turkish social scientists both in Ankara, London and Canterbury. Only one US trained Turkish anthropologist, Emine Onaran İncirlioğlu,[6] worked with Stirling during his fieldwork in Turkey in 1986. The commonality between these anthropologists is that almost all Western trained Turkish anthropologists of the post-1980s did long term fieldwork in and out of Turkey.

FROM ANTHROPOLOGY DEPARTMENTS TO
INTERDISCIPLINARY CENTERS

It is possible to observe some new formations with respect to conducting qualitative, critical and reflexive research. Besides the bureaucratic structure and rigidly defined research fields within the hierarchical structure of the classical departments, there has been a shift since the late 1990s toward research centers both in the public and private universities based in Ankara and Istanbul. In these centers, there are interdisciplinary and cross-cultural studies on migration, women, political, and region oriented research (see Erdemli 2000). Women and cultural studies require especially more attention when compared to others, with respect to their emphasis on developing a critical perspective in the social sciences in an institutionalized way. These centers are part of nationwide and worldwide networks and financed by independent national and international resources due to their international connections. It is through these centers that a breaking away from positivism, hierarchy and patriarchy could be observed to a certain extent.

Women studies have been carried out in Turkey since the early 1990s; at present, there are thirteen women studies programs in public universities, though the ones in Ankara and Istanbul are more active (see <http://kasaum.ankara.edu.tr>). These programs promote qualitative and interdisciplinary research on various aspects of economic, social, and political issues related with the status of women in society, and the development of academic feminism. According to Sancar (2003), academic feminism with its interdisciplinary and critical approach could help other social sciences to overcome their "scientific blindness." Ethnography and participant observation are not dominated by anthropologists anymore. Particularly in the field of women studies, sociologists extensively do reflexive anthropology, but it is still not possible to speak of the existence of a feminist anthropology in Turkey. However, this break from positivism has added a gender dimension to the work of anthropological studies, which was missing before the 1970s.

Cultural studies constitute another break from positivism toward critical studies. The emergence of cultural studies in Turkey dates back to the late 1990s as an undergraduate program at Sabanci University (Schneider 2002), and at the graduate level at Bilgi and Bogazici Universities, in Istanbul and at Middle East Technical University in Ankara. According to Pultar and Kirtunc (2004: 129): "It must be said that cultural studies seems to have been invented especially for Turkish society as its emphasis on examining issues of power and social difference makes it a particularly apt approach to exploring and critiquing the decidedly hierarchical and patriarchal character of the latter." The formation of the Group for Cultural Studies in Turkey (see <http://www.cstgroup.org>) in 1999 by a majority of women academics from diverse universities is an alternative formation for anthropology departments. This group promotes new approaches and understandings toward the study of cultural diversity in Turkey. Its ambitious task was described by Pultar and Kirtunc as follows:

> The inter-university Group set for itself from the beginning an agenda that was meant to seek ways to apply cultural theory to the cultures of Turkey (Turkish, Jewish, Greek, Armenian, Circassian, Laz, Kurdish and others such as the Romans), and Turks (in Turkey, in Europe and the West in general, in the former Ottoman territories in the Balkans and the Middle East, and in the former Soviet territories in Central Asia and the Caucasus, and in Iran and China); and if possible to generate new theory and methodology. (2004: 140)

Even if this breathtaking geographical inclusiveness of the group's scope remains to be seen in practical terms, its ambition to revitalize and renew the already existing studies on culture might serve as an inspiration for future studies and help to free the encapsulated Turkish anthropological studies.

Migration studies are mostly conducted outside the anthropology departments in Turkey and either by sociologists or anthropologists. Political science, sociology, and international relations departments as well as recently established migration research centers[7] constitute the institutional and organizational logistics to the studies in migration. It should be also noted that Turkish anthropologists[8] who are employed in various European universities conduct extensive fieldwork among the Turkish immigrants in Europe. It may be argued that Turkey is a country of people in motion. International emigration, transnational connections, internal migration, refugee, and transit flows constitute diverse patterns of human mobility in Turkey. The study of the diverse form of this mobility is crucial for local and global dynamics. In the Turkish context, there is a focus on urban anthropology, ethnographic researches in the squatter settlements (Erman 1998; Erder 1996), as well as quantitative studies (see *Internal Migration in Turkey* 1998).

Fieldwork in the neighboring countries requires financial and bureaucratic support. Due to the geopolitical location of Turkey, the study of the region is of the utmost importance in political and social sciences. Field research conducted in the Balkan countries, Central Asian countries, Ukraine, and Russia is sustained by the Center for Black Sea and Central Asia, founded in 1993 at the Middle East Technical University, a state university based in Ankara. The director of the Center, who is a British trained social anthropologist, Ayşe Ayata (2000), describes the activities of the Center as follows:

> We are trying to send to these countries the young researchers as much as possible. We make sure that our students learn the language of the countries on

which they are studying. For example, a student who we send to Uzbekistan learns both Uzbek and a little Russian there. Moreover, he/she lives there for a considerable span of time ... One should acquire knowledge not only by reading about the place, but being there. Until now our studies are concentrated mostly on the subjects of family, family culture, women, youth, juvenile culture. We have conducted a study on the local culture in Uzbekistan, as well as in Turkmenistan, Azerbaijan and Ankara, Turkey. We have conducted a series of comparative research on family. Another important issue for us was the phenomenon of migration. It is highly important for Turkey. We are working on both the international emigration and migration from urban to rural areas. For instance, we tried to find answers to the questions where do Ahiska Turks live and whence they immigrate? (Ayata 2000)

The above mentioned examples of interdisciplinary studies, among others, provide an opportunity for young academics, as prospective researchers, to undertake non-positivistic, agency oriented, qualitative research opportunities as compared to the positivistic research tradition that is still dominant in the universities of the country in general. The limited number of these formations and their affiliations to private universities located in the urban areas might confine interdisciplinary, critical, and ethnographic research to more a internationalized, English-speaking, and economically well-off academics and students. In other words, anthropological research still remains in the periphery of the periphery.

CONCLUDING REMARKS

Anthropological practice in Turkey is to a great extent a university based scholarly activity. Turkish anthropologists are dispersed among diverse social science departments in and out of Turkey. It is a small, fragmented, and silent discipline having no or low impact in public debates, macro politics, and mass media. There is an encapsulation of Turkish anthropologists within the academic milieu. Fieldwork and ethnographic research seem to be sponsored mostly by private enterprises or by the universities with international connections. Variances in epistemological and methodological approaches are not only confined to different generations, but also to the patterns of Western and Turkish anthropology training. If one of the ways of defining anthropology is the study of the other through which one reflects on his/her own society, this reflexive approach seems to be a lonely activity in the Turkish case. On the other hand, beyond the limits of departmental boundaries, there are new openings toward more non-positivist, qualitative, critical, and reflexive social research. I do not think that it would be fair to

reduce all the above mentioned debates and developments as a peculiarity of Turkish anthropology. From a comparative perspective, there are more similarities than differences between us and them. Maybe it is time to protect our "good" authentic sides against some "bad" erosions of globalization.

NOTES

1. I will use anthropology to refer to social and cultural anthropology throughout the text.
2. In 1983, I took a fourth year elective course, a seminar on women and society, offered by Nükhet Sirman, a female anthropologist teaching in the Department of Sociology at Middle East Technical University in Ankara. After the "grand narratives" of my department of political science, it was extremely interesting to learn about social anthropology. My term paper was on the Turkish peasant women handicrafts and their symbolic meanings. When I decided to study folklore at the graduate level, I found myself in the Anthropology Department at Hacettepe University. I was accepted with two warnings; first, I should not get married and leave the field, and second, I should hold fast to folklore due to its unpopularity among the students. However, I both married and shifted to social anthropology. I did my field research among Turkish migrants residing in a multicultural district in Oslo between 1989 and 1991. At present, I am teaching in the Department of Political Science at Bilkent University and offering courses from an anthropological perspective on transnational cultures, interculturalism and Europe, among others (see Tandoğan 1999 and 2004 for related publications).
3. There are eight anthropology departments today: in Ankara, at Hacettepe and Ankara Universities; in Istanbul, at Yeditepe and Istanbul Universities; in Sivas, at Cumhuriyet University; in Hatay, at Mustafa Kemal University; and in Van, at Yuzuncu Yil University.
4. From email correspondence on 28 October 2004, translated by Zerrin Tandoğan.
5. Paul Stirling did his doctoral fieldwork in two villages, Sakaltutan and Elbasi, in Kayseri, a small city located in the southeast of Ankara, between 1949 and 1951. The book, which is based on this research, was *Turkish Village,* published in 1965. He revisited and restudied the same villages after thirty-five years had passed, together with a team of Turkish anthropologists. For his ethnographic data and archives, see <http://lucy.ukc.ac.uk.Stirling/>.
6. US trained female anthropologist, Emine Onaran Incirlioglu, did fieldwork together with Paul Stirling during his "Thirty-five Years of Transformation in Central Anatolia" project from January 1986 to August 1986. See Incirlioglu (1994) for more details.
7. There are two migration research centers based in Istanbul; one at Bilgi University launched in 2002 (see <http://www.goc.bilgi.edu.tr/>, and the other at Koc University, opened this year (see <http://www.ku.edu.tr/~mirekoc/>.

8. See Ayse Simsek-Caglar (2003) and Lale Yalcin-Hekmann (2003) for related studies.

REFERENCES

Atay, Tayfun. 2000–1. "Erken Bir Doğumdan Gecikmiş Bir Büyümeye. Türkiye'de Antropoloji, Bir Kongrenin Cağrıstırdıkları" [From a Premature Birth to a Suspended Growth: Impressions from a Congress]. *Folklor/Edebiyat* VI, 21.
——. 2000–2. "Kavramlar Kargaşası, Bilimdalları Çatışması: Dünyada ve Türkiye'de 'Sosyal İçerikli' Antropolojiyi Adlandırma Sorunu" [Confusion of Concepts, Clash of Disciplines: The Problem of Naming Anthropology with a "Social Content" in Turkey]. *Folklor/Edebiyat* VI, 22.
Ayata, Ayşe. 2000. From the interview conducted by Erol Mutlu in Eurosia -Turkey radio program. <http://pc12.soc/metu.edu.tr.ars.html> (accessed November 2004).
Aydın, Suavi. 1998. "Eksigil'in Yazısı Vesilesiyle Türkiye'de Antropolojinin Eni-Boyu Üzerine" [In Connection with Eksigil's Article and the Scope of Anthropology in Turkey]. *Toplum ve Bilim* 77, Summer.
——. 2000–2. "Arkeoloji ve Sosyolojinin Kıskacında Türkiye'de Antropolojinin 'Geri Kalmışlığı' [The Underdevelopment of Anthropology in Turkey Beneath Archaeology and Sociology]. *Folklor/Edebiyat* VI, 22.
——. 2004. "Türkiye'de Sosyal Bilimlerin Değeri ve Sınırları: Peter Andrews'un calışmaları ve yeni yayınlanan bir 'ansiklopedi' üzerinden bir değerlendirme" [The Limits and the Value of Social Sciences in Turkey: An Evaluation Through the Works of Peter Andrews and a Recently Published "Encyclopaedia"]. *Toplum ve Bilim* 100, Spring 2004.
Başgöz, İlhan. 1998. "Türkiye'de Halk Bilimi Calışmaları ve Milliyetcilik" [Nationalism and Folkore Studies in Turkey]. *Folklor/Edebiyat* no. 14.
Birkalan, A. Hande. 2000–4. "Türkiye'de Halkbilimi ve Bazı Türk Halkbilimcileri" [Folklore in Turkey and Some Turkish Folklorists]. *Folklor/Edebiyat,* vol. VI.
Çağlar, Şimşek Ayşe. 2004. "İki Elde Bir Sehpa" [One Coffee Table in Two Hands]. In *Kültür Fragmanları* [Culture in Fragments], D. Kandiyoti et al., eds. Istanbul: Metis.
Erdemli, Özgül. 2000. "A Guide to Research Centers in Turkey," *Turkish Studies,* Vol. 1, No. 2.
Erdentuğ, Aygen. 1985. "Bibliography of Anthropology (1935–1983)." *Antropoloji* no. 12.
——. "The Pioneering Anthropologists of Turkey: Personal Profiles in Socio-Political Context." *The Turkish Studies Association Bulletin* vol. 22, no. 2.
Erdentuğ, S. Aygen, and Paul J. Magnarella. 2000–2. "Türkiye'deki Üniversitelerde Sosyal Antropolojinin Dünü ve Bugünü: Biyo-bibliyografik Bir Degerlendirme" [The Past and Present of "Social Anthropology" in the Universities of Turkey: A Bio-biographical Evaluation]. *Folklor/Edebiyat* vol. VI, no. 22..

——. 2001. "Turkish Social Anthropology Since the 1970s." *The Oriental Anthropologist* vol. I, no. 1.

Erder, Semra. 1996. *Istanbul'da Bir Kent Kondu: Ümraniye* [A Shantytown ın Istanbul: Ümraniye]. Istanbul: Iletişim.

Erman, Tahire. 1997. "Göç Olgusunda Kalitatif Yöntem Olarak Etnografik Araştırma: Bir Gecekondu Araştırmasının Düşündürdükleri" [Ethnographic Research as a Qualitative Methodology on the Phenomenon of Migration). In the conference proceedings of *Türkiye'de İçgöç* [Internal Migration in Turkey]. Istanbul: Yurt Yayınları.

Gürsoy, Akile. 1998. "Kimliğimizi daha iyi tanıyabilirdik" [We could have known our identity better]. From the interview in *Milliyet*, <http://www.milliyet.com.tr/ 1998/06/20/entel/entel.html>, accessed in November 2004.

Guvenc, Bozkurt. 1971. "Etnolojik ve Sosyal (Kültürel) Antropolojik Araştırmalar" [Ethnological and Social (Cultural) Anthropological Studies in Turkey]. In Türkiye'de Sosyal Araştırmalarin Gelişmesi [Development of Social Research in Turkey]. Ankara: Hacettepe University Publication.

Hannerz, Ulf. 1982. "Twenty Years of Swedish Social Anthropology." *Ethnos* 47: 1–11.

Heckmann, Yalcin Lale. 2003. "Kimlikler Üzerine Pazarlik" [Bargain on Identities]. In *Kültür Fragmanları* (Culture in Fragments), D. Kandiyoti et al., eds. Istanbul: Metis.

İncirlioğlu, Onaran Emine. 1994. "Negotiating Ethnographic Reality: Team Fieldwork in Turkey." In *When History Accelerates: Essays on Rapid Social Change, Complexity and Creativity*, ed. by Chris M. Hann. London: Athlone.

Icduygu, A., et al. 1997. *Türkiye'de İçgöç* [Internal Migration in Turkey]. Conference proceedings. Istanbul: Yurt Yayınları.

Kağıtçıbaşı, Çiğdem. 1986. "Sosyal Psikoloji Arastırmaları: Geleceğe İlişkin Öneriler" [Studies in Social Psychology: Prospective Suggestion]. In *Türkiye'de Sosyal Bilim Araştırmalarının Gelişimi* [Development of Social Science Studies in Turkey], S. Atauz , ed. Ankara: Turkish Social Science Association.

Kıray, Mübeccel. 1986. "Toplum, Bilgi ve Türkiye" [Society, Knowledge and Turkey]. In *Türkiye'de Sosyal Bilim Araştırmalarının Gelişimi* [Development of Social Sciences in Turkey], S. Atauz , ed. Ankara: Turkish Social Science Association.

Magnarella, J. Paul and Orhan Türkdoğan. 1976. "The Development of Turkish Social Anthropology." *Current Anthropology* 17, 2.

Nalbantoglu, Ünal. 2003. "Üniversite A.Ş.'de bir 'homo academicus': 'Ersatz' yuppie akademisyen" ['Homo academicus in Joint-stock Company University: 'Ersatz' Yuppie Academics]. *Toplum ve Bilim* 97, Summer 2003.

Öncü, Ayşe. 1986. "Sosyoloji Araştırmaları Oturumu Üzerine Yorum" [Comments on the Sociological Researches Session]. In *Türkiye'de Sosyal Bilim Araştırmalarının Gelişimi* (Development of Social Sciences in Turkey), S. Atauz, ed. Ankara: Turkish Social Science Association.

Özbudun, Ergun. 1993. "State Elites and Democratic Political Culture in Turkey." In *Political Culture and Democracy*, Larry Diamond, ed. Boulder and London: Lynne Rienner.

Özdalga, Elisabeth. 1997. "Türkiye'de Bir Sosyolog Olmak Üzerine" [To Be a Sociologist in Turkey]. *Toplum ve Bilim* 48/49.

Özmen, Abdurrahim. 2000-2. "Öteki'ni Anlama(ma)nın Bilimi: Türkiye Antropolojisinin Sorunları" [A Science of Understanding (and not Understanding) the Other: Problems of Turkish Anthropology]. *Folklor/Edebiyat* 22: 125-34.

Pultar, Gönül and Ayşe Lahur Kırtunc. 2004. "Cultural Studies in Turkey: Education and Practice." *The Review of Education, Pedagogy, and Cultural Studies* 26: 129-53.

Sancar, Serpil. 2003. "Universitede Feminism? Bağlam, Gündem ve Olanaklar" [Feminism in the University? Context, Agenda and Possibilities]. *Toplum ve Bilim* Fall 97.

Sirman, E. Nükhet. 2002. "Antropoloji: Olanla Olması Gerekenin Arasında Bir Bilim" [Anthropology: A Science Between Is and Ought]. In *Bilgi Toplumuna Geçiş* [Transition to Information Society], Tekeli et al., eds. Ankara: Turkish Academy of Sciences.

Schneider, Annedith. 2002. "The Institutional Revolutionary Major? Questions and Contradictions on the Way to Designing a Cultural Studies Program in a New Turkish University." *International Journal of Cultural Studies* 5, 4: 393-404.

Tandoğan, G. Zerrin, with E. Onaran Incirioglu. 1999. "Cultural Diversity, Aesthetics and Power." *European Journal of Intercultural Studies* 10, 1: 51-63.

——. 2004. "Academics in Motion: Cultural Encapsulation and Feeling at Home." *City and Society* 16, 1: 99-114.

Tekeli, Ilhan. 1977. "Ideological Problems Concerning Social Sciences in the Peripheral Countries." In *Seminar on Approaches and Methods in Social Sciences in Turkey.* Ankara: METU.

Timuroğlu, Vecihi. 1995. "Pertev Naili Boratav: Türk Halkbiliminin Kurucusu" [Pertev Naili Boratav: The Founder of Folklore in Turkey]. *Folklor/Edebiyat* 2: 104-10.

Chapter 6

Committed or Scientific? The Southern Whereabouts of Social Anthropology and *Antropología Social* in 1960–70 Argentina*

Rosana Guber

INTRODUCTION

Since 1984, Social Anthropology has become the main branch of Argentine anthropology. Many anthropologists celebrate this position, first, as a reply to a fifty-year long intrusion of right wing ideology in academia and of conservative theory in anthropology, and second, as evidence of the anthropologists' involvement into the fate of their social subjects. Thus, Argentine social anthropologists still depict Argentine *antropología social* as the "committed" (Alberti 1962), "militant," and "persecuted" discipline (Herrán 1990; Garbulsky 1991–92), the democratic orientation (Ratier & Ringuelet 1997), and as the "weak" and "marginal" branch of anthropology (Bartolomé 1980; Vessuri 1989). Thus, *antropología social* has been both a victim of ideological repression and academic exclusion, and a political agent battling against official anthropology, the State and the powers that be.

The ways in which Argentine academics were molded by, and helped mold, the particular relationship between politics and academia, have been crucial in rendering *Antropología Social* as a meaningful category in Argentina (L'Estoile et. al. 2002). Such meanings are not given, but resulted from a fifty-year long process of political and theoretical struggles in the humanities and the social sciences. Here, I will show two notions of *antropología social* as they unfolded in the *porteño* academia of Buenos Aires between 1956 and the early 1970s. I call these two ways of theoretical and political practice social anthropology and *antropologia social*. In order to root such notions, I will analyze the contexts, trajectories, and thoughts of two *porteño* anthropologists self-ascribed as *"antropólogos sociales."* The cases of Esther Hermitte (1921-1990) and Eduardo Menéndez (ca. 1930) illuminate the similarities and differences underlying the meanings of socioanthropological theory and practice in Buenos Aires.[1] Hermitte and Menéndez became acquainted with anthropology at the University of Buenos Aires; both resigned to their teaching posts after the "Night of the Long Batons," when the Police Infantry broke into the University in July 1966; both were banned after the new intervention of the Executive Power to national universities in July 1974, a prologue to the latest military dictatorship of 1976. Menéndez has lived in México City ever since, whereas Hermitte remained in Argentina teaching social anthropology at a small institute, the *Instituto de Desarrollo Económico y Social* (IDES), in Buenos Aires city.

Though not alone, these two anthropologists helped shape the two major perspectives in *antropología social* that evolved in Argentina between the mid 1960s and the mid 1970s, and more importantly, the main definitions of the current anthropology. Despite their disagreements, they strove to root social anthropology in specific articulations of theory and practice,[2] and of academic and political practice. Here, I will show the sources and stances underlying these two perspectives.

MODERN AND SCIENTIFIC

Antropología social developed in 1957 at the University of Buenos Aires.[3] Until the late 1950s, Argentine anthropology only dealt with the past and with what anthropologists and most state agents conceived of as survivals of pre-Hispanic and pre-modern times—archaeology, ethnology, and folklore. This was in fact the orientation when the brand new degree—*licenciatura*—in *Ciencias Antropológicas* was launched in 1958–59 in Buenos Aires (the *licenciatura* at La Plata University started a year before). The professionalization of anthropology, hitherto an auxiliary branch of history, seemed to demand neither social nor cultural anthropology.

Antropología social entered Buenos Aires from the United States, but along two lines: one was introduced by an Argentine woman trained as a History professor at the Ethnographic Museum, the home of anthropological and archaeological research and teaching since 1904; the other was cultivated by the neighboring department of Sociology (a degree in Sociology was launched in 1957). Both lines were relatively independent, although familiar to each other.

As to the first source, it was Esther Alvarez, shortly married to Raúl Hermitte, who started to talk about social anthropology once she returned to the Museum in 1956. In 1947, she quit the university under a pro-Peronist intervention, although in 1950 she managed to get her degree as a History professor, the program which she started in 1941. Between 1947 and 1950 Esther Hermitte traveled twice to the University of Chicago, where she was introduced to social anthropology. Later on, while striving for a grant to pursue graduate studies at Robert Redfield's department, Hermitte started a short research project on the social relations in a mining complex. El Aguilar had extracted lead, zinc, and silver since about 1926. Hermitte's fieldwork was short but intensive: she traveled to the Puna desert at 4,000m above sea level, in northwest Argentina, in January and February of 1957 and 1958, with a field assistant. There she wandered and observed, and she surveyed and interviewed Bolivian and Argentine miners and white collar employees about their families, networks, jobs, houses, illnesses, casualties, leisure, domestic economy, religion, and ceremonies. Hermitte was not looking for culture or tradition, but rather for social relations among Bolivian and Atacameño miners, and the company agents. Although her final report is still missing, her work became known to her Argentine contemporaries as "*antropología social,*" or, as Hermitte also put it, "applied anthropology."[4]

In 1958, she left to pursue a Ph.D. in Anthropology at Chicago, the beachhead of British Anthropology in the United States. Radcliffe-Brown's stay between 1931 and 1937 gave rise to a more "scientific" and "strictly non-historical" method to study society, and a departure from the humanities cultivated by Sapir and the Boas school. Radcliffe-Brown's search of "laws governing the synchronic functioning of human society" left deep marks in the Chicagoan school of anthropology, namely the fall of ethnological studies, the subordination of culture to social structure and the primacy of area studies and extended case studies (Stocking 1979: 21; Wax 1970).

Even though Redfield had just died and US anthropology was becoming increasingly Parsonian (Stocking 1979; Handler 1995; Kuper 1999), the influence of British social anthropology was still alive in an interdisciplinary project. The project "Man-in-Nature" started in 1956 and was chaired by Norman McQuown. Fieldworkers, mostly MA and Ph.D. candidates, were coordinated by Evans Pritchard's former student Julian Pitt-Rivers. The Chicago-Chiapas Project looked for social and cultural change among Tzeltal and Tzotzil Indians (Pitt-Rivers & McQuown 1964: 5–7)˙ After spending twenty-four months in an Indian quarter (1959–61), Hermitte wrote up her MA thesis (1962) on the Indian social mobility of the *revestidos,* those Indians who adopted the *ladino* dress and the way of life. Her doctoral dissertation (1964) dealt with the Indian uses of supernatural beliefs and forces in order to exert social control upon their Indian fellows. Nahualism and witchcraft were allies of a political organization that *Pinolteco* Indians had "moved up" to the supernatural sphere, whereas *ladino* people ruled "down here" (1970/ 2004). Both her MA and Ph.D. theses received important awards, but de spite this success and after serving as research assistant to David Schneider's project "American Kinship System," she returned to Argentina in 1965, looking for a teaching position and a research location.

Once in Buenos Aires she was able to enter the Sociology Department where a course on Social Anthropology was being taught since 1962. Gino Germani, known as the founding father of modern Argentine sociology, included this course in the degree of Sociology which he created in 1957. However, Social Anthropology was taught for the first time in 1962 by Ralph Beals, who was hired for just one semester.[5] The syllabus included several topics familiar to the American and British traditions: fieldwork, culture, function and structure, theories of kinship, politics, cultural ecology, evolutionism, adaptive system, urban studies, national cultures, acculturation, culture, and personality. English and North American traditions were dominant in the reading list,[6] and many titles had already been translated for a broader audience.[7] Also, a large part of these materials were part of other courses, such as Germani's Introduction to Sociology and Systematic Sociology (Guber & Visacovsky 2006).

The inclusion of Social Anthropology in the Anthropology program was probably imposed by the university reformers of the post-Peronist era, who vowed for a modern and applied social science. Although their hand did not reach the Department of Anthropology itself, still devoted to reconstruct the origins of the American Man, they seemed to assume that Social Anthropology was a social science that would become the practical branch of anthropology.

These two routes to British and American Social Anthropology in Buenos Aires were cultivated with some discontinuity. *Ciencias Antropológicas* started during Hermitte's absence, and only two professors—Palavecino and Cortazar—taught some social anthropologists. However, it was the Sociology Department that took the lead in the instruction of British and American social anthropology. Interestingly enough, Hermitte was assigned to a seminar on modern Mayas, already as part of the degree in *Ciencias Antropológicas,* instead of being appointed to the course on Social Anthropology at Sociology. Once back at the Museum, she met scholars who had just graduated as *Licenciados* and young students. One of them, Carlos Herrán, began as her field assistant and performed new research on *poncho* weavers and *pimentón* growers in the northwestern province of Catamarca. The *porteño* think tank in the Social Sciences *Instituto Torcuato Di Tella* appointed Hermitte as the chair of the Social Anthropology section, almost at the same time as the military coup of the so-called *Revolución Argentina* entered the university and jailed students and professors. As a result, most teaching assistants—including young anthropologists—resigned from their posts. Hermitte was the only professor in anthropology to do so.

Based in Buenos Aires city, she also gathered a research team to work on "The social meaning of illness" in 1965. Four junior anthropologists—Mirtha Lischetti, Hugo Ratier, and Eduardo Menéndez, of the first cohort, and María Rosa Neufeld, of a later one—started to work on the notion of illness, healer-patient relations, and social class in a *porteño* neighborhood. Some theoretical work and fieldwork was done, including participant observation and deep and semi-structured interviews to doctors and nurses, patients and their relatives, social workers, and students at local primary schools. In 1968, the team was analyzing data (AA 1968: 14–15), but for some reason this research rendered no publication. In its members' memories, a theoretical clash occurred, although in Hermitte's view more ethnographic fieldwork had to be done. The team dissolved after a while.

Meanwhile, she continued to work in Catamarca along the political economic critique that anthropologists like Eric Wolf and Sidney Mintz posed to Redfield's approach (Bartolomé & Gorostiaga 1974). Her findings showed that officially sponsored cooperatives did not help create social equality; they rather strengthened the inequality between the well-off and the dependent and poor weavers and peasants (Hermitte 1972; Hermitte & Herrán 1970). Hermitte was certainly not alone in her findings. Young graduate students doing intensive fieldwork for their doctoral degrees in social anthropology abroad, such as Hebe Vessuri in Oxford, Eduardo Archetti in Paris, and Leopoldo Bartolomé in Wisconsin, followed the same lines. In 1974, Hermitte managed to gather with them and other social anthropologists from the North, Central and South America under the notion of "social articulation."[8] This group was affiliated to CLACSO, the Latin American Council of Social Sciences for the autonomous development of social sciences in Latin America. Its aim was to set a forum for theoretical debate founded in intensive fieldwork and social anthropology, rather than in culturalist approaches such as "acculturation" and "transculturation." But this was not the only song that Social Anthropology sang in Buenos Aires.

COMMITTED TO TRANSFORMATION

Those who had enrolled in *Ciencias Antropológicas* in 1959 were not as young as other students of other degrees. Many came from the school of History professors at the *Facultad* and most of them had a job out of academia. Since 1962, they started to graduate as *licenciados* with an orientation in Folklore, Ethnology, and Archaeology. Yet, they called themselves "anthropologists" and paid no attention to whether they were acknowledged as "folklorists" or "ethnologists." "Social Anthropology" was not a category in use at that time in the Museum. What mattered to young anthropologists was to take care of the "real world" out there. In a journal called *Anthropologica,* which only had two issues, they presented anthropology as a discipline "committed" to development and to social change, since:

> The modern anthropologist becomes, because of the circumstances, an active militant in the 'battle for welfare' that countries in the making must face and he must give his diagnosis and his advice. The modern anthropologist operates on reality with a 'militant commitment,' and fosters change. (Alberti 1962: 6)

Although they used some notions taught by the Department of Sociology, they never recalled Sociology as their main source of socioanthropological inspiration. Militant, grassroots, committed anthropologists were part and parcel of a national and global process of politicization, including the radicalization of anthropological critique and of the Argentine youth. The university was led by open-minded intellectuals and updated scientists, in the midst of a restricted democracy, the banning of Peronism, and supported by the policies of the Alliance for Progress and the National Security Doctrine throughout Latin America. Popular youth took part in the Peronist *resistencia* that strove for Perón's return, whereas anthropology students demanded a new plan closer to "real Argentine society." In 1965, they asked for a fourth orientation on "Social Anthropology," a professional and scientific discipline devoted to the study of the "here and now," not bound to study primitive people, but rather to understand "our own society according to the stage of transformations that our country is going through" (AA 1968: 1).

A leading character in this move was Eduardo Menéndez, who had graduated from the first cohort in the ethnological orientation under the advice of the charismatic Italian anthropologist Marcelo Bormida. However, Menéndez quitted Bormida's circle and contacted Hermitte for academic advice. Hermitte—the only Ph.D. in social anthropology in Argentina—became his research director in a CONICET project on European migrants to the Littoral interior of Entre Ríos. He also took part in the Di Tella group of medical anthropology, as already noted. Nonetheless, by 1968 he left Hermitte's influence and went on with his own academic career.

Devoted mainly to the theoretical critique of colonialism and racism, Menéndez gained visibility in the humanities and social sciences. Together with other colleagues, he advocated for an *antropología social* interested in "non-traditional ecosocial areas" and topics (Menéndez 1968: 49), with a committed perspective against colonialism and racism. His theoretical interlocutors were also political and ideological ones. The target was functionalism and structural functionalism, structuralism and culturalism, and the culture historical and phenomenological orientations which prevailed at *Ciencias Antropológicas* even after 1966. His critique revolved around the ahistoricism and isolationism of such stances, as well as their involvement into different kinds of political and cultural oppression and discrimination.

Menéndez consolidated his critique into the MAC or "Anthropological Classic Model" (*Modelo Antropológico Clásico,* 1967–8).[9] Still taught today in introductory courses to anthropology, the manuscript was finished in 1968 but never reached publication. Menéndez featured the "classic" anthropologist perception of "sociocultural reality" as based on the "variables" of objectivity, authenticity, quality, relativism, totality, and homogeneity. Within this model, Menéndez lumped together most of the theoretical trends that had developed along 150 years of anthropological history. To support his model, Menéndez picked up examples from the ethnographic literature of American and British modern anthropology. Based on Franz Fanon's rhetoric on the power of colonialism to shape and dominate their subject's daily lives, values, and beliefs, Menéndez conceived of the anthropologist as an agent of imperialism who gained access to people's lives by means of long term fieldwork. This enterprise, he asserted, was undertaken by hanging around in supposedly isolated communities bound by close social ties. In fact, Menéndez's points were part of a growing movement of the anthropological Left shared by many anthropologists in Argentina, Latin America, the US, and Western Europe. His rhetoric also tied colonialism to anthropology, as in Talal Asad, Orlando Fals Borda, Pablo González Casanova, Rodolfo Stavenhagen, and Peter Worsley, and culturalism to traditional peasant studies, as the critiques posed by Sidney Mintz, Eric Wolf, Charles Wagley, and Marvin Harris (Bartolomé & Gorostiaga 1974).

But Menéndez's points were not uttered in a colonial setting. Argentina had been an independent country since 1816, with a unified central State since 1853. What Argentina did have at the time of Menéndez's critiques, was a military dictatorship suffused by the National Security Doctrine, the ban on Peronism, the most popular political force, and the rise of guerrilla movements mirroring the Cuban experience. Actually, in Argentines' current talk, colonialism amounted to authoritarianism, and the Armed Forces to an occupation army. This view was not only imported by the Left, but by doctrinarian nationalism and right wing Anti-Britanism, critical of Argentine compliance to the United Kingdom, the owner of Argentine commodities and public services until Perón's nationalization. Perón's rhetoric was also marked by anti-Britanism and later on by anti-Americanism. Such standpoints had their representatives in anthropological theory at the Ethnographic Museum. Most professors under Perón's administration were of a non-liberal creed, namely the chair of Anthropology between 1947 and 1955, Italian anthropologist Giuseppe Imbelloni, and two other researchers who entered the Museum in 1948, Austrian prehistorian Oswald Menghin and Roman junior anthropologist Marcelo Bormida. In 1955, the university modernizers tried to restore both political and academic liberalism. However, in Anthropology, only Imbelloni and archaeologist Casanova were forced to resign.

Many students of anthropology and young graduates in *Ciencias Antropológicas* were neither *Peronistas* nor liberals, but the rereading of the Peronist experience from the Left and Latin American anti-imperialism became intertwined when the *Libertadora* Revolution proved its authoritarian character. Liberal did not equate to being democratic, at least in Argentina. To make matters worse, the overlapping of the military coup, self-labeled as the *Revolución Argentina* of 1966, with the scholarly reaction to the bloody coup and Bormida's promotion as chair of the Department, brought to an end the project of Social Anthropology as the degree's fourth orientation, a project junior anthropologists and students vied for. *Antropología social* was ready to become an anti-institutional field, although no kind of social anthropology would apply.

From an unorthodox Marxist perspective, Menéndez analyzed the crisis or "ideologization" of the socio-cultural sciences, in which he included "anthropology." In his contribution, "Ideology, science and professional practice," to the edited volume *Social Sciences: ideology and national reality,* Menéndez warned that the social sciences and social anthropology had become "ideological" devices because theories ignored the historical contexts of scientific production. Lévi-Straussian structuralism was the utmost representation of ahistorical theory. Ahistoricism uncovered, to Menéndez, scholarly alienation from intellectual work. Likewise, methodology and fieldwork techniques were accomplices of such alienation. Sociologists had first split up the knowing process between patrons or analysts, between employees or fieldworkers, and second, anthropologists and sociologists had taken life history as a commodity, thus alienating it from its direct producer and the conditions of production (Menéndez 1970: 114–5). This led to what mattered most to Menéndez and to many scholars at that time—not just the production, but the appropriation of knowledge.

The Project Camelot was instituted by the US State Department on the Chilean territory to get information about insurrectional activities through information provided by social scientists. Along with denunciations by American anthropologists at the American Anthropological Association against anthropologists involved in American counter-insurgency in Thailand and Vietnam (Wakin 1992; Patterson 2001), Menéndez warned against those who had the power to use anthropological knowledge effectively, and against those organizations such as CLACSO and the Di Tella Institute, Hermitte's academic homes, which provided information for the sake of the US hemispheric security (Menéndez 1970: 106).

Menéndez recommended that scholars and intellectuals no longer follow the mirage of free, autonomous, and apolitical knowledge. Instead, they must attend to what "objectively" stood out as "crucial for the objective requirements of this transforming project," "the highest task to tend to." Argentine intellectuals had to gain access to the knowledge produced elsewhere and relate it to their own goals and priorities in order to exercise power. As a case in point, Menéndez quoted the use of participant observation by young Vietnamese scholars who learned local values by living in a peasant community. Local knowledge would be "applied," not for the Empire's ends, but rather to resist the American invasion and to achieve revolution (ibid.: 119–20). Finally, Menéndez raised a pledge for an "counter-system science" (ibid.: 123).

Throughout this period, Menéndez was one of the most influential anthropologists and was widely known in and out of the anthropological field. He had passionate discussions with sociologists and anthropologists, he entered into the powerful realm of psychoanalysis, and he proclaimed anthropology the cradle of modern theories such as evolutionism and neo-evolutionism, functionalism, structuralism, and structural-functionalism. In 1971, Menéndez managed to create a degree in *antropología social* at the University of the Buenos Aires Province at Mar del Plata. The faculty came largely from the department of social anthropology from Buenos Aires. Though short-lived, this *licenciatura* was very important to visualize *antropología social* as an institutional stance devoted to transformation and theoretical critique. In turn, ethnographic fieldwork was not as successful since it was visualized as intertwined with partisan activities, something hard to achieve without serious implications. In 1974, students and scholars began to be kidnapped and murdered by death squads (the Argentine Anticommunist Alliance), a task that the military government had systematized since March 1976.

THEORETICAL OR POLITICAL?

I decided to call s*ocial anthropology* and *antropología social* the two versions that Argentine scholars usually acknowledge under the single label of *"Antropología Social."* I chose Hermitte and Menéndez as two anthropologists who developed these two standpoints even though many other colleagues also shared the two views since they were not mutually exclusive. Moreover, Hermitte never advocated for an isolated community, since her *catamarqueño teleras* and her *tzeltal* Indians were always embedded in social relations entailing political and economic inequality (Hermitte & Bartolomé 1977). Menéndez acknowledged the relevance of ethnographic fieldwork, for it provided the best and most accurate information concerning a community, a neighborhood or a social stratum (Menéndez 1970: 121). And even though Hermitte was not a Marxist, her approaches were close to it, similar to many radical anthropologists in the northern hemisphere of the late 1960s. Menéndez claimed to be a Marxist, but of a special kind, looking for agency and subjectivity in the social process.

Concerning these two characters of Argentine social anthropology, it looks as if their disagreements came not just from theoretical turns, but rather from a different experience of the relationship between politics and the social sciences. Hermitte had been socialized in the liberal climate of the Argentine University in the early 1940s, when the faculty claimed to be apolitical and strictly academic, that is, fully liberal. As a student at the school of History professors, Hermitte was fond of her professor of Argentine and American Archaeology Francisco de Aparicio, also a liberal archaeologist, ethnohistorian, and geographer, who chaired the Museum and the Argentine Society of Anthropology between 1939 and 1947. Aparicio left the University of Buenos Aires after signing a letter which protested Perón's bold intervention into the university. He died shortly after and thus never returned to the Museum, but Hermitte did. In turn, Imbelloni (1885–1967) took over Aparicio's posts. He had arrived in Argentina before the First World War and started working as a journalist writing right wing articles vowing for war (Garbulsky 1987). In 1920, Imbelloni received his Ph.D. in Natural Sciences at Padua and returned to Argentina for a hasty academic career in *porteño* anthropology. In 1947 and throughout the Peronist era, he was appointed director of the Institute of Anthropology and of the Ethnographic Museum to continue developing the science of the American Man or *Americanística.* In 1948, he invited Austrian prehistorian Oswald Menghin, and a former balilla and still young Roman bachelor in Natural Sciences, Marcelo Bormida (1925–1978) as regular professors (Fígoli 1995). In 1955 and after the *Libertadora* Revolution which ousted Perón, Imbelloni was removed from all academic positions and left the University of Buenos Aires for good. Menghin and Bormida stayed.

The Peronist intervention in the universities founded a lasting relationship which the modernizers reproduced (Neiburg 1997), by which academics could serve politics for particular social and ideological ends. However, political standpoints and theories had their own ways of being interpreted. Bormida was molded by Imbelloni's philosophical contours, namely his devotion to Gianbattista Vico and his notion of history as *corsi* and *recorsi,* and the Crocian background he acquired in Italy. He also took from Menghin the bases of the Culture-Historical school. Anthropology was part of the humanities born out of Universal History, rather than of the social sciences. In his courses, Bormida taught Central European literature on diffusionism, popular culture and religion, from extensive irrational phenomenology (Mircea Eliade, Rudolf Otto, R. Volhardt), and diffusionism. On the other side, Bormida grouped evolutionists and materialists, such as Frederick Engels, Lewis Morgan, and neoevolutionists Leslie White and Julian Steward, together with "sociological masters" such as Marcel Mauss and Emile Durkheim, Malinowski and Radcliffe-Brown, which he dismissed for their "sociological reductionism," empiricism, a-historicism, and linear forms of explanation (Bormida 1961: 486). Bormida's main criticism to social anthropology was its lack of historicism and its reduction of culture to applied sociology. The fact that "social anthropology" was taught by the neighboring department seemed to confirm its sociological, that is, non-anthropological character.

When the first anthropology students met Bormida, not only did they praise him as "a good teacher (who) planned each class" (Ratier in Gurevich 1989b), but also as "the only professor with an ideological and political project" (Alberti in Gurevich 1989a). This allowed students to reread Bormida's premises as Marx had done before. "He (Bormida) tried to formulate a Universalist theory based on Hegel. And from Hegel it is quite possible to jump to the critique of Hegel by means of the idea of historical and cultural totality" (ibid.: 5). Interestingly enough, this job paralleled the left wing youth's reinterpretation of the Peronist years. Besides Bormida's fascism, he also taught some heavyweights of European idealism—Hegel, Husserl, Benedetto Croce—and a sensitive mind of the Left.

Italian ethnologist Ernesto de Martino (1908–1965) graduated in Letters (1932) and devoted to the history of religions and folklore. De Martino's observations and reflections revolved around the Southern Question that also became a focus in the writings of another amateur ethnologist and folklorist, the founder of the Italian Communist Party, Antonio Gramsci (1891–1937).

Both De Martino, himself a Socialist and later a Communist, and Gramsci, jailed in 1926 until his death, were most influential in Italian Anthropology, following Benedetto Croce's historicism (1866–1952). Although they shifted to materialism, they always maintained Croce's radical immanence and historicity of human life (Saunders 1993: 876). De Martino differed though, since he did not deny the historicity of primitive people, as Croce did.

Menéndez somehow reproduced this relationship. Besides his approaches to Gramsci and with many Communist dissidents at the time, Menéndez still regards De Martino as an ethnographic exemplar (Menéndez 2002: 9), which he acknowledges as Bormida's legacy: "I read De Martino thanks to a Fascist" (Conference at FLACSO, Buenos Aires, 2003). Whereas Bormida read *Naturalismo e storicismo nell' Etnologia, Morte e pianto rituale,* and *Il Mondo Magico* as examples of a non-materialist version of popular culture and of historical *Verstehen* (Guber & Visacovsky 2006), Menéndez took them as approaches to a kind of Marxism moved by social agents, not by the abstract forces of structure. This theoretical search of social agency benefited from anthropology, as the later Gramscian move of the 1980s would show.

Political and academic developments and debates certainly put young anthropologists self-labeled as "social anthropologists" at odds with Bormida and official anthropology. As Blas Alberti recalled, the students began to notice "the disjunction between that theory and our own. So we started to criticize it and we broke away radically from Bormida's perspective." Nonetheless, he "went on with that tradition of European thought, which I consider to be more rooted in the totalizing perspective" (Gurevich 1989a: 4), meaning "more rooted" than the Anglo-Saxon tradition.

This specific articulation between "science" and "politics" marked by "anti-Britanism," had two sources: a political, theoretical, and counter-institutional left, and a political, institutional, and theoretical right. It also had two targets: Social Anthropology taught by the Department of Sociology, and that practiced at the Social Anthropology section of the Di Tella Institute, chaired by Hermitte between 1965 and 1974. In this light, Menéndez regarded *antropología social* more as a political *cum* theoretical critique to the social sciences and to official anthropology at the Buenos Aires University and at Di Tella, rather than as an avenue to empirical research which he started to develop in Mexico.[10] Meanwhile, Hermitte used the term *antropología social* in the British way, vowing for intensive fieldwork. She despised "abstract theorization" and anthropology's subservience to aims other than those of the discipline, most likely as a reaction to local politics and to the memories of the Peronist era. In fact, she never recalled her experience in the US as marked by McCarthyism, nor did she warn against the uses of applied anthropology for political ends. In her view, anthropology was a neutral discipline and most of her critiques pointed at the lack of fieldwork and of updated (or at least, structural-functionalist) perspectives away from culturalism and diffusionism. Her contribution was unique and expanded the horizons of Argentine anthropology as the study of social relations, beyond *volkskunde* and *volkerkunde* traditions.

In spite of their diversity, both versions were banned from the *porteño* academic setting between 1966 and 1973, and between 1974 and 1983; both went through some kind of (internal or external) exile and both went back to the University in 1984. Was it because they were committed or rather because they were scientific? Nobody knows, but as Argentine anthropologists have it, social anthropology is far from a transparent notion, probably as everywhere else.

NOTES

* I thank the late Eduardo Archetti, Beatriz Heredia, Diana Milstein, Verena Stolcke and SergioVisacovsky, for their comments on an earlier draft.

1. There are, to be sure, other anthropological centers such as La Plata, Olavarría, Rosario, Córdoba, Tucumán, Posadas. Each developed different branches of anthropology at different points in time.

2. Cecilia Hidalgo (1997/8) quotes Hermitte and Menéndez as two lines of *porteño* social anthropology.

3. In the late 1940s, "Antropología Social" was also referred by Branimiro Males in Tucumán, as an applied expertise of Anthropology related to the State, yet it was never applied after Perón's fall (Lazzari 2004).

4. Hermitte's two field assistants, Amalia Sanguinetti and Ana María Mariscotti, published a short article in *Runa,* the Museum journal, where they called Hermitte an "expert in *Antropología Social*" (1958–59: 195). In 1958, Hermitte presented a paper called "*Antropología aplicada and its future in Argentina*" at the regular meeting *Semana Antropológica* of the *Sociedad Argentina de Antropología.*

5. Ralph Beals (1901–1985) was the first Ph.D. in anthropology at the University of California, Los Angeles, in 1936. He chaired the *American Anthropological Association* in 1950. In 1958, he became President of the Southwestern Anthropological Association. His main contributions dealt with the warfare of native peoples in Northern Mexico. He retired in 1969 (Patterson 2001).

6. Lowie, Malinowski, Nadel, Radcliffe-Brown, Evans-Pritchard, Linton, Steward, White, Lewis, Redfield, Benedict, Mead, Durkheim, and Lévi-Strauss are cases in point (*Programa de Antropología Social* 1962).

7. Translations into Spanish were already available, as Mexican publisher Fondo de Cultura Económica published Linton's *Culture and Personality* and *The Study of Man* (1945); Klukhohn's *Anthropology* (1949), Herskovits's *The Man and His Work* (1952), and Nadel's *Fundaments in Social Anthropology* (1955).

8. The group included, besides the aforementioned Argentine social anthropologists, Roberto Cardoso de Oliveira and Guillermo Bonfil Batalla, Beatriz Alasia de Heredia, Jorge Dandler, Blanca Muratorio, Sidney Greenfield, Moacir Palmeira, Roberto Ringuelet, Guillermo Ruben, Lygia Sigaud, Kristi-Anne Stolen, and Arnold Strickon, among others.
9. Since the original manuscript seems lost, I rely on one of Menéndez's friends and colleagues, Mirtha Lischetti, and her description of the "*El Modelo Antropológico Clásico*" (Lischetti 1987, 1998).
10. Menéndez had some fieldwork experience in Argentina, such as Buenos Aires city and Entre Ríos province. However, he never published his conclusions. In turn, he managed to publish several theoretical articles between 1962 and 1971.

BIBLIOGRAPHY

AA. Actualidad Antropológica. 1968. "Antropología Social, aquí y ahora," 1–3. Olavarría, Provincia de Buenos Aires.
Alberti, Blas. 1962. "La Antropología del desarrollo." *Anthropologica* 1. Buenos Aires.
Bartolomé, Leopoldo. 1980. "La Antropología en Argentina: Problemas y Perspectivas." *América Indígena* 40, 2: 207–15.
Bartolomé, Leopoldo, and Enrique Gorostiaga, eds. 1974. *Estudios sobre el campesinado latinoamericano. La perspectiva de la antropología social.* Buenos Aires: Editorial Periférica.
Bormida, Marcelo. 1961. "Ciencias Antropológicas y Humanismo." *Revista de la Universidad de Buenos Aires* 6, 3: 470–90.
Garbulsky, Edgardo. 1987. "José Imbelloni, positivismo, organicismo y racismo." *Cuadernos de la Escuela de Antropología* 3 (87). Universidad Nacional de Rosario, Facultad de Humanidades y Artes.
——. 1991–92 "La antropología social en la Argentina," *Runa* 20: 11–34.
Guber, Rosana, and Sergio E. Visacovsky. 2006. "The Birth of Ciencias Antropológicas at the University of Buenos Aires, 1955–1965," in Regna Darnell and Frederic W. Gleach, eds., *Histories of Anthropology Annual,* Vol 2. Lincoln: University of Nebraska Press.
Gurevich, Estela. 1989a. *Interview with Blas Alberti.* Ms.
——. 1989b. *Interview with Hugo Ratier.* Ms.
Handler, Richard, ed. 1995. *Schneider on Schneider.* Durham: Duke University Press.
Hermitte, M. Esther. 1968. "La movilidad social en una comunidad bicultural." *Revista Latinoamericana de Sociología* no. 1.
——. 1970. *Poder sobrenatural y control social.* México: Instituto Indigenista Interamericano.
——. 1972. *Asistencia técnica en materia de promoción y asistencia de la comunidad en la provincia de Catamarca.* Buenos Aires: Consejo Federal de Inverciones.
Hermitte, M. Esther, and Carlos A. Herrán. 1970. "¿Patronazgo o cooperativismo? Obstáculos a la modificación del sistema de interacción social en una comunidad del noroeste argentino." *Revista Latinoamericana de Sociología* 2: 293–317.

Hermitte, M. Esther, and Leopoldo J. Bartolomé, eds. 1977. *Procesos de articulación social.* Buenos Aires: Amorrortu.

Herrán, Carlos A. 1990. "Antropología Social en la Argentina: apuntes y perspectivas." *Cuadernos de Antropología Social* 2, 2: 108–15.

Hidalgo, Cecilia. 1997/1998. "Antropología del mundo contemporáneo. El surgimiento de la antropología de la ciencia." *Relaciones de la Sociedad Argentina de Antropología* 22–23: 71–82.

Kuper, Adam. 1999. *Culture: An Anthropologists' Account.* Cambridge, MA: Harvard University Press.

L'Estoile, Benoit de, Federico Neiburg, and Lygia Sigaud, eds. 2002. *Antropología, Impérios e Estados Nacionais.* Rio de Janeiro: Relume/Dumará.

Lischetti, Mirtha, ed. 1987. *Antropología.* Buenos Aires: EUDEBA.

McQuown, Norman, and Julian Pitt-Rivers. 1964. *Man in Nature.* Ms, University of Chicago.

Menéndez, Eduardo L. 1968. "Correo antropológico." *Actualidad Antropológica* 3: 48–51.

———. 1970. "Ideología, ciencia y práctica profesional." In *Ciencias sociales: ideología y realidad nacional,* pp. 101–24. Buenos Aires: Tiempo Contemprorráneo.

———. 1967/1968. *El modelo antropológico clásico.* Ms.Buenos Aires.

———. 2002. *La parte negada de la cultura. Relativismo, diferencias y racismo.* Barcelona: Librería Santa Fe.

Neiburg, Federico G. 1997. *Los intelectuales y la invención del peronismo.* Buenos Aires: Alianza.

Lazzari, Axel. 2004. "Antropología en el Estado: el Instituto Etnico Nacional." In Federico Neiburg and Mariano Plotkin, eds., *Intelectuales y expertos. La constitución del conocimiento social en la Argentina,* pp. 203–29. Buenos Aires: Paidós.

Patterson, Thomas C. 2001. *A Social History of Anthropology in the United States.* Oxford: Berg.

Ratier, Hugo E., and Roberto R. Ringuelet. 1997. "La antropología social en la Argentina: un producto de la democracia," *Horizontes Antropológicos* 3, 7: 10–23.

Sanguinetti, Amalia C., and Ana M. Mariscotti. 1958/1959. "Notas para el estudio de la cultura de la Puna." *Runa* 9, 1–2.

Saunders, George R. 1993. "'Critical Ethnocentrism' and the Ethnology of Ernesto De Martino." *American Anthropologist* 95, 4: 875–93.

Stocking, George A., Jr. 1979. *Anthropology at Chicago.* Chicago: The University Library.

Vessuri, Hebe M.C. 1989. "Las ciencias sociales en la Argentina: diagnóstico y perspectivas." In Enrique Oteiza, ed., *La política de investigación científica y tecnológica argentina. Historia y Perspectivas,* pp. 339–363. Buenos Aires: Centro Editor de América Latina.

Visacovsky, Sergio E., and Rosana Guber, eds. 2002. *Historias y estilos de trabajo de campo en Argentina.* Buenos Aires: Antropofagia.

Wakin, Eric. 1992. *Anthropology Goes to War: Professional Ethics & Counterinsurgency in Thailand.* Madison: Center for Southeast Asian Studies.

Chapter 7

Themes and Legacies: Anthropology's Trajectories in Cameroon

Jude Fokwang

INTRODUCTION

Located between West and Central Africa, Cameroon offers a unique setting both geographically and culturally, serving as a powerful attraction to the ever growing number of scholars, especially anthropologists, who have interacted intimately with its amazing peoples and landscapes. Indeed, it is now a widely held opinion that Cameroon ranks among the few African countries that attract the most foreign anthropologists (Gausset 2004: 223). Often described as "Africa in miniature" owing to its exceptional geographies, ethnic diversity,[1] and intricate histories, Cameroon is also easily known as the source and origin of the Bantu group that migrated over a thousand years ago towards the east and then southwards, occupying most of central and southern Africa today (Nkwi and Warnier 1982).

In July 1884, Cameroon (Kamerun) officially became a German protectorate, although the German colonial hold over the territories was short-lived, owing to its defeat in the First World War. Subsequently, its territories were divided between Britain and France.[2] Few anthropological or ethnological works that emerged during the German colonial period are hardly known. One such work is a publication in 1898 of the cross country expedition of Max Esser, a German merchant banker, which began in 1896. Although it contains little of anthropology, the author's observations and accounts have interesting historical and anthropological insights, some of which have been illuminated using contemporary materials by historian, E.M. (Sally) Chilver, and anthropologist, Ute Röschenthaler (Chilver and Röschenthaler 2001). The partition of Cameroon into British and French territories following the defeat of Germany created not only an enabling environment for the penetration of more foreign anthropologists, but it also made the country a veritable theatre for competing anthropological traditions whose legacies remain apparent until today. This chapter examines the particular experience of anthropology as it has evolved in the country, especially in the former Southern Cameroons,[3] which in October 1961 gained its independence by joining the already independent Republic of Cameroon (French-speaking Cameroon).

In this chapter, I seek to sketch the contours of anthropological practice as it has developed in modern Cameroon. I argue that although many anthropologists have secured a solid foothold in the country in terms of field sites, the discipline itself has largely remained at the margins of academic practice. However, I also maintain that anthropology's legacies and its practices are not limited to those who are trained or professional anthropologists. As a matter of fact, the growing number of short stories, novels (see for example Jumbam 1980), and travelogues (Murphy 1989) that capture the challenges of everyday life in cultural contexts have critical relevance to local anthropology. Indeed, if one were to think of social-cultural anthropology in a broad perspective as the study of humankind, and particularly so of "marginal" lives or peoples, then anthropology's shape, substance, and configurations have assumed deeply nuanced attributes in Cameroon, drawing on local experiences as well as the traditions that characterize the discipline in Western scholarship, thus enriching the discipline in terms of its claims and rewards.

Although I have as my general objective a critical appraisal of anthropological practice in Cameroon as a whole, I will pay particular attention to the Anglophone region, partly because of my knowledge of the area and its anthropological endeavors, and partly because it would take more than the scope of this brief chapter to explore the vast terrain of anthropological expressions in the country as a whole. This I reserve for another project. I therefore limit myself primarily to the Anglophone region of the country, with a particular bias for the area known to the German imperialists as the *graslands*[4] or grassfields, which today cover the North West and Western Provinces, where most of my own anthropology is anchored. Often described as a microcosm of Cameroon's diversity, this area has attracted the bulk of foreign anthropologists who conduct research in Cameroon. In fact, since colonial times, the grassfields has been host to German, British, French, Dutch, and, increasingly, American anthropologists, a diversity reflected in both their scholarship and the training offered to the growing number of local anthropologists.

PIONEERS: PATHWAYS TO ANTHROPOLOGY IN CAMEROON

The anthropological enterprise in Cameroon accompanied and proceeded the colonizing project, the most important of which was the integration of local economic histories into a capitalist framework (Mudimbe 1988). Hence, anthropology's object tended to focus on the transformations experienced by the natives and the impact of capitalist initiatives on native lives and customs. In addition to professional ethnographers, there were colonial civil administrators who had received training in ethnographic skills as evinced by the archives in Bamenda and Buea, which bear testimony to the anthropological tinge of countless "area or assessment reports" and confidential files in which District Officers (DOs) made painful efforts to give elaborate accounts of the cultures and beliefs of each "tribal" group under their jurisdiction. It therefore seems to me that besides a host of German anthropological initiatives of which little is known, it would be fair to assert that British colonial administrators were the foremost pathfinders of what I term anthropological practice in Anglophone Cameroon. Although not advanced compared to the Germans, the British colonial administrators, in collaboration with missionaries, created working conditions for professional anthropologists who soon arrived and began an enterprise that has continued to attract scholars of different anthropological persuasions even today.

As noted above, few professional ethnographers are known to have conducted research during the German colonial period. Bernhard Ankermann is known to have been the first professional ethnographer to tour the western grassfields between 1907–1909. Gulla Pfeffer, the Berlin Museum ethnographer, visited the Northern areas of the grasslands in the 1920s, notably the Aghem and Fungom districts, taking photographs of their material culture. During the 1930s, Agathe Schmidt caried out fieldwork on "village life and gender roles in the small chiefdom of Nsei (Bamessing) in the Ndop Plain" (Chilver 1988: 1). Schmidt's ethnography was published in 1955, but her publications have remained largely unknown even among contemporary anthropologists.

Of the earliest English ethnographers who published extensively on the grasslands, M.D.W. Jeffreys remains the most famous. Jeffreys was both a scholar and administrator in charge of the Bamenda Division between 1936 and 1945. His fieldwork took him to many areas of the Bamenda grassfields, resulting in the publication of a substantial number of historical papers and ethnographies covering topics on linguistics, coronation rites among the Bamum, Tikar history, the Bali of Bamenda, and the cultural perceptions of twins in the region. He was the first ethnographer to research on a range of themes, and many that came after him acknowledge his pioneering role. His archives are located at the University of the Witwatersrand in Johannesburg, where he returned after his service in the British Cameroons (Shirley Ardener, personal communication).

Not often has the history and anthropology of a region owed so much to so few a host of scholars. Two female English scholars in particular have bestridden the grasslands with colossal familiarity. The first of these, Phyllis Kaberry (1910–1977), famous for her ethnography *Women of the Grassfields* (1952), trained as an anthropologist at the London School of Economics under Audrey Richards. Kaberry was invited by the colonial government to study the economic position of women in the Bamenda region after concern had been expressed about the "low status of women," "lag in girls' education … and by medical officers concerned about the high rate of infant mortality in the trust territory" (Chilver 1988: 1). She made two trips between 1945 and 1948, during which she carried out fieldwork on women in the Bamenda region as a whole, focusing specifically on women in the Nso chiefdom—then and still the largest chiefdom in the entire region. She revisited the Bamenda grasslands in 1958, 1960, and 1963, when she investigated a range of issues including traditional political institutions, farmer-grazier disputes, gender relations, and land tenure systems, especially in the Nso chiefdom. During her third trip to the Bamenda region in 1958, she travelled with Mrs. Elizabeth M. Chilver, a historian and archivist who was to describe herself later as "an apprentice historian in stout boots" (Ardener 1996: xii). At 90, she remains one of the most important pillars and living archives of grassfields history. A more comprehensive account of Chilver's biography has been published by Mitzi Goheen and Eugenia Shanklin (1996), both of them renowned anthropologists and life students of grassfields cultures. The following account of the circumstances of Chilver and Kaberry's meeting and their careers as research collaborators is drawn from Shirley Ardener (1996).

As secretary of the Colonial Social Science Research Council, a key sponsor of overseas research, Mrs. Chilver came into contact with many anthropologists, including Phyllis Kaberry, and later, Edwin Ardener. At the time of their meeting, Kaberry was completing the draft of her book, *Women of the Grassfields.* Inspired by exciting stories about Africa, most likely from the British Cameroons, Chilver resolved to take a trip to Africa by accompanying Kaberry for a ten week visit to the Bamenda grassfields in 1958. The

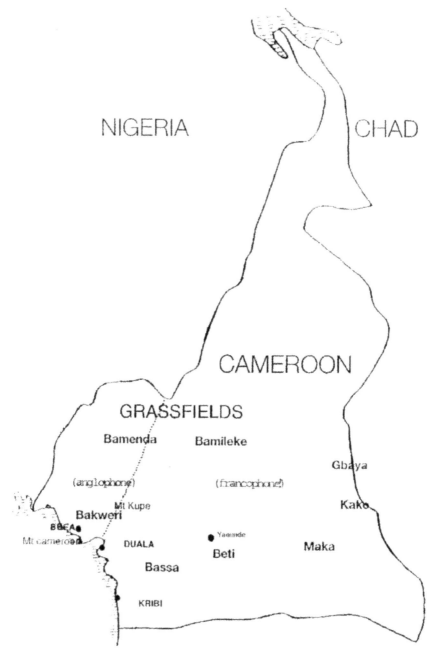

Map 2: Map of Cameroon, adapted from Geschiere 1997.

duo returned for further research in 1960 and 1961, when they studied the transformations experienced by indigenous political institutions owing to German and British colonial rule, and the ways in which these institutions had been manipulated by colonizing forces. Kaberry and Chilver authored numerous publications. Both of them, especially Chilver, made further trips to the Bamenda grassfields in the post-independence era and has kept in touch with local scholars and dignitaries ever since.

Part of Sally Chilver's job at the Colonial Social Science Research Council also included "implementing the policy of establishing research institutes in East and West Africa (The East African Institute for Social Research [EAISR] and The West African Institute for Social and Economic Research [WAISER], now The Nigerian Institute for Social and Economic Research [NISER])" (Ardener 1996: xii). As noted earlier, it was at her job that she came into contact with many social anthropologists working in Africa. Soon after meeting Kaberry in 1951, she also met Edwin and Shirley Ardener, who had just returned from a research trip among the Igbo, sponsored by a grant from the Council. The Ardeners first set foot in the Southern Cameroons in 1953 as part of a team from WAISER to study the impact of plantations on native life (Shirley Ardener, personal communication). The outcome of this research was the publication of a book, *Plantation and Village in the Cameroons* (1960) co-authored by the Ardeners and W.A. Warmington. Edwin and Shirley Ardener carried out extensive research among the Bakweri, the principal ethnic group occupying the coastal territories of the present South West Province. Even after Edwin Ardener's death, Shirley continued to conduct research in this region of Cameroon and, most recently, co-edited a publication on gender studies in Cameroon. Age and a tight academic schedule at Oxford have still not prevented her from making short visits to Buea in most years. The Ardeners, both individually and collectively, have made lasting contributions to the anthropology of Cameroon, and the Bakweri in particular. Shirley's continuous involvement with Cameroon studies and her collaboration with Sally Chilver (both are based at Oxford) are indications of their passionate commitment to the scholarship of this region.

Kaberry and Chilver have inspired a growing number of expatriate anthropologists who have published extensively on different areas of the Bamenda grassfields. Mitzi Goheen for instance, inspired by Kaberry's *Women of the Grassfields,* returned to Nso to investigate women's position in Nso society, half a century after Kaberry's study. Her ethnography, *Men Own the Fields, Women Own the Crops* (1996), is a powerful analysis of the continuities and transformations of gender relations in a typical Bamenda chiefdom. Some of Kaberry's students, such as Richard Fardon and Ian Fowler, followed after her and have conducted fieldwork in the Bamenda grasslands since the 1970s.

A growing number of local historians and anthropologists have been motivated by the efforts of Kaberry and Chilver, whose published and unpublished materials remain critical sources and basis for further research. In fact, the formation of two local historical societies in the 1960s, one in Nso and another in Bali Nyonga, were conceived to stimulate debate and research on local histories and to position the findings and analysis of expatriate researchers with local experiences and memories. In fact, in 1960, the Bali Historical society became the focus of Kaberry and Chilver in their investigations about Bali history and political institutions (Fardon 1996: 35). These developments and even more recent ones have prompted me to examine some grassroots initiatives undertaken to promote anthropological practice among locals. One such initiative was the creation of the Kaberry Research Centre (KRC), which in my mind deserves its place in the anthropology of Cameroon.

CAMEROONISING ANTHROPOLOGY:
THE KABERRY RESEARCH CENTRE

The Kaberry Research Centre (KRC) was created in 1988 as an offshoot of the Association for Creative Teaching (ACT). The latter was an element of a Yaounde University based project known as the Guelph-Yaounde Project, whose aim was to promote creative teaching among teachers, particularly among primary school teachers. It aimed further to assist teachers and learners to collect and use local stories, literatures, folklore, and histories. It also had the lofty objective of promoting research on local history and cultures in order to acquaint teachers with the diversity of cultures and proper understanding of their local environment. In order to achieve the last objective, some members of the ACT executive, led by the late Patrick Mbunwe, resolved to create a research wing whose primary and exclusive objective would be to carry out research on local history and anthropology (KRC 1989). Upon arriving at the decision to set up a grassfields research center, various members of the nascent association began to communicate with Sally Chilver (since Kaberry died from a stroke in 1977), who contributed significantly toward the collection of a remarkable quantity of historical and anthropological materials, both published and unpublished. However, the decision to name the center after the anthropologist, Phyllis Kaberry, was based on another rationale. According to the founding members of the KRC:

> ... the most endearing aspect of her contribution to research in this area was her insistence that everything she learnt should eventually be returned to the people to whom that knowledge belonged. Prompted by this humanistic consideration, we set out to secure literature on the Western Grassfields from her

colleagues and friends. Consequently at one of our discussion sessions, it was agreed that in appreciation of her singular contribution, the proposed Centre be named in her honour. (KRC 1989: 4)

Such was the birth of a brilliant idea to promote anthropological research. Although the idea was spearheaded and implemented by individuals who had received no formal anthropological training, they showed remarkable zeal and potential in their efforts, sometimes with the collaboration of expatriate anthropologists. Regrettably, most of these works are not widely accessible, due to poor marketing by local publishers, while some of them remain unpublished.

In order to facilitate research among its members, individuals were appointed to study selected themes from their chiefdoms or clans of origin, or where they had lived for a significant length of time. Once the allocation of research sites had been accomplished, the enthusiastic scholars set to work on the classic anthropological theme—rites of passage—which culminated in a publication of the first volume of their ethnography entitled, *Rites of Passage and Incorporation in the Western Grassfields of Cameroon* (1993). Various elements covered in the project included delivery and naming rites of infants as well as the initiation rites of children into adolescence. The project was carried out among the Nso, Yamba, Wimbum, Bafut, Bali Nyonga, Oshie, Oku, Bamunka, Aghem, Kom, Batibo, and the Fulani. A second volume, which remains unpublished, addressed a different category of persons, adults. The unpublished volume covered ritual practices on marriage and funeral rites, among others.

Leadership crisis soon left the KRC in wreckage, which partly accounts for why the second volume of *Rites of Passage* remains unpublished. However, by 2004, several individuals (myself included), together with the Canadian, Elizabeth Cockburn, who had been involved in both the Yaounde-Guelph Project and the KRC, began to rally interested persons for a revival of the defunct research center. There was overwhelming enthusiasm among local scholars and several former members who responded positively to a meeting aimed at reviving the center. The center has been operational since February 2005, and counts among its current membership historians, geographers, English and drama teachers, educators, literary critics, medical and legal practitioners, sociologists, journalists, freelance writers, and, of course, anthropologists.

ANTHROPOLOGY AND ANTHROPOLOGISTS OF CAMEROON

Compared to its cousin discipline sociology, anthropology has occupied quite marginal ground in Cameroon, especially in regard to the teaching and training of local anthropologists. But anthropological practice has not been the exclusive terrain of those who pass for professional anthropologists. In fact, many scholars who received some measure of anthropological training in the 1970s and 1980s preferred to identify themselves as historians, sociologists, political scientists, and philosophers, largely because of anthropology's detested status as a handmaid to imperial rule. While these claims are abundantly patent and familiar in many academic circles, things have changed and a growing number of scholars trained as anthropologists are today defining themselves as such, except among those who remain frozen in the past.

Paul Nkwi was the first Anglophone Cameroonian to obtain a Ph.D. in Social Anthropology in 1975, from the University of Fribourg in Switzerland. He joined the department of Sociology at the then University of Yaounde in 1976, which at the time was dominated by French anthropologists (Nkwi, personal communication). Until the early 1990s, anthropology, in the words of Paul Nkwi, "had very little visibility" as it was taught as a complementary subject to sociology. Anthropology only succeeded to establish a separate department at Yaounde University during the 1992/93 academic year and since then, it has awarded B.A. and postgraduate degrees.

When the Cameroon government decentralized its university system in 1992 by raising former university centers to fully fledged universities, two more anthropology departments were created—one at the University of Ngaoundere in the Adamawa province, and another at the University of Buea in the South West province. The latter is the only public university whose official medium of instruction is in English. Based in the former capital of what used to be the Southern Cameroons, the University of Buea promised new opportunities for many scholars and students of English expression who, for many decades, had endured various sorts of discrimination at the Francophone-dominated University of Yaounde. At Buea, anthropology was established as a joint program with sociology and since 1997, has awarded joint B.A. degrees.

Graduates from Yaounde and Buea have gone on to pursue further studies in anthropology abroad. The Netherlands, the USA, South Africa, and more recently, Switzerland have proved particularly attractive. Their training in these different countries has the potential to reproduce or, perhaps, transform the legacy of diverse anthropological traditions in Cameroon. However, compared to their Francophone counterparts, there are still relatively few Anglophone anthropologists, which accounts partly for the dearth of anthropological works; a void that arguably has been filled by other kinds of intellectual works that have relevance for anthropology or better still, have drawn on anthropological methods and concepts (see for example, Fonlon's enunciations on the concept of culture, Fonlon 1967). Research in the anthropology of Cameroon remains dominated by expatriate anthropologists, although in more recent years substantial contributions have emerged from local anthropologists. In the following paragraphs, I will consider just a few of the popular themes that have attracted scholarship both among local and expatriate anthropologists. They include ethnohistory, identity and ethnic politics, chieftaincy, and, lastly, witchcraft in the contemporary era.

One of the key challenges encountered by researchers of predominantly non-literate societies is to document and reconstruct the histories of these societies. This claim is particularly true of African and other non-Western societies, which by dint of their non-literate past, provides invaluable opportunity for the intersection of history and anthropology (cf. Fowler and Zeitlyn 1996: 6). To this end, a huge, perhaps, ever growing amount of literature has been produced in the domain of ethnohistory. Some of the key areas include Tikar history and identity (Chilver 1970; Chilver and Kaberry 1967; Jeffreys 1964), which has generated a great deal of debate in the past decade (see Fowler and Zeitlyn 1996 for a summary). The pre-colonial history of many Western grassfields groups have also attracted a tremendous scholarship, as seen in the works of Paul Nkwi (1982) and the French anthropologist, Jean-Pierre Warnier (1985). Their works, both individually and collectively, reveal a strong cultural historical tradition, grounded and steeped in local histories, which, interestingly, echoes the intellectual collaboration between Chilver (a historian) and Kaberry (an anthropologist). A more recent contribution comes from Emmanuel Yenshu (2001), which focuses on inter-community relations between the Kedjom Keku and its neighbors in the pre-colonial and colonial history of the grassfields. Yenshu has taken issues with the ways Kedjom history is presented in the works of Kaberry, Chilver, Nkwi, and Warnier. Yenshu's contributions reveal the ways in which knowledge produced by indigenous anthropologists link up with and differ from those of expatriate scholars and even with other local anthropologists.

Another theme deals with ethnicity, identity, and what has come to be known as "the politics of belonging." This domain is particularly attractive, partly because anthropology finds profound excitement with the ways in which "others" are produced and contested by social actors. The introduction of democratic reforms in the early 1990s in Cameroon, for example, provoked new obsessions with belonging and ethnicity, especially in the coastal areas of the country that are host to substantial numbers of migrants from the Western grassfields, known by various names as "settlers" or "cam no go." Although these issues have occupied prominence in political circles, they have also had ripple effects in the religious spheres as brilliantly depicted and analysed by Konings (2003). Stated simply, ethnic politics has had a long history in the body politic dating from the era of Ahmadou Ahidjo, the first president of Cameroon (1960–1982). But its more recent expressions under the present regime of Paul Biya have assumed deeply divisive, violent, and exclusionary proportions, most often teleguided and championed by members of his regime (Geschiere and Gugler 1998; Geschiere and Nyamn-joh 2000; Nyamnjoh and Rowlands 1998).

Since colonial times, traditional leadership has remained a fascinating issue with anthropologists, precisely because it has shown remarkable resil-ience and adaptation to successive colonial and postcolonial regimes (Nkwi 1976; Nyamnjoh 1985). In fact, scholars have given attention not only to the ways traditional leadership have been influenced by different colonial regimes—German, British and French (Geschiere 1993)—but also to their position in the modern state and their relationship with the new elites (Fisiy 1995; Jua 1995; Konings 1999). It should also be noted that traditional lead-ership features conspicuously in many ethnographies on Cameroon (see, for example, Geschiere 1997; Goheen 1996), largely because chiefs play decisive roles in the lives of their subjects, such as resolving witchcraft disputes, land conflicts, participating in development projects or initiating them, co-opting the new elite, and getting involved in modern politics both at national and local levels. My own research has shown that contrary to claims about the in-compatibility of chiefs and democracy, the reality is that political transition in Cameroon produced contradictions which created space for chiefs to fill, but on the condition that they were able to draw from different kinds of le-gitimacy and had not been discredited by their past or present involvement with the postcolonial state. In Cameroon, this claim could be substantiated by the fact that the emergence of the discourse of autochthony provided space for the resurgence of chiefs in regional and national politics. By pos-ing as the protectors or guarantors of the rights of their subjects, some chiefs have appropriated the discourse of democracy and autochthony to secure advantages for themselves and their regions or chiefdoms (Fokwang 2003).

Lastly, witchcraft remains a domain that has consistently received an-thropological attention, and increasingly among local researchers, precisely because people seem to be concerned that witchcraft has become even more pervasive and destructive in the modern society. Concerns about witchcraft are not limited to so-called ordinary people as it has also made significant and sometimes shattering inroads among the powerful elites and government circles (see, for example Rowlands and Warnier 1988, about the elite's fear of witchcraft and Nyamnjoh 2002 for accusations against leading govern-ment officials' involvement with witchcraft). Geschiere (1997) draws heavily on data from Cameroon, and he is indeed one of the leading researchers of this phenomenon in the country. Researchers have also drawn our attention to the diverse ways in which witchcraft issues are dealt with in different parts of Cameroon, with emphasis on regional trajectories and their implications for societal harmony (cf. Fisiy and Geschiere 1996). Tatah Mbuy, a catholic priest of the Archdiocese of Bamenda, has also been involved in research on witchcraft, both from an academic perspective as well as for pastoral concerns. Mbuy's writings about witchcraft have raised eyebrows even among church circles (Mbuy 2000), which tend to dismiss witchcraft issues as a sign of backwardness and lack of faith among Christians. Certainly, witchcraft will remain a critical theme for research, insofar as misery, despair, and dictatorship remain key companions both to the downtrodden as well as the rich and powerful.

The above themes are far from exhaustive as scholars continue to make inroads into research domains that were previously unexplored. Anthropologists are now looking at women and the (in)formal economy (Niger-Thomas 2000), youth identity and their relationship to the state (Fokwang 2003), as well as *feymania* (Malaquais 2001), a phenomenon associated with fraudulent schemes involving the use of deceit and trickery to dispossess people of their savings and property.

ANTHROPOLOGY'S FUTURE

Anthropological training in Cameroon has shifted its bearing to the realm of applied studies, with the aim of at arming students with necessary skills to be competitive in the job market upon graduation. The reasons for this are varied. First, very few students take up anthropology at the postgraduate level because, according to local perceptions, its economic or practical value leaves much to be desired. This is not entirely unique to Cameroon, as this seems to be a widely held belief in many African countries. Hence, recent anthropological training in Cameroon is tailored to meet the needs of students who intend to join the civil service, work in NGOs or in the communication sector. Whilst this initiative seems not only necessary, there remains the risk of sacrificing the theoretical merits of the discipline at the altar of practicality, in which case it is crucial to aim at reasonable balance in regard to the courses designed for undergraduates.

Already the consultancy syndrome has made significant inroads into academia and, in some cases has led to a compromise of academic standards and practices. This is more so with local anthropologists, for whom research grants are extremely rare, and remains a vexing concern. Thus, a shift in the kinds of training offered to undergraduates might not be a function of foresight only, but also arises from the scholars' own experiences in both the academic and economic worlds. Given this trend, comparatively little ethnographic work in the nature of "thick description" and prolonged field-work might be undertaken by local scholars. However, this is not to insist that scholarship counts as anthropological only when its data are obtained through specific methods such as prolonged fieldwork. As argued earlier, the production of anthropological knowledge in Cameroon has not been the prerogative of trained anthropologists only. However, in my mind, three categories of researchers continue to occupy a constituency which I see as crucial for the practice of anthropology in Cameroon.

First, there remains the crying need for indigenous anthropologists, who, for job-related factors, live abroad, to continue researching and pub-lishing about Cameroon. There is a modest number of Cameroonian an-thropologists trained in Western universities who have opted to remain in the West, either practicing anthropology or involved in other professional ventures that might have significant bearing on anthropological practice in Cameroon. To this category, I add the growing number of Cameroonian graduate students training for doctoral degrees in anthropology, especially in Western countries, whose research projects are carried out in the country. They also have it in their disposition to shape the paths of anthropology in this region.

Second, I anticipate a more assertive and productive role for local re-search bodies such as the KRC. With specific reference to the KRC, I see an enthusiasm among local researchers which promises exciting times and discussions on a range of themes. The KRC is made up of people who are not formally trained as anthropologists, but whose experiences and inter-ests have significant consequences for the anthropology of Cameroon. Their participation in the knowledge production enterprise might raise questions about insider-outsider positionalities, which constitute a major area of de-bate in contemporary anthropology. The KRC, prior to its untimely demise, had already demonstrated its potential to carry out quality and publishable research. Its revival is a welcome initiative and will carry on the task of promoting local research by locals, as well as networking with expatriate scholars of this region.

Lastly, there is promise that the grassfields will continue to attract an ever-growing number of expatriate anthropologists whose academic influ-ences remain indelible. Drawn from several traditions, especially the Anglo-American, French, and Dutch, it is apparent that the grassfields—indeed, Cameroon as a whole—will continue to be host to diverse anthropological traditions, which in real terms will continue to enrich the practice of anthro-pology in a so divergent and sometimes disparate country. In fact, many expatriate anthropologists remain connected in various ways to this region, either through their close-knit networks abroad, or by making short regular trips. This raises the very interesting issue if anthropologists ever really leave the field—given their deep involvement in matters of the region even when not physically present in their field sites.

CONCLUSION

Since the early twentieth century, Cameroon has emerged as a strategic locus for anthropological practice. It is on this grand theater that diverse anthropological traditions have mingled, perhaps competed against each other for the understanding and articulation of native livelihoods and customs. This seems almost apposite, given Cameroon's triple colonial history. The country's geographical, historical, and cultural diversity have made it "a true African crossroads, a microcosm of the continent" (Fowler and Zeitlyn 1996: xviii). Of course, Nigel Barley (1982, 1986) has done his fair share of bringing Cameroon to a rather odd limelight through his absurd but hilarious account of certain mountain "tribes" in the north of the country. His *innocence*, notwithstanding, Cameroon seems to have established fairly intimate relationships with anthropology and anthropologists.

The Bamenda grassfields in particular, described as a "microcosm of this microcosm," has been the subject of a huge number of ethnographies emerging from the country. These works go a long way to celebrate the legacy of the pioneers such as Jeffreys, Kaberry, and Chilver, and indeed, the lives of those who inhabit the rugged territories of the grassfields. The pioneers whose works and legacies I have examined in brief have remained indispensable among Cameroonian and Cameroonist historians and anthropologists. Usually, many pioneers do not enjoy the glorification that seems to be endowed on them by virtue of being the first to set foot on a region or the first to write about a people's lives. But if anything, most of the pioneer anthropologists examined above have immortalized their names, due to their insightful and fascinating studies in Cameroon. The growing number of local anthropologists also promises exciting times for anthropology in this region. Their own contributions, it is anticipated, will foster the kinds of conversations that stimulate and propel intellectual networking to the benefit of both locals and expatriates.

NOTES

1. The country is composed of over 150 ethnic groups and counts more than 200 languages for a population of 16 million.

2. About eighty percent of the territory was allocated to French rule, and the remaining portion was administered as part of Eastern Nigeria until the mid 1950s.

3. Anglophone Cameroon constitutes two of the ten provinces in Cameroon. During the past decade, several pressure groups such as the Southern Cameroons National Council (SCNC) have emerged within this region of the country, advocating the restoration of their independence from Francophone-dominated Cameroon.

4. I use grasslands and grassfields interchangeably. Originally coined by the Germans to describe the vast territories of what constitutes the present West and North West provinces, it has come to assume derogatory connotations, especially as used by coastal peoples to depict people from the hinterlands as more traditional and backward.

REFERENCES

Ardener, E., S. Ardener, and W.A. Warmington. 1960. *Plantation and Village in the Cameroons: Some Economic and Social Studies.* Oxford: Oxford University Press.

Ardener, S. 1996. "The Catalyst: Chilver at the Crossroads." In *African Crossroads: Intersections between History and Anthropology in Cameroon,* eds. Ian Fowler and David Zeitlyn, pp. ix–xvi. Oxford: Berghahn.

Chilver, E.M. 1970. "Chronology of the Bamenda Grassfields." *Journal of African History* 11: 249–57.

——. 1988. "Women Cultivators, Cows and Cash-Crops: Phyllis Kaberry's Women of the Grassfields Revisited." Paper presented at the The Political economy of Cameroon: historical perspectives, African Studies Centre. Leiden.

Chilver, E. M., and P. Kaberry. 1967. *Traditional Bamenda: The Precolonial History and Ethnography of the Bamenda Grassfields.* Buea: Government Printer.

Chilver, E. M., and U. Röschenthaler. 2001. *Cameroon's Tycoon. Max Esser's Expedition and Its Consequences.* Oxford: Berghahn.

Fardon, R. 1996. "The Person, Ethnicity and the Problem of 'Identity' in West Africa." In *African Crossroads: Intersections between History and Ethnography in Cameroon,* eds. I. Fowler and D. Zeitlyn. Oxford: Berghahn.

Fisiy, C.F. 1995. "Chieftaincy in the Modern State: An Institution at the Crossroads of Democratic Change." *Paideuma* 41: 49–62.

Fisiy, C. F., and P. Geschiere. 1996. "Witchcraft, Violence and Identity: Different Trajectories in Postcolonial Cameroon." In *Postcolonial Identities in Africa,* edited by Richard Werbner and T. Ranger. London: Zed Books.

Fokwang, J. 2003a. "Ambiguous Transitions: Mediating Citizenship among Youth in Cameroon." *Africa Development* 28: 76–104.

——. 2003b. *Chiefs and Democratic Transition in Africa: An Ethnographic Study in the Chiefdoms of Tshivhase and Bali.* MA Thesis, University of Pretoria.

Fonlon, B. 1967. "Idea of Culture (Ii)." *ABBIA: Cameroon Cultural Review* 16: 5–24.

Fowler, I., and D. Zeitlyn. 1996a. "The Grassfields and the Tikar." In *African Crossroads: Intersections between History and Anthropology in Cameroon,* edited by I. Fowler and D. Zeitlyn, pp. 1–16. Oxford: Berghahn.

——. 1996b. "Preface." In *African Crossroads: Intersections between History and Anthropology in Cameroon,* edited by I. Fowler and D. Zeitlyn, pp. xvii–xxvii. Oxford: Berghahn.

Gausset, Q. 2004. "Richesse Et Défis Des Études Camerounaises." *Social Anthropology* 12, 2: 223–26.

Geschiere, P. 1993. "Chiefs and Colonial Rule in Cameroon: Inventing Chieftaincy, French and British Style." *Africa* 63, 2: 151–75.

——. 1997. *The Modernity of Witchcraft: Politics and the Occult in Postcolonial Africa.* Charlottesville: University of Virginia Press.

Geschiere, P., and J. Gugler. 1998. "The Politics of Primary Patriotism (Special Issue)." *Africa* 68, no. 3.

Geschiere, P., and F.B. Nyamnjoh. 2000. "Capitalism and Autochthony: The Seesaw of Mobility and Belonging." *Public Culture* 12: 423–52.

Goheen, M. 1996. *Men Own the Fields, Women Own the Crops: Gender and Power in the Cameroon Grassfields.* Madison: University of Wisconsin Press.

Jeffreys, M.D.W. 1964. "Who Are the Tikar?" *African Studies* 23, 3/4: 141–53.

Jua, N. 1995. "Indirect Rule in Colonial and Postcolionial Cameroon," *Paideuma* 41: 39–47.

Jumbam, K. 1980. *The White Man of God.* London: Heinemann.

Konings, P. 1999. "The 'Anglophone Problem' and Chieftaincy in Anglophone Cameroon." In *African Chieftaincy in a New Socio-Political Landscape,* eds. E.A.B. van Rouveroy van Nieuwaal and R. van Dijk, pp. 181–206. Hamburg: LIT Verlag.

——. 2003. "Religious Revival in the Roman Catholic Church and the Autochthony-Allochthony Conflict in Cameroon." *Africa* 73: 31–56.

KRC. 1989. "A Publication of the Centre on the Western Grassfields." *KRC Bulletin* 1, 1: 1–48.

Malaquais, D. 2001. *Anatomie D'une Arnaque: Feymen Et Feymania Au Cameroun.* No. 77: CERI.

Mbunwe-Samba, P., P.N. Mzeka, M.L. Niba, and C. Wirmum, eds. 1993. *Rites of Passage and Incorporation in the Western Grassfields of Cameroon Vol. 1.* Bamend: Kaberry Research Centre.

Mbuy, T. 2000. *The Mysterious World of the Tikar: Fighting with Witches among the Tikar of the Bamenda Grassfields.* Bamenda.

Mudimbe, V.Y. 1988. *The Invention of Africa: Gnosis, Philosophy and the Order of Knowledge.* London: James Currey.

Murphy, D. 1989. *Cameroon with Egbert.* London: Arrow Books.

Niger-Thomas, M. 2000. *'Buy Futures': The Upsurge of Female Entrepreneurship Crossing the Formal/Informal Divide in South West Cameroon.* Leiden: CNWS.

Nkwi, P.N. 1976. *Traditional Government and Social Change: A Study of the Political Institutions among the Kom of the Cameroon Grassfields.* Fribourg: University Press Fribourg.

Nkwi, P.N., and J.P. Warnier. 1982. *Elements for a History of the Western Grassfields.* Yaounde: University of Yaounde.

Nyamnjoh, F.B. 1985. *Change in the Concept of Power Amongst the Bum.* Yaounde: Unpublished Maîtrise Dissertation. FHSS, University of Yaounde.

Nyamnjoh, F.B., and M. Rowlands. 1998. "Elite Associations and the Politics of Belonging in Cameroon." *Africa* 68, 3 : 320–37.

Rowlands, M., and J.P. Warnier. 1988. "Sorcery, Power and the Modern State in Cameroon." *Man* 23, 1: 118–32.

Warnier, J.P. 1985. *Échanges, Développement Et Hiérarchies Dans Le Bamenda Pré-Colonial (Cameroun).* Stuttgart: Frantz Steiner Verlag.

Yenshu Vubo, E. 2001. *Itinerant Craftsmen, Highland Farmers and Royal Herdsmen: An Interpretation of Kedjom Historical Traditions.* Limbe: Design House.

Chapter 8

Japanese Anthropology and Desire for the West

Kaori Sugishita

INTRODUCTION

The disciplinary system of anthropology is geared to investigation of "different cultures/societies" in the world. As a logical extension, the system investigates its own diversification into "national anthropologies" (Gerholm and Hannerz 1982). It can be fairly argued that anthropology takes different forms in different "nations" as distinctive socio-cultural entities, not to mention as polities. However, it should be remembered that distinctiveness of a nation, society or culture is a product of geopolitics in which anthropology itself is involved, namely the differentiation of "we/here" from "others/there" (Gupta and Ferguson 1992). The investigation of national anthropologies plays along with the same politics, reaffirming the socio-cultural boundaries that have been negotiated in the field of power relations. Hence, my inquiry into "Japanese anthropology" starts by delineating the geopolitical circumstances of "Japan" as an anthropological "we/here."

Historically, "the West" as a putative socio-cultural entity has been the "we/here" of anthropology, a unified subject who explores "others/there" (Gupta and Ferguson 1992: 14). Accordingly, American, British, French, and, to a lesser extent, German anthropologies constitute "international anthropology" that dominates the "world order of anthropology" (Gerholm and Hannerz 1982: 6–7). Yet, of course, a "non-Western nation" such as Japan, which is the "others/there" for the West, can be regarded as a "we/here" of anthropology in its own right. In the postcolonial world, it is argued (Moore

142

1996) that non-Western scholars should be recognized as producers of knowledge on equal terms with their Western counterparts. Japanese anthropologists could then justifiably challenge the "Western academic hegemony" in producing knowledge about, at least, Japan (Kuwayama 2004). Furthermore, given the multiplicity of anthropological "we/here," Japanese anthropologists could envisage "Asia" to be another, non-Western, unit of international anthropology (Shimizu 2001: 192–94). However, as "we" all fear: "Western social science consistently repositions itself as the originary point of comparative and generalizing theory" (Moore 1996: 3). The West thus remains the centre of anthropological knowledge production, subordinating its periphery as the locus of derivative or "distinctively cultural" production that has little relevance to itself. I make an issue of Japanese anthropology at the risk of reinforcing such a marginal position of Japan as an anthropological "we/here," with its otherness/thereness vis-a-vis the West reasserted.

Despite the risk involved, it is worth questioning how the Japanese, as the non-Westerners by definition, are engaged in anthropology, the disciplinary system of Western origin. Japanese anthropologists rarely address this question; they normally regard themselves as practicing "anthropology" rather than "Japanese anthropology" (Yamashita 1998: 4). This is to say that Japanese anthropologists tend to affiliate themselves with anthropology, or rather, Western international anthropology, as a universal system of knowledge production that transcends national particularities (Shimizu 2001: 172).[1] My intention is to counteract this tendency by exploring how anthropology has operated in and developed along modern history, politics, and the economy of Japan as a non-Western nation. The socio-cultural dichotomy between the West and the non-West has surely dictated the formation of anthropology and the modern world. Japanese anthropology should reflect on itself with regard to the workings of this dichotomy. Insofar as it fails to do so, Japan deserves to be marginal in the world order of anthropology, being not so much "we/here" in its own right as "others/there," which uncritically identifies itself with the dominant "we/here." the West.

THE OBSERVER AND THE OBSERVED

Japanese anthropology is fairly established and large in scale, with Japanese, the national language, used as the default medium. Reflecting the size of academia, the Japanese Society of Cultural Anthropology (formerly the Japanese Society of Ethnology) consists of more than 2,000 members at present. Also sizable is the scope; Japanese anthropology covers almost every corner of the world, and is far from being limited to Japan. Such an extensive interest in "others/there" is not shared by all national anthropologies, although it is a feature of Western international anthropology. As a matter of fact, "we/here" is the central concern of anthropology in many nations, particularly non-Western nations that were colonized by imperial powers and currently constitute the so-called Third World (Gerholm and Hannerz 1982: 23; Shimizu 2001: 185–86).[2] It is likely that the anthropology of "we/here," i.e., "native anthropology," has special relevance to these nations for its aspect as a countermeasure against the Western academic hegemony (Kuwayama 2004: 1). Apart from that, it is undeniable that exploration of "others/there" is the prerogative of "we/here" that is politically and economically dominant, which applies to not only the West but also to Japan. Focusing on this point, I will give a brief survey of the history of Japanese anthropology.

Japan entered a period of "enlightenment" and "civilization" upon the restoration of imperial rule (1868); the nation strived to catch up with the West, giving up a policy of isolationism that had been stipulated by the previous regime of Tokugawa shogunate. Anthropology was introduced to Japan during this period, then undivided into physical and socio-cultural domains, through the mediation of Western investigation into the "origins of the Japanese." The main catalyst was Edward Morse, an American zoologist, who initiated anthropological research in Japan by examining ancient shell-mounds in a suburb of Tokyo (Morse 1879). This work was vigorously followed up by Western scholars first; among the foci of the debate was its controversial claim that cannibalism was practiced in prehistoric Japan (Askew 2002: 85). Motivated by such a flowering of Western discourses on Japan, younger generations of Japanese scholars started to engage in anthropology, with the assistance of a modernized/westernized education system (Askew 2002: 91–92). The birth of Japanese anthropology thus accompanied a "shocking realization" by the Japanese that they were indeed "the objects of Western observation" (Shimizu 1998: 115).

In 1884, Shōgorō Tsuboi and his fellows formed the first anthropological association in Japan, called the Friends of Anthropology (renamed the Tokyo Anthropological Society shortly afterwards). They inquired into the origins of the Japanese in opposition to Western investigation, while drawing on the vocabulary imported from the West, most importantly the notion of "race"; their focus was on prehistoric interaction of different "races" from which the "modern Japanese" has emerged (Askew 2002: 80, 90–93). It can be fairly argued that such inquiries were part of the search for a Japanese "national" identity, of the modern attempt to forge the unity of Japan as a "nation-state" (Askew 2003: 138). The impetus for this process was not only Japan's centralization under the restored imperial rule, but also its encounter with the West as a dominant "racial" and socio-cultural entity. Against a backdrop of the emergent world order centred on the West, Japanese anthropologists traced the origins of "we/here" back to various "others/there" in the north and the south. In doing so, they were most likely affected by the growing ideology of imperialism, according to which "we/here" was superior to "others/there," including the West (Askew 2003: 136–37).

Toward the beginning of the twentieth century, Japan joined the West in imperialist power competitions, starting with the Sino-Japanese war (1894–95) that resulted in Japan's annexation of Taiwan. Later, Japan won a part of Sakhalin in the Russo-Japanese war (1904–05), and went on to annex Korea (1910) and Micronesia (1918). As the territory of Japan thus expanded, Japanese anthropology became concerned with not only prehistoric, but also contemporary "others/there." Pioneering overseas research, Ryūzō Torii, a renowned disciple of Tsuboi, explored the Liaodong Peninsula in 1895; thereafter he extended his research to as far as Eastern Siberia and Southern China, following the footsteps of the Japanese Empire (Askew 2003: 141–47; Sasaki 2003: 113–15). Torii focused on cultural rather than physical traits of different "races," arguing for the separation of socio-cultural anthropology (then called ethnology) from physical anthropology (Shimizu 1998: 116). On the other hand, he remained interested in the origins of the Japanese, and implicitly justified Japan's territorial expansion by establishing a prehistoric relationship between the colonizer and the colonized (Askew 2003: 143). Japanese anthropology thus started to develop alongside imperialism. At this point, Japan was no longer a passive object of Western observation, having obtained the power-based prerogative to observe "others/there" (Shimizu 1998: 117).

Japanese imperialism intensified in the 1930s and then collapsed in the following decade; Japan established a puppet state in Manchuria (1931), made further advances on China (1937), and participated in the Second World War (1939–45), which ended in defeat. Throughout this period, the Japanese government was eager for the information that would serve colonial administration and military operations (Nakao 2000a: 32). In addition, the general public were interested in the foreign peoples and lands targeted by the Japanese Empire (Shimizu 1998: 119). Accordingly, "ethnology" flourished and its institutionalization proceeded in Japan.

In 1934, the Japanese Society of Ethnology was founded separately from the Tokyo Anthropological Society (the latter came to focus on physical anthropology and grew into the present Anthropological Society of Nippon). Ethnology also became separate from folklore studies, as demonstrated by the foundation of the Folklore Society of Japan in 1935. By then, ethnology had been introduced to the systematic colonial research conducted at Taihoku Imperial University (Taiwan), Keijo Imperial University (Korea), and the South

Sea Islands Government Office (Micronesia). Further, between 1943 and the following year, the Institute of Ethnology (mainland Japan), the Institute of Northwestern Studies (China/Inner Mongolia), and the Institute of Southern Studies (Taiwan) were founded as part of the war effort. Affiliated to these byproducts of imperialism, many Japanese ethnologists pursued their academic careers in the wartime: Masao Oka, Eiichirō Ishida, Tōichi Mabuchi, to mention a few well-known figures (Nakao 2000b; Shimizu 1998: 118; Sofue 1961: 174–75, 191–95). Apparently, their research received only a "meager recognition" in Japan at that time (Nakane 1974: 68). However, there is little doubt that imperialism facilitated, if not co-opted, ethnology by not only securing access to "others/there," but also providing the discipline with a rationale. It is worth noting that the scope of the Japanese Empire was conceived as a "Great East Asian Coprosperity Sphere," reflecting a self-righteous idea that Japan shall release other nations from Western colonial rule.

Upon the end of the Second World War, Japan was occupied by the victorious Allied Forces led by the United States of America. During the occupation (1945–52), Japan transformed itself into a "democratic" and "pacifist" nation under American supervision, with the Emperor defined as a "symbolic head" of the new nation. The Institute of Ethnology and other war related research establishments met the fate of immediate closure. Besides, as Japan lost overseas territories, ethnologists were deprived of access to "others/there." Hence, many of them turned to researching in rural Japan and cooperating with American anthropologists at a civil section of the occupation forces (Sofue 1961: 175–76). American anthropology thereby exerted direct influence on Japanese ethnology; particularly influential was Ruth Benedict's analysis of the "patterns" of Japanese culture (Benedict 1946). Meanwhile, the old interest in the origins of the Japanese resurfaced under the influence of German/Austrian cultural diffusionism (e.g., Ishida et al. 1949). Japanese ethnology thus shifted its focus onto "we/here," taking part in the reconceptualization of Japan in the aftermath of a failed imperialism. However, ethnology was in disgrace; the discipline was closely associated with imperialism, to the extent that ethnology was introduced to the postwar university education under a new name, "cultural anthropology," leaving its tainted past behind (Nakane 1974: 57 n. 2; Nakao 2000a: 32–33). Nevertheless, the Japanese Society of Ethnology retained its name; it was not until 2004 that the association was renamed the Japanese Society of Cultural Anthropology.[3]

With sovereignty regained, Japan embarked on the road to global economic power, drawing on its alliance with the United States in the postwar world order. Corresponding to the nation's high economic growth, Japanese anthropologists resumed their exploration of "others/there." By the end of the 1960s, previously unexplored areas such as Africa came into the scope of

Japanese anthropology. In contrast, the inquiry into "we/here," particularly its origins, started to decline (Shimizu 1998: 121; Uchibori 2003: 45–46). In the 1980s, according to a study (Eades 1994: 12), Japan featured in only 20 percent of the articles published in the *Japanese Journal of Ethnology;* the rest concerned Southeast Asia, South Asia, Europe (15% each), Africa (12%), China (10%), Oceania, South America (5% each), Korea, and North America (3% altogether). Ethnographic diversification aside, Japanese anthropology kept following theoretical trends in Western international anthropology; needless to say, French structuralism attracted due attention and elaboration (e.g., Yamaguchi 1975). Japan thus became a locus of anthropology comparable to the West in terms of ethnographic and theoretical range. However, Japanese anthropology has had little international influence; it has been practiced mostly in the national language, with translations of Western scholarship abundantly supplied, thanks to the size of Japanese academia and readership (Kuwayama 2004: 57–58; Gerholm and Hannerz 1982: 8–9). That is to say, Japanese anthropology, "unlike the Japanese economy, imports too much and exports too little" (Yamashita 1998: 4).

While striving to keep up with Western international anthropology, current Japanese anthropology is not necessarily bound by the political and economic interests of contemporary Japan (Shimizu 1998: 121). In fact, the Japanese government does not seem to have recognized anthropology as a "useful science," despite a move toward "internationalization" of the Japanese politics and economy in the 1980s (Aoki 1985: 116–17). Still, internationalism serves as an ideological patron of Japanese anthropology in the same way in which imperialism did, although the former is apparently devoid of the latter's sinister orientation to subjugating the world. It is obvious that contemporary Japanese anthropologists are privileged to observe "others/there" because of Japan's success in international politics and the economy, including a huge investment in the "Third World," which has made the nation into a honorary member of the West. Given the situation, it is not surprising that Japan itself is not in the foreground of Japanese anthropology. However, even if "others/there" is the central concern, anthropology (be it national or international) should objectify its "we/here," the putative socio-cultural entity in which it is embedded. I explore this point next with a view to revealing the problems of anthropology as the study of "different cultures/societies."

UNASKED QUESTIONS

During the 1970s and the following decade, Western international anthropology intensively reflected on itself in response to the official end of the colonial relationship between "we/here" and "others/there." This self-reflection encompassed the historiography of national anthropologies, the "postmodern" redefinition of ethnography, and the inquiry into the collusion between anthropology and colonialism (e.g., Kuper 1973; Clifford and Marcus 1986; Asad 1973). A crucial point was thus recognized: anthropology has been an "epistemological dictatorship reflecting the real political relations between the society that studies and societies that are studied" (Fabian 1983: 140). In this context, anthropology is problematized for the way in which the disciplinary system has operated in the West. However, the system's operation has been equally problematic in the non-West, at least in Japan, as illustrated by the history of Japanese anthropology. On the one hand, Japan has been subjected to the epistemological dictatorship of the West. On the other, the nation has joined the West in exercising the same dictatorship. It is only recently (and not quite prominently) that Japanese anthropology began to reflect on itself by taking account of such complicated relationships between Japan, the West, and the rest of the world.

The postcolonial currents in Western international anthropology, including the so-called postmodernism, started to influence Japanese anthropology in the 1990s. In keeping with Japan's twofold involvement in the dictatorial system of anthropology, the inquiry into Japanese colonial anthropology was initiated simultaneously with the search for a counterbalance to the West-centred knowledge production (Nakao 2000; Ota 1998; Kuwayama 2004). These lines of investigation are necessarily connected with reflections on Japan as an anthropological "we/here." However, this is not always the case with Japanese adoption of Western postcolonial thoughts on anthropology.

To begin with, many Japanese anthropologists dealt with postmodernism from a purely epistemological perspective, overlooking its political implications for anthropology in the postcolonial world, and specifically Japan as the periphery of the West (Ota 1998: 175-246). While postmodernism as an apolitical epistemology has lost currency in Japan as well as in the West, it remains that Japanese anthropologists hardly make an issue of Japan as a particular locus of postcolonial anthropology (Sugishima 2001). This means they are inclined to accept Western international anthropology as it often represents itself, that is, as universal/unmarked anthropology (Shimizu 2001: 173–74). It can be argued that anthropology in general is questioned under postcolonial conditions. The disciplinary system is likely to entail political/epistemological problems wherever it operates; the end of colonialism by no means eradicated the inequalities between socio-cultural entities composing the world. However, Japanese anthropology should see its burdens in the historical context of Japan in particular, as Western international anthropology has identified its own by objectifying the West as "we/here." In this connection, a tricky question arises: What is "Japanese modernity," the particular conditions under which imperialism, colonialism, and anthropology were nurtured in the non-West?

When Western international anthropology exhausted the issue of "postmodernity," what emerged as the real issue was "modernity" itself, or rather, its multiplicity (Comaroff and Comaroff 1993). The Western conception of "modernization" as a universal process of cultural convergence was called into question, thereby starting the inquiry into "different modernities" coexisting in the world. This kind of investigation has proven to be fruitful (e.g., Knauft 2002), coupled with a caution against the "meta-narratives of modernity" that account for "others/there" as a variant of the West (Englund and Leach 2000). The issues pertaining to modernity thus constitute a major focus of Western international anthropology at present. One might speculate that the West has emerged from postcolonial self-reflection by postulating the multiplicity of modernities to be the basis for anthropology as the study of "different cultures/societies." For Japanese anthropology, this Western/international trend is an opportunity to finally take a postcolonial turn based on self-reflection by posing the question of modernity with regard to not only "others/there," but also to "we/here." In fact, Japanese modernity is not a new issue for Japanese intellectuals; anthropologists' engagement with the issue is long overdue.

While "the world has not been reduced to sameness" (Comaroff and Comaroff 1993: xi), it is undeniable that "modernization" is synonymous with "westernization" in the non-West, and certainly in Japan. As mentioned earlier, Japan strived to catch up with the West (to modernize/westernize itself) upon the restoration of imperial rule, which gave birth to anthropology in the country. It was such a desire to join the West or, interchangeably, to "get out of Asia" that propelled Japan into imperialism (Shimizu 1998: 113), alongside which anthropology developed. At the peak of imperialism, many Japanese intellectuals (philosophers, literary critics, historians, etc.) addressed the question of how Japan went beyond the modernity that has been achieved through westernization. In so doing, they largely endorsed the devastating consequence of Japanese modernity, i.e., the war over Asia-Pacific regions as fought against the West (Harootunian 1988: 449–53; Sakai 1988: 487–96). Apparently, anthropologists (ethnologists) did not take part in such discussions, while involving themselves in the war effort. Absorbed in "others/there," they failed to problematize the actuality of "we/here," particularly its modernization/westernization, the byproduct of which was their scholarship (Yamaguchi 1966: 23–24). By contrast, folklorists were absorbed in "we/here," for which they parted from anthropologists and established their own association in the mid 1930s. Hence, it is illuminating to take account of folklorists, especially Kunio Yanagita, who is not only the founding figure of Japanese folklore studies, but also an outstanding intellectual of imperial Japan.

Yanagita mediated the interaction between folklorists and anthropologists in the late 1920s, although he became increasingly dismissive of cultural comparison by limiting his perspective to Japan (Shimizu 1998: 118–19). According to him, only "natives" can "understand" their culture, which means that the comparison of cultures is impossible until "primitive people" who are represented by "foreigners" learn to study themselves (Kuwayama 2004: 69–71). Furthermore, he considered the Japanese to be "civilized people" who do not require "foreigners," particularly Western anthropologists, to represent themselves, even though his "analytical understanding" of Japanese culture largely drew on Western scholarship (Kuwayama 2004: 13–14, 72–73, 81–85). Yanagita was thus imbued with not only a nationalist ideal of folklore studies, but also a patronizing view on the people whom the Japanese or Westerners had colonized and subjected to anthropological studies. However, such "imperial consciousness" did not prevent him from criticizing the status quo, as demonstrated by his evocation of "original" life in rural Japan "under threat" of the state-sponsored process of modernization/westernization (Barshay 1996: 222–24). To be sure, the emergence of folklore studies was itself a "phenomenon" of Japan's modernization/westernization, as was the case with anthropology (cf. Yamaguchi 1966: 23). Attesting to this point is Yanagita's academic nationalism and his search for the "originally Japanese" as opposed to the modern/the Western. The difference between folklore studies and anthropology was that the former refused to accept Japanese modernity, while the latter took it for granted.

Japan's defeat in the war against the West over the Asia-Pacific led Japanese intellectuals to reconsider the wartime proposition of overcoming the modern/the Western. A current of modernism prevailed among them, postulating that Japan had yet to achieve modernity, and was far from overcoming it (Koschmann 1988: 507–8). Anthropologists, on the other hand, continued to ignore the question of modernity. Their research on rural Japan failed to deal with the issues that other social scientists had broached in defining Japanese modernity, such as absolutism, capitalism, and land ownership (Yamaguchi 1966: 26–27). Modernity was also not the issue for the inquiry into the origins of the Japanese, another focus of postwar Japanese anthropology (Yamaguchi 1966: 27–28). It can be said that anthropologists were reconceptualizing Japan in their own ways. However, if they had addressed the question of modernity, their scholarship could have been more relevant to postwar Japanese society and more critical about itself; anthropology was implicated in imperialism, the most repugnant problem of Japanese modernity. They largely ignored this implication until recently, perhaps out of concern for their predecessors who had to compromise their academic interests with Japan's wartime agendas (Nakao 2000a: 31–33). Apart from such concern, anthropologists have been too uncritical about their scholarship, a kind of knowledge production enmeshed with the problems of Japanese modernity.

It is difficult to say whether contemporary Japan has overcome the modern/the Western. When postmodernism set the scene for this kind of discussion, Japan turned out to be a global economic power threatening the hegemony of the West. Hence, it was possible to discuss the postmodernity of Japan as if it had gone beyond modernity and even surpassed the West. However, such discussions inevitably brought back a "fateful decision" that Japan made a century ago, the decision to transform itself "in the image of Western 'enlightened' wealth and power" (Miyoshi and Harootunian 1988: 397). It seems that Japan has largely completed this transformation, with its desire to join the West satisfied in the field of economy at least (Shimizu 1998: 114). Consequently, Japan almost identifies itself with the West, with Japanese and Western modernities (and, for that matter, postmodernities) barely distinguished from each other. Such identification might be a solution to the modern dichotomy between the West and the non-West. However, it might also be a "repeat performance of the archetypal colonial gesture," yet another expression of Japan's lust for membership in the West, the "first world," or the "utopian sanctuary" (Miyoshi and Harootunian 1988: 391). This point does not seem irrelevant to contemporary Japanese anthropology, even if its identification with Western international anthropology derives from a desire to share not only prerogatives, but also burdens with the West.

CONCLUSION

Japanese anthropology is inseparable from Japan's desire to join the West as the dominant socio-cultural entity with enormous wealth, power, and knowledge. This desire has been the driving force behind the making of Japan throughout the periods of modernization, imperialism, postwar reconstruction, and internationalization. It is important to note that Japan's pursuit of membership in the West has been not so much an egalitarian crusade against Western dominion over the world as a relentless attempt to obtain as much autonomy as possible in the West-centred world order. This applies not only to Japanese imperialism, which was aimed at establishing Japan's control over the Asia-Pacific, but also Japanese internationalism, which is little more than a pro-American foreign policy aimed at maximizing Japan's economic opportunity. Japan has thus contributed to the inequalities between socio-cultural entities which anthropology as the study of "different cultures/societies" draws on. However, Japanese anthropology hardly makes an issue of this point; it seems that Japan as anthropological "we/here" is yet to become fully aware of its unfair privilege to explore "others/there." I therefore suggest that Japanese anthropology, despite its ethnographic and theoretical sophistication, does not compare with Western international anthropology, which has internalized critical perspectives on the political, economic, and academic dominance of the West.

The lack of self-reflection in Japanese anthropology largely owes to Japan's identification of itself with the West, which is a continuation of its modern desire to join the West. This is neither to say that Japanese anthropology should look for the "originally Japanese" buried under the modern/the Western, nor that it should aim for "distinctively Japanese" scholarship in opposition to the Western one. As we recall, Japanese folklore studies entertained such nationalist ideals, which was not only the self-defeating dismissal of the West's intellectual achievements (Kuwayama 2004: 61–62), but also a futile reaction against Japan's irreversible modernization/westernization. My view is that Japanese anthropology should objectify Japan as "we/here" that has involved "others/there" in its desire for Western power, wealth, and knowledge. This kind of self-reflection is a prerequisite for Japanese anthropology to share burdens with Western international anthropology, including the search for a counterbalance to the West-centred knowledge production.

It is tempting to consider that Japanese anthropology represents a new form of anthropology, namely the study of "other" cultures/societies by the non-West, which has overcome the limitations of Western epistemology as well as the dominance of the West as the "observer" (Shimizu 1998: 124, 127). However, such self-congratulation seems untenable, given that Japan has neither been anthropological "we/here" in its own right, nor been as conscious as the West of the political/epistemological problems involved in the observation of "others/there." Also untenable is the view that Japanese anthropology is situated outside the world order of anthropology centered on the West (Shimizu 2001: 188). Japanese anthropology is by no means free from the influence of Western international anthropology, even though the former's employment of the national language precludes its incorporation into the latter. Surely, Japan cannot be identified with the West. However, it is misleading to claim that Japan stands outside the West; historically and geopolitically, Japan is "implicated" in the West (Sakai 1988: 495).

I thereby repeat that Japanese anthropology ought to reflect on the complicated relationship between Japan, the West, and the rest of the world. Unless based on such reflections, any Japanese intervention in the Western academic hegemony, which would necessarily involve Asia, could be reminiscent of the modern attempt to create the "Great East Asian Coprosperity Sphere," an imperialist venture disguised as an egalitarian crusade.

NOTES

1. Japanese anthropologists thus resist their production of knowledge to be regarded as "distinctively cultural" in comparison with Western "universal" production. As they do so, Japan as anthropological "we/here" often escapes their attention, which applies to my own works (e.g., Sugishita 2006). I am grateful to Aleksandar Bošković, the editor of this volume, who gave me an opportunity to investigate "Japanese" anthropology, and many others who assisted me in this effort, especially Kawori Iguchi and Masako Igarashi. I also express my gratitude to the University of the Witwatersrand, which provided me with funding to present a draft of this essay at the 2004 Conference of the European Association of Social Anthropologists.
2. I am aware that "we/here" recognizes "others/there" within itself, most notably ethnic minorities. Such "internal others/there" often feature in national anthropologies oriented to "we/here." In this essay, however, I focus on "external others/there" in order to highlight the relationship between socio-cultural entities that exclude each other from their respective unity.
3. The Japanese Society of Ethnology, on the other hand, started to consider renaming itself only in the 1990s. By then, the term "cultural anthropology" had gained more currency than "ethnology" in the Japanese education system, making the Society's name incongruous (Aoki 1985: 115). The name was even disadvantageous in view of the negative association between "ethnology" and imperialism (Kuwayama 2004: 59). Another impetus for renaming was that members of the Society had decreased their interest in ethnological issues, specifically the origins of the Japanese (Uchibori 2003: 45–46). Thus, after a prolonged debate, the Society had decided to adopt the term "cultural anthropology," which became effective in 2004.

REFERENCES

Aoki, Tamotsu. 1985. "Minzokugaku (bunka jinruigaku) no kiki" [A Crisis of Ethnology/Cultural Anthropology]. *Minzokugaku Kenkyū* [Japanese Journal of Ethnology] 50, 1: 115–17.

Asad, Talal, ed. 1973. *Anthropology and the Colonial Encounter.* London: Ithaca Press.

Askew, David. 2002. "The Debate on the 'Japanese' Race in Imperial Japan: Displacement or Coexistence?" *Japanese Review of Cultural Anthropology* 3: 79–96.

——. 2003. "Empire and the Anthropologist: Torii Ryūzō and Early Japanese Anthropology." *Japanese Review of Cultural Anthropology* 4: 133–54.

Barshay, Andrew E. 1996. "Toward a History of the Social Sciences in Japan." *Positions* 4(2): 217–51.

Benedict, Ruth F. 1946. *The Chrysanthemum and the Sword: Patterns of Japanese Culture.* Boston: Houghton Mifflin.

Clifford, James, and George Marcus, eds. 1986. *Writing Culture: The Poetics and Politics of Ethnography.* Berkeley: University of California Press.

Comaroff, Jean and John. 1993. "Introduction." In *Modernity and its Malcontents: Ritual and Power in Postcolonial Africa,* eds. J. and J. Comaroff, pp. xi–xxxvii. Chicago and London: University of Chicago Press.

Eades, Jeremy. 1994. "Gaikoku kara mita nihon no bunka jinruigaku" [Japanese Cultural Anthropology Viewed from Outside]. *Bunka Jinruigaku* [Cultural Anthropology Newsletter] 1: 12–13.

Englund, Harri, and James Leach. 2000. "Ethnography and the Meta-narratives of Modernity." *Current Anthropology* 41, 2: 225–48.

Fabian, Johannes. 1983. *Time and the Other: How Anthropology Makes its Object.* New York: Columbia University Press.

Gerholm, Tomas, and Ulf Hannerz. 1982. "Introduction: The Shaping of National Anthropologies." *Ethnos* 47, 1–2: 5–35.

Gupta, Akhil, and James Ferguson. 1992. "Beyond 'Culture': Space, Identity and the Politics of Difference." *Cultural Anthropology* 7, 1: 6–23.

Harootunian, H. D. 1988. "Visible discourses/Invisible ideologies." *South Atlantic Quarterly* 87, 3: 445–74.

Ishida, Eiichirō, Namio Egami, Masao Oka, and Ichirō Yawata. 1949. "Nihon minzoku-bunka no genryū to nihon kokka no keisei" [Origins of the Japanese People/Culture and the Formation of the Japanese State]. *Minzokugaku Kenkyū* [Japanese Journal of Ethnology] 13, 3: 11–81.

Knauft, Bruce M., ed. 2002. *Critically Modern: Alternatives, Alterities, Anthropologies.* Bloomington and Indianapolis: Indiana University Press.

Koschmann, Victor J. 1988. "Maruyama Masao and the incomplete project of modernity." *South Atlantic Quarterly* 87, 3: 505–23.

Kuper, Adam. 1973. *Anthropology and Anthropologists: The Modern British School.* London: Routledge and Kegan Paul.

Kuwayama, Takami. 2004. *Native Anthropology: The Japanese Challenge to Western Academic Hegemony.* Melbourne: TransPacific Press.

Miyoshi, Masao, and H. D. Harootunian. 1988. "Introduction." *South Atlantic Quarterly* 87, 3: 387–99.

Moore, Henrietta L. 1996. "The Changing Nature of Anthropological Knowledge: An Introduction." In *The Future of Anthropological Knowledge,* ed. H. L. Moore, pp. 1–15, London: Routledge.

Morse, Edward S. 1879. *Shell Mounds of Omori.* Tokyo: University of Tokyo.

Nakane, Chie. 1974. "Cultural Anthropology in Japan." *Annual Review of Anthropology* 3: 57–72.

Nakao, Katsumi. 2000a. "Joron: Shokuminchi jinruigaku no shatei" [Introduction: The Scope of Colonial Anthropology]. In *Shokuminchi Jinruigaku no Tenbō,* ed. K. Nakao, pp. 15–44, Tokyo: Fūkyō-sha.

——. 2000b "Nairiku Asia kenkyū to Kyōto gakuha: Seihoku Kenkyūjo no soshiki to katsudō" [The Study of Inner Asia and the Kyoto School: Organisation and Activities of the Northwest Institute]. In *Shokuminchi Jinruigaku no Tenbō*, ed. K. Nakao, pp. 211–58. Tokyo: Fūkyō-sha.

Nakao, Katsumi, ed. 2000. *Shokuminchi Jinruigaku no Tenbō* [A Prospect of Colonial Anthropology]. Tokyo: Fūkyō-sha.

Ota, Yoshinobu. 1998. *Transposition no Shisō: Bunka Jinruigaku no Sai-Sōzō* [Transposition: Reconceptualization of Cultural Anthropology]. Kyoto: Sekaishisō-sha.

Sakai, Naoki. 1988. "Modernity and its Critique: The Problem of Universalism and Particularism." *South Atlantic Quarterly* 87, 3: 475–504.

Sasaki, Shirō. 2003. "Anthropological Studies on Ethnic Minorities in Siberia and the Russian Far East by Nineteenth- and Twentieth-Century Japanese Anthropologists and Ethnologists." *Japanese Review of Cultural Anthropology* 4: 107–132.

Shimizu, Akitoshi. 1998. "Nihon no jinruigaku" [Japanese Anthropology]. In *Bunka Jinruigaku no Susume* [An Encouragement of Cultural Anthropology], ed. T. Funabiki, pp. 111–33. Tokyo: Chikuma Shobō.

——. 2001 "Nihon no jinruigaku: Kokusai-teki ichi to kanōsei" [Japanese Anthropology: Its Position and Potential in the International Stage]. In *Jinruigaku-teki Jissen no Sai-kōchiku: Postcolonial Tenkai Igo,* ed. T. Sugishima, pp. 172–201, Kyoto: Sekaishisō-sha.

Sofue, Takao. 1961. "Anthropology in Japan: Historical Review and Modern Trends." *Biennial Review of Anthropology* 2: 173–214.

Sugishima, Takashi, ed. 2001. *Jinruigaku-teki Jissen no Sai-kōchiku: Postcolonial Tenkai Igo* [Reconstruction of Anthropological Practice: After the Postcolonial Turn]. Kyoto: Sekaishisō-sha.

Sugishita, Kaori. 2006. "Transgression for Transcendence?: On the Anthropologist's (Dis) Engagement in the Politics of Meaning." In *Celebrating Transgression: Method and Politics in Anthropological Studies of Culture,* eds. U. Rao and J. Hutnyk. Oxford and New York: Berghahn Books.

Uchibori, Motomitsu. 2003. "Tracing Ourselves Back to 'Ethnologie': Ethnographic Works by Japanese Anthropologists on the Peripheries of Insular Southeast Asia." *Japanese Review of Cultural Anthropology* 4: 45–74.

Yamaguchi, Masao. 1966. "Jinruigakuteki ninshiki no sho-zentei: Sengo nihon jinruigaku no shisō jōkyō" [Conditions of Anthropological Perception: Anthropological Thoughts in Postwar Japan]. *Shisō* [Thought] 508: 21–33.

——. 1975. *Bunka to Ryōgisei* [Culture and Ambiguity]. Tokyo: Iwanami Shoten.

Yamashita, Shinji. 1998. "Introduction: A Viewing Anthropology from Japan." *Japanese Review of Cultural Anthropology* 1: 3–6.

Chapter 9

Anthropology in Unlikely Places: Yugoslav Ethnology Between the Past and the Future[1]

Aleksandar Bošković

INTRODUCTION

Ethnology in the Balkans is the product of nineteenth century romanticism, coupled with the wish to understand the "Spirit of the People" (*Volksgeist*) and its mysterious doings (cf. Vermeulen 1995; Bratanić 1976; Kulišić 1961). Within the Balkans, and all of its obsession with ideology (Nixon 1997), my emphasis here is on anthropology in the former Yugoslavia—taking my examples from Serbia, but with some comparisons with Croatia, Slovenia, and Macedonia. I take Serbia as my primary example because it has had an interesting ethnological tradition since at least 1884, but also because it had an institutionalized ethnology before the Second World War (with a proper University Department, a national journal, etc.). Furthermore, some of the debates about the future of the discipline in the region are well reflected in Serbia, with the confusion between ethnology and anthropology after the 1990s, as well as different positioning of scholars in various faculties and departments.

In all countries of the former Yugoslavia, social scientists (and this includes ethnologists and would-be anthropologists) traditionally longed for a wider recognition both by the public and by the state (Halpern and Hammel 1969)—but they were also part of specific nation-building projects. Being such, they were also in the forefront of the explanations of the conflicts of 1990s—explaining or justifying the position of "their people" in tumultuous times (Baskar 1999; Muršič 2000; Naumović 1995, 1999; Povrzanović 2000; Pusić 1995). Some of them were engaged in a more specific ethnographic work (Brumen 1997, 1998) or more general attempts to deconstruct the uses and abuses of nationalism (Bakić-Hayden and Hayden 1992; Rabrenović 1997; Godina 1998), or more complex issues of disciplinary boundaries and methodologies (Godina 2002; Muršič 2002; Rihtman-Auguštin 1996, 1998a, 2000; Prica 2005; Urh 2003); I will return to some of these issues later.

In order to make my position clear, I take ethnology to be similar to (and derived from) the German concept of *Volkskunde*—"the science of the people"—a national science that is primarily oriented towards studying and understanding one's own ethnic group (or "nation"). On the other hand, by anthropology, I mean social or cultural anthropology, a much broader field of research that studies all aspects of social and cultural communication in a comparative perspective, especially when it comes to the relationship between society and culture. It could also be said that this kind of anthropology is "a comparative study of common sense, both its cultural forms, and the social consequences it produces" (Herzfeld 2001: x).

In the first part of this chapter, I will briefly outline some crucial moments for the development of ethnology in Serbia, from the nineteenth century until the end of the Second World War. I will outline work of the three key figures for this development (Cvijić, Đorđević, and Erdeljanović), who were all crucial for the establishment of ethnology as a scientific discipline.

In the second section of the paper, my main focus is on the attempts at distinguishing between ethnology (and ethnography) and anthropology, and here I introduce some examples and references from Slovenia and (to a much lesser extent) from Macedonia and Croatia. In terms of time frame, I trace some of the debates from the pre-Second World War Serbian examples (like Erdeljanović's distinction between ethnography and ethnology) to the developments after the fall of communism throughout the Eastern Europe. As departments of ethnology throughout the region received new names, there were also attempts to redefine the discipline's methodology, subject matter, and scope. My main point is that it takes more than just wishful thinking to establish a new discipline—and would-be anthropologists in the region have always been oblivious to one of the crucial methodological components of social and cultural anthropology: the comparative method.

In the final and concluding section of the paper, I discuss some of the key problems that ethnology and would-be anthropology in the region face in the years to come—from the issues dealing with power and local politics, to the practical problems connected with the institutional reorganization. It is my belief that if social and cultural anthropology are going to be established in the countries of the former Yugoslavia, they will not be based on the idea of the "national science" (nor a part of the "nation-building" endeavor), but on the strict methodological and conceptual rules, and in tune with the more global developments.

THE "GOLDEN AGE" OF SERBIAN ETHNOLOGY

Serbian ethnology appears as a part of the national project of building the Serbian state ("The Kingdom of Serbia" from 1882; Serbia was internationally recognized at the International Congress in Berlin in 1878) in the early twentieth century. However, the need and importance to emphasize the study of folk life and customs was already made public in Serbia in 1867, and ethnology (then called "ethnography") is actually amalgamated with the so-called "human geography" in the early 1880s, and the first lecturer who taught it academically was also one of the most important and influential Serbian (and Balkan) scientists (cf. also Kovačević 2001, Vol. 2).

Jovan Cvijić (1865–1927) was a geographer who held many important posts, including the President of the Serbian Royal Academy. He was also a member of the state delegation at the Versailles Treaty in 1918, but his interest in anthropology ("human geography" or "anthropogeography" at the time) resulted in a monumental work *The Balkan Peninsula,* published first in French in 1918. In this work, and based on his researches into the interdependency of culture and environment, Cvijić developed a theory of different "character types" of the Balkan peoples (Ćulibrk 1971), concluding in an evolutionist (and even racist) way that the most developed (advanced) type was the one that inhabited the central regions of Serbia ("Dinaric type of the Šumadija variety"). This was immediately picked up by many Serbian authors (like Stanoyevich 1919), but was for obvious reasons rejected by non-Serbs (Tomasic 1941). Cvijić was the very first person to lecture on a course in "ethnography"–but as a part of general course in *geography*–in Belgrade in 1884, and he was the most important influential factor in the establishment of the Department of Ethnology in 1906, having before that recommended Jovan Erdeljanović, another key figure, for a hefty state stipend in 1902.

After completing his Ph.D. in Munich (in 1902), Tihomir Đorđević (1868–1944) was appointed the first Lecturer and Chair of Ethnology at the University of Belgrade, and in his very first lecture, on 18 September 1906, stressed the importance of ethnology in studying the inevitable progress of humanity (Đorđević 1906: 521). He also noted differences between this new science and others (like anthropology–perceived as *physical* anthropology–psychology, geography, sociology, cultural history, folklore, and others). Đorđević did relatively little fieldwork, and from contemporary perspective, one could say that he was very much into what is today known as "cultural history." Đorđević was very much interested in systematizing the new discipline, and he was also instrumental in establishing the teaching of ethnology at the University of Skopje (Macedonia) in 1923. (Unfortunately, he remained very much a prisoner of the prejudices of his own time—rejecting even a possibility that there could be a Macedonian nation.) Đorđević remained at the University of Belgrade until 1938, having been elected Professor in 1921. He was also a member of the Serbian Royal Academy.

Some of Đorđević's social evolutionist ideas were subsequently criticized (for the criticism of his glorification of the Serbian peasants, see Čolović 1995), but the period of his work is frequently referred to as "the Golden Age" of Serbian ethnology.

Another very important figure of this period is Jovan Erdeljanović (1874–1944), a former student and protégé of Cvijić who also began working at the University of Belgrade in 1906, having obtained his Ph.D. a year earlier in Prague. Erdeljanović studied in Vienna, Berlin, Leipzig, and Prague, and his career followed a similar trajectory to that of Đorđević—elected Professor in 1922, and remaining at the University until the Second World War.

Erdeljanović did much more fieldwork than Đorđević; he was interested in the problems of ethnicity (especially in his native region of Vojvodina), as well as in religion (he claimed that animism was the primordial religion). He was also interested in the establishment of ethnology as a scholarly discipline, and wrote at least one very accessible textbook about it (Erdeljanović 1932). On the theoretical level, Erdeljanović is quite interesting because his works (for example, 1932, 1938) represent excellent examples of *evolutionism*— even when evolutionism is almost completely absent from and discredited in international scholarship. Erdeljanović also tried to make a clear distinction between ethnology (as a very general science) and ethnography (as "the science of peoples").

These attempts made a lasting impact on later considerations of the different terms and concepts in Serbian and other Yugoslav ethnologies (see Slavec 1988; Supek 1988). Throughout the post-Second World War period, when the Communist Party was ruling Yugoslavia (1945–1990), *ethnology* (at universities) and *ethnography* (at museums and research institutes) were developed as clearly distinct from *anthropology*—seen as a Western (bourgeois) construct (Kulišić 1961, 1967). Things only gradually began to change after the fall of communism throughout Eastern Europe, when the need to be in tune with the developments of "the West" (see Godina 2002: 1–3 for an interesting account of the local "discovery" of the discipline much before the mainstream historians of anthropology became aware of it) increased and significantly influenced academic developments in the whole region.

FROM ETHNOLOGY TO ANTHROPOLOGY

Following the Second World War, besides Croatia and Serbia, different ethnological traditions began to develop in other parts of Yugoslavia—especially Slovenia. However, an interesting situation arises when it comes to the distinguishing between ethnology and anthropology. On the one hand, many practitioners declared that these are (and were) one and the same and that there is no difference between the two. However, as ethnology was established in all parts of the former Yugoslavia as a part of the *national project,* a *comparative perspective,* so crucial for the theoretical development of social and cultural anthropology elsewhere, was absent. Furthermore, it is difficult to see how some people could simply wake up one day and decide that they have become anthropologists.

Suddenly, "ethnology" became a politically suspicious term, while "anthropology"—so prominent in "the West" to which the new elites throughout the region began to aspire—became politically correct. Just like with some other key terms (like "the Balkans," which no one wants to be part of any more—Karakasidou 2002; Todorova 1997; Rihtman-Auguštin 1998b, 1999; Bakić-Hayden and Hayden 1992), new constellation of powers became crucial for issues such as personal promotions (in the former Yugoslavia, it was always based on personal alliances—not on quality of research!) and application for grants and fellowships. The issues of methodology, institutionalization, and actual research topics became largely irrelevant. Although proponents of the continuity (from ethnology to anthropology) frequently referred to the historical considerations of authors like Vermeulen (1995), they also failed to take into account some specificities of the development of the discipline in their proper regions (or countries).

This distinction becomes crucial following the political changes of the late 1980s, as throughout the former Eastern Europe departments of ethnology literally overnight changed their names into Departments of Ethnology *and Cultural Anthropology.*[2] Yugoslavia already entered the global anthropological map when Zagreb (Croatia) hosted the 12th International Congress of Anthropological and Ethnological Sciences in July 1988. The presence of so many foreign scholars in one place was an exciting opportunity for Yugoslav scholars to exchange views and opinions with their colleagues. There were very few scholars who conducted studies abroad (for example, Erlich 1966 is a publication of her Ph.D. from the University of California at Berkeley), but due to a deep distrust of the Yugoslav communist authorities, very few foreigners ventured to conduct fieldwork in Yugoslavia—as they were mostly considered "spies" (among notable exceptions was Halpern and his groundbreaking work in the Serbian village of Orašac).

Anthropology did have a period of slow emergence in Yugoslavia, but mostly as a product of individual endeavors. In Ljubljana (Slovenia), Professor Božo Škerlj (biological anthropologist by training and a great proponent of eugenics before the Second World War) began teaching "social anthropology" at the Faculty of Philosophy in the early 1950s. Another self-taught anthropologist, Professor Stane Južnič, began teaching "cultural anthropology" at the Faculty of Social Sciences a decade later, and one of his first students, Vesna Godina, started working in a postgraduate program in Anthropology there following her M.A. degree in 1983 (Godina 2002: 15; see also Godina 1990 for a "who is who" in this program in the late 1980s). On the other hand, ethnology was taught since 1940, and the Department of Ethnology was established after the Second World War.[3]

In Belgrade, also at the Faculty of Philosophy, two very prominent scholars, Professors Dragoslav Srejović (an archaeologist renowned for his groundbreaking work on Neolithic sites along the Danube, as well as for his work on several sites from the Roman period) and Zagorka Golubović (a sociologist, formerly affiliated with the *Praxis* philosophy circle) established the interdisciplinary postgraduate program in Social Anthropology. Just like in Slovenia, this program had very little to do with the Department of Ethnology, as it was formally part of the (then) Program (now Department) of Sociology. This program first suffered a severe blow when Golubović was banned from teaching by the state (communist) authorities in 1981 and expelled from the University. A decade later, she was able to return, but Srejović died in late 1996, and she subsequently retired (still currently working part time as Professor Emerita). Hence, the future of the only place where one could get *some* education in social anthropology in Serbia is in serious doubt.

The situation was aggravated by the wars and destruction of the 1990s, when ethnological research in Serbia was practically stripped of all state funding–there were some important projects on nationalism and values conducted since then, but they were the result of the private initiative and enthusiasm of some researchers (like Golubović and Prošić-Dvornić). In recent years, a course in political anthropology was also introduced at the Faculty of Political Sciences. (This is not to be confused with Čolović, who never held an academic position, and who always considered himself as an *ethnologist,* despite occasionally characterizing his field of research as *political anthropology*–cf. Čolović 1997.)

The wars and the destruction of Yugoslavia in the 1990s brought it to the attention of international scholars (as well as the angry responses to some of them, like Baskar 1999). While this is neither time nor place to evaluate many excellent works that resulted from fieldwork in troubled places, I would like to mention a recent work by Brown (2003) dealing with Macedonia. There, Brown skillfully explores the construction of nationhood in this country, along with the complexities of studying shifting identities anthropologically. Macedonia presents a good example of the place whose very existence has been denied in the last decade (as well as the existence of its Slavic Macedonian inhabitants), so there is a level on which reasserting a Macedonian identity has been a constant struggle. National projects throughout the region present excellent opportunities for research, but these are not taken up easily. One of the key problems is the relation of foreign scholars with the "native" ethnologists and anthropologists, who had some interesting situations of miscommunication with their Western colleagues during the troublesome 1990s (a good example is provided by Van der Port 1999; for a very critical perspective on local [Serbian] scholars, like Prošić-Dvornić and Čolović, see Naumović 2002).

Macedonia is also interesting for the fact that the very existence of ethnology in the country (as mentioned before, established from Serbia—who ruled what is today the Republic of Macedonia between 1913 and 1941) has also been somewhat problematic, and it is located within Geography, and the Faculty of Natural Sciences of the University of Skopje (cf. also Godina 2002: n. 17).

The only part of the former Yugoslavia where real debates about the relationship between these two disciplines took place seems to be Croatia (Godina 2002: n. 18), and in the mid 1990s, Rihtman-Auguštin (1998a) created the term "ethno-anthropologist" to describe a particular situation in which she (as well as many of her colleagues) suddenly found herself. However, Croatian ethnology also had a period of very distinctive development after the Second World War, with one of its chief representatives (Gavazzi) very much insisting on the methodology that (in contemporary perspective) can be more appropriate to "cultural studies." Therefore, the shift from ethnology to anthropology that occurred in Croatia can be seen much more as a shift in terms of a specific historical and topical development, than elsewhere in the region.

CONCLUSION: BETWEEN THE POLITICS AND
THE FUTURE OF THE DISCIPLINE

In previous sections of this chapter, I pointed out to some elements that characterize the development of ethnology in Serbia, as well as to certain debates that marked the shift from ethnology to anthropology in Serbia and Slovenia. It is somewhat paradoxical that the recent interest of foreign scholars in the region (Bosnia and Herzegovina, Macedonia, Serbia) did not translate into greater influence of some contemporary anthropological ideas. I would like to conclude with examples that are characteristic not only for the former Yugoslav (and Balkan) ethnologies, but that can be put in a wider context of the global developments of ethnology and anthropology. While these terms are used interchangeably throughout the region (with the possible exception of Croatia), I still take them to refer to distinctive (although related) scholarly disciplines. Whether *anthropology* will actually be established remains to be seen, although I believe that there are some grounds for cautious optimism.

When writing about the relationship between anthropology and ethnology in the former socialist countries, Vesna Godina (2002) points to the discrepancies and blurring of the distinctions between the various terms. Throughout her paper, Godina also refers to the forty-three questionnaires that she administered in 1996–97, asking people from eleven countries to comment on the "state of the art" of the discipline in their countries. One of the conclusions is that there was a considerable difference in opinions between the scholars educated in "the West" and the ones "at home"—one of the more practical consequences being that the "respondents possessing Ph.D.s in Anthropology from western universities have not found places either in university teaching or in university-based research" (Godina 2002: n. 20).

This is at least partially a remnant of the "it takes one to know one" attitude—among the local ethnologists or anthropologists, it is considered as self-evident that only an "insider" knowledge is possible. When studying abroad, people from the former Yugoslavia break this "golden rule"—being exposed to "foreign" influences is seen as potentially corrupting, destructive for the "national cause" that the discipline is trying to protect and explain, and definitively something that separates "us" and "them." Therefore, the regeneration of the departments (along with teaching, key concepts, ideas, and methodologies) is seen as a process in which the younger scholars first work as assistants for the more senior professors, and then eventually replace them when these retire. The basic idea is (and was) that these younger scholars will essentially replicate what their distinguished predecessors did and thought. The institution of job advertisements is still unknown in the region, and a young colleague from Belgrade assured me that it is quite unrealistic to expect it for at least another four to five years.

Another somewhat paradoxical situation is that, even with the increased openness and possibilities for international cooperation and communication in recent years, scholars in the region are usually acquainted with a very limited range of anthropological traditions—usually, only the Anglo-

American and French ones. This severely limits some important theoretical considerations—for example, when it comes to issues like "anthropology at home," some knowledge of the rich tradition of India (where practically all anthropology has been "anthropology at home") would definitively help. Another interesting example is a tendency to write about the "crisis" of anthropology—again, in total disregard of other traditions (like Brazil—see Peirano, this volume), or of the fact that the actual "crisis" could refer only to one (limited) segment of American anthropology—*not to all of anthropology,* whether in the US, or elsewhere.

Having said all that, however, I do not want to sound too pessimistic about the possibilities for the development of the discipline in the countries of the former Yugoslavia. While I do believe that the assumption that *there is a developed anthropology in the region* represents a kind of wishful thinking, the prospects for serious research are there, as well as many well-trained scholars intellectually capable of introducing new ideas. This is particularly the case with the institutionalization of the discipline in Croatia. The work of my Slovenian colleagues in recent years has also been extremely encouraging. In Macedonia, the situation is unfortunately clear, as there are no possibilities for the institutionalization of anthropology yet. The situation in Serbia is more complicated, as the power vacuum within the institutions is greater, and the state shows absolutely no intention of supporting any ethnological or anthropological research. However, in the limited contacts I had with students and some younger colleagues from Belgrade, the impression is that there is a willingness to learn and to develop, and there is eagerness to get in contact with new concepts and new ideas. Whether this willingness and eagerness will actually translate into the development of *anthropology,* we will still have to see.

NOTES

1. My interest in the former Yugoslav ethnologies was sparked by the fascinating conversations with the late Dr. Dunja Rihtman-Auguštin in early 2001. I am indebted to Ms. Sanja Potkonjak and Dr. Renata Jambrešić Kirin for inviting me to present a version of this paper at the Department of Ethnology and Cultural Anthropology of the University of Zagreb in late March 2005. I found the comments of Dr. Vjera Bonifačić and Dr. Tomislav Pletenac especially illuminating. I am also very grateful to Mr. Miloš Milenković for providing me with copies of many relatively inaccessible articles. Over the years, I have enjoyed the hospitality and many intellectually stimulating encounters in Slovenia, for which I am particularly grateful to Professors Vesna V. Godina, the late Borut Brumen, and Rajko Muršič. A special thanks goes to Ms. Maja Petrović, Dr. Jana Urh,

and my brilliant students at the Faculty of Social Sciences of the University of Ljubljana. This, however, does not mean that any one of them would agree with anything written here.

2. See also Elchinova, this volume. The situation is different in Croatia, where at the University of Zagreb, Departments of Ethnology and Cultural Anthropology are actually part of different Faculties. The Faculty of Philosophy of the University of Rijeka is at present (late 2004) trying to establish studies of cultural anthropology as a part of their new Program in Cultural Studies.

3. For the insider's view of the recent developments at this department—somewhat different from the perspective that I am taking—see Brumen 2001. Brumen saw the conflict and changes in Slovenia in terms of the issue between different generations. He also points to the fact that one of the key determinants in the switch or addition to "Cultural Anthropology" in his department was the fact that "Social Anthropology" was already "taken" (both by Sociology and by the Faculty of the Social Sciences)—hence, this term was also politically unproblematic, as there was no infringement into anyone's "territory." Muršič, who was one of the key participants (and a very strong advocate of the "anthropological turn") of these debates in Slovenia, recently described "the situation with anthropology in Slovenia" as "rather comical" (Muršič 2002: 157).

REFERENCES

Bakić-Hayden, Milica, and Robert M. Hayden. 1992. "Orientalist Variations on the Theme 'Balkans': Symbolic Geography in Recent Yugoslav Cultural Politics." *Slavic Review* 51, 1: 1–15.

Baskar, Bojan. 1999. "Anthropologists Facing the Collapse of Yugoslavia." *Diogenes* No. 188, 47, 4: 51–63.

Bratanić, Branimir. 1976. "Pogled na 200 godina etnološke znanosti" [A Look at the 200 years of Ethnological Science.]. *Izvješća* V and VI. Zagreb.

Brown, Keith. 2003. *The Past in Question: Modern Macedonia and the Uncertainties of Nation.* Princeton: Princeton University Press.

Brumen, Borut. 1997. "Cambio en los conceptos de tiempo y espacio de los pueblos eslovenos a causa de la nueva frontera estatal." *Política y Sociedad* 25: 77–86.

——. 1998. "Grenzen, lokale Identitäten und interkulturelle Kommunikation im istrianischen Dorf Sv. Peter." In C. Giordano, R. C. Dougoud, and Elke-Nicole Kappus, eds., *Interkulturelle Kommunikation im Nationalstaat,* pp. 183–205. Munich: Waxmann Verlag.

——. 2001. "'Refolucija' slovenske etnologije in kulturne antropologije" [The 'Refolution' of Slovenian ethnology and cultural anthropology]. *Glasnik SED* 41, nos. 1–2: 8–16.

Čolović, Ivan. 1995. "Selo i grad u delu Tihomira Đorđevića" [The village and the city in the work of Tihomir Đorđević]. *Bulletin of the Ethnographic Institute SASA* 44: 23–30.

——. 1997. *Politika simbola. Ogledi o političkoj antropologiji* [The Politics of Symbol in Serbia, London, 2002]. Belgrade: Samizdat B92.

Ćulibrk, Svetozar. 1971. "Cvijić's Sociological Research into Society in the Balkans." *British Journal of Sociology* 22, 4: 423–40.

Cvijić, Jovan. 1918. *La Péninsule balkanique: géographie humaine.* Paris: Armand Colin.

Đorđević, Tihomir. 1906. "O etnologiji" [On ethnology]. *Srpski književni glasnik* 17, 7: 520–32.

Erdeljanović, Jovan. 1932. *Osnovi etnologije* [Basics of Ethnology]. Belgrade: Narodna štamparija Mirko Drobac.

——. 1938. "Etnologija kao nauka" [Ethnology as a Science]. *Bulletin of the Ethnographic Museum in Belgrade* 13: 9–22.

Erlich, Vera. 1966. *Family in Transition: A Study of 300 Yugoslav Villages.* Princeton: Princeton University Press.

Godina, Vesna V. 1998. "The Outbreak of Nationalism on Former Yugoslav Territory: A Historical Perspective on the Problem of Supranational Identity." *Nations and Nationalism* 4, 3: 409–22.

——. 2002. "From Ethnology to Anthropology and Back Again: Negotiating the Boundaries of Ethnology and Anthropology in Post-Socialist European Countries." In Peter Skalník, ed., *A Post-Communist Millenium: The Struggles for Sociocultural Anthropology in Central and Eastern Europe*, pp. 1–22, Prague: Set Out.

Godina, Vesna V., ed. 1990. *Antropološki zvezki 1: Zbornik socioantropoloških besedil* [Anthropological Notebooks: A Collection of Essays in Social Anthropology]. Ljubljana: Faculty of Social Sciences.

Halpern, Joel M., and E. A. Hammel. 1969. "Observations on the Intellectual History of Ethnology and Other Social Sciences in Yugoslavia." *Comparative Study in Society and History* 11, 1: 17–26.

Herzfeld, Michael, ed.. 2001. *Anthropology: Theoretical Practice in Culture and Society.* Oxford: Blackwell.

Karakasidou, Anastasia. 2002. "The Burden of the Balkans." *Anthropological Quarterly* 75, 3: 575–89.

Kovačević, Ivan. 2001. *Istorija srpske etnologije,* 2 vols [A History of Serbian Ethnology]. Belgrade: Srpski genealoški centar.

Kulišić, Špiro. 1961. "Glavni pravci i neka osnovna teorijska pitanja u etnologiji" [Main Currents and Some Basic Theoretical Issues in Ethnology]. *Bulletin of the Ethnographic Museum in Belgrade* 24: 5–24.

——. 1967. "Osvrt na razvitak naučne misli u srpskoj etnologiji" [An Outline of the Development of Ethnological Science in Serbia]. *Bulletin de Musée de la republique Socialiste de Bosnie Herzégovine à Sarajevo* 22: 197–206.

Muršič, Rajko. 2000. "The Yugoslav Dark Side of Humanity: A View from a Slovene Blind Spot," in Joel M. Halpern and David A. Kideckel, eds., *Neighbors at War: Anthropological Perspectives on Yugoslav Ethnicity, Culture, and History*, pp. 56–77, University Park: Pennsylvania State University Press.

——. 2002. "In the Arms of the Sublime Objects of Desire: On Politics and Anthropology/Ethnology in Slovenia." In Peter Skalník, ed., *A Post-Communist Mille-*

nium: The Struggles for Sociocultural Anthropology in Central and Eastern Europe, pp. 147–65. Prague: Set Out.

Naumović, Slobodan. 1995. "Srpsko selo i seljak: između nacionalnog i stranačkog simbola" [Serbian Village and Serbian Peasant: Between the Symbol of the Nation and the Symbol of the Party.]. *Bulletin of the Ethnographic Institute SASA* 44: 114–28.

——. 1999. "Instrumentalised Tradition: Traditionalist Rhetoric, Nationalism and Political Transition in Serbia, 1987–1990." In Miroslav Jovanović, Karl Kaser, Slobodan Naumović, eds., *Between the Archives and the Field: A Dialogue on Historical Anthropology of the Balkans.* Belgrade: Association for Social History.

——. 2002. "The Ethnology of Transformation as Transformed Ethnology: The Serbian Case." *Ethnologia Balkanica* 6: 7–37.

Nixon, Paul J. 1997. "Ideology in Balkan Anthropological Research." *Anthropology Today* 13, 2: 17–18.

Povrzanović, Maja. 2000. "The Imposed and the Imagined as Encountered by Croatian War Ethnographers." *Current Anthropology* 41, 2: 151–62.

Prica, Ines. 2005. "Autori, zastupnici, presuditelji. Hrvatska etnologija u paralelizmima postsocijalističkog konteksta" [Authors, Representatives, Judges: Croatian Ethnology in Parallelisms of the Post-Socialist Context.]. In *Proceedings of the Ethnographic Institute SASA* 21: 29–44. Belgrade: Serbian Academy of Sciences and Arts.

Prošić-Dvornić, Mirjana. 1998. "The Topsy-Turvy Days were there Again: Student and Civil Protest in Belgrade and Serbia 1996/1997." *The Anthropology of East Europe Review* 16, 1. <http://condor.depaul.edu/~rrotenbe/aeer/aeer16_1.html>

Pusić, Vesna. 1995. "Uses of Nationalism and the Politics of Recognition." *Anthropological Journal of European Cultures* 4, 1: 43–61.

Rabrenović, Gordana. 1997. "The Dissolution of Yugoslavia: Ethnicity, Nationalism, and Exclusionary Communities." *Dialectical Anthropology* 22: 95–101.

Rihtman-Auguštin, Dunja. 1996. "A National Ethnology, its Concepts and its Ethnologists." *Ethnologia Europaea* 26, 2: 99–106.

——. 1998a "An Ethno-anthropologist in His Native Field: To Observe or to Witness." *Anthropological Journal of European Cultures* 7: 129–44.

——. 1998b "Kroatien und der Balkan. Volkskultur–Vorstellungen–Politik." *Österreichische Zeitschrift für Volkskunde,* N. s. 101, 2: 151–68.

——. 1999. "A Croatian Controversy: Mediterranean-Danube-Balkans." *Narodna umjetnost* 36, 1: 103–19.

——. 2000. *Ulice moga grada. Antropologija domaćeg terena* [The Streets of my City: Anthropology of the Home Terrain]. Belgrade: XX vek.

Slavec, Ingrid. 1988. "Slovenian Ethnology between the Past and the Present." *Ethnological Review* (Belgrade) 23/24: 37–59.

Stanoyevich, Milivoy S. 1919. "The Ethnography of the Yugo-Slavs." *Geographical Review* 7, 2: 91–97.

Supek, Olga. 1988. "Ethnology in Croatia." *Ethnological Review* (Belgrade) 23/24: 17–35.

Todorova, Maria. 1997. *Imagining the Balkans.* New York: Oxford University Press.

Tomasic, Dinko. 1941. "Sociology in Yugoslavia." *American Journal of Sociology* 47, 1: 53–69.

Urh, Jana. 2003. *Oblast in politična imaginacija na prizoriščih Balkana* [Power and Political Imagination in the Balkans]. Unpublished Ph.D. Diss., FDV, University of Ljubljana.

Van der Port, Mattijs. 1999. "'It Takes a Serb to Know a Serb': Uncovering the Roots of Obstinate Otherness in Serbia." *Critique of Anthropology* 19, 1: 7–30.

Vermeulen, Han F. 1995. "Origins and Institutionalization of Ethnography and Ethnology in Europe and the USA, 1771–1845." In Han F. Vermeulen and Arturo Alvarez Roldán, eds., *Fieldwork and Footnotes: Studies in the History of European Anthropology,* pp. 39–59. London: Routledge.

Chapter 10

The Otherness of
Norwegian Anthropology

Thomas Hylland Eriksen

INTRODUCTION

It is debatable whether Norwegian anthropology merits inclusion in a book about "other" anthropologies. A criterion for "otherness"–the main criterion, one might say–is that the subject has, in the country in question, followed an itinerary separate from the Anglophone and French mainstream, building on theories and intellectual impulses unfamiliar to mainstream anthropology, or facing empirical challenges which give direction and shape to the work of local anthropologists as well as the domestic anthropological discourse, that make it in important ways distinct from dominant trends.

   A promising case could be made for the otherness of Norwegian anthropology before the mid to late 1950s, when, under the influence of German *Völkerkunde* as well as the more sprawling varieties of North American four-field anthropology, it purported to be a broad and comprehensive "science of man." The leading light of Norwegian anthropology at the time, Professor Guttorm Gjessing at the Ethnographic Museum of Oslo, was an engaged intellectual who was an enthusiastic defender of *samnorsk,* a radical hybrid language fusing the two main varieties of Norwegian, *nynorsk* and *riksmål.* He was also a committed environmentalist and a founding member of the Socialist People's Party, branching off from the left wing of the Labour Party in the early 1960s. Gjessing's rich and varied writings in anthropology revealed a synthesizing intellectual who saw few limitations to the possibilities of anthropological knowledge. Whether writing about the Sami, ecological adaptation or comparative politics, Gjessing rarely relinquished an opportunity to draw inferences about implications for politics and critical self-examination. His anthropology was truly a cultural critique, if not quite along the lines envisioned by Marcus and Fischer (1986).

However, the influence of colorful iconoclasts and maverick intellectuals like Gjessing was not destined to last. At the Oslo Ethnographic Museum, advanced students were, by the early 1950s, quickly absorbing the latest British social anthropology, correctly seen as the most dynamic and innovative branch of anthropology at the time. *Primus inter pares* in the museum attic, the young Axel Sommerfelt convinced his fellow students, *pace* Fortes and Gluckman, that anthropology was tantamount to the comparative study of social forms, and in particular, legal and political forms, and that the vastly ambitious anthropology of the likes of Gjessing was far too imprecise and, at the end of the day, amateurish to count as scientific. Soon afterwards, a young and very energetic Fredrik Barth appeared in the museum attic, and the rest is, as they say, history; or more precisely, the rest is the history of Norwegian social anthropology. Effectively erasing the memory of earlier Norwegian anthropologies and refusing them a place in our genealogy, students never even get to hear about these anthropologies. Mary Bouquet (personal communication) recalls sitting in the Ethnographic Museum in the mid 1990s studying the history of Norwegian anthropology (Bouquet 1996), with Professor Axel Sommerfelt separating the pages of a book by Ole Solberg with a pen-knife as he simultaneously translated from it. The book, written by Gjessing's contemporary and predecessor as Professor at the museum—in his day, an important voice against the racist pseudoscience defended by a very different kind of anthropologist, namely the physical—had been sitting on its shelf for half a century without being read once. Such was the extent of willed amnesia when the majority of Norwegian social anthropologists (both of them—the subject was small back then) decided to narrow and sharpen the discipline, dissociate them from the earlier history of Norwegian anthropology, and set up shop as a subsidiary of Oxbridge.

Thus, Norwegian anthropology in the last forty years can, only a tad simplistically, be described as that of a branch of British social anthropology. By and large, Norwegian anthropologists tend to see themselves, and to be seen, as matrilateral relatives of their British colleagues (with Barth playing the part of the mother's brother). The location of the country has nonetheless given it the autonomy of the remote province, and it is possible that theoretical orientations among Norwegian anthropologists are more varied than what is the case in the UK.

Be that as it may, Norwegian anthropologists publish most of their scholarly work in English, do fieldwork all over the world, and take part in the English language public sphere of academic anthropology. Thus the question raised initially: What is "other" about it?

Norwegian anthropology is unusual in two respects: it has a very large number of practitioners and enormous student numbers; and it is highly visible in the public sphere, domestic anthropologists contributing actively to all the constituent parts of it—cultural journals, newspapers, books and magazines, radio, television, internet, and public meetings. This chapter sets itself the task of outlining the untypical situation of Norwegian anthropology, and trying to account for it.

DEMOGRAPHY AND RECRUITMENT

Like in many other European countries, social anthropology has grown very fast in Norway since the 1960s, with an accelerated growth rate in the 1990s. It is taught at all levels at four universities (Oslo, Bergen, Trondheim, and Tromsø), the Oslo and Bergen departments being the largest with a permanent staff of about 15 each, in addition to dozens of Ph.D. students and temporary lecturers. A considerable number of anthropologists, moreover, work at research institutes and colleges around the country; in some places, such as Nordlandsforskning in Bodø and NOVA in Oslo, the number of anthropologists exceeds half a dozen.

The number of people qualified as anthropologists in Norway is very high in proportion to the population, possibly more than a thousand in a total population of four and a half million. Partly, this high number is a result of the system of higher education, which was transformed only in 2003 due to the so-called Bologna Process. Until now, it was possible to graduate as a social anthropologist without a doctoral degree. The lower degree, which took seven or eight semesters, was roughly equivalent to (but slightly superior to) a B.A., while the higher degree, which typically took three or four years more, was clearly superior to the M.A. Entitled *cand. polit. (candidatus politicarum)* in the social sciences, it involved fieldwork sometimes lasting a year or more, and a dissertation which was often in the 250 page range. An older degree, *mag. art. (magister artium)*, maintained along with the *cand. polit.* system for many years, was considered slightly superior, and in fact, many university academics born before 1940 never took a doctoral degree because the *mag. art.* was considered to be almost equivalent to it.

Access to the *cand. polit.* programs was much easier than access to a doctoral program anywhere. Taking loans to finance their studies, supplemented by government grants of varying size, several hundred students carried out fieldwork, more often than not overseas, and completed their *cand.*

polit. or *mag. art.* degree in social anthropology between 1970 and 2003. They could now entitle themselves, and had a self-identity as, anthropologists. Some of the best *cand. polit./mag. art.* dissertations were published.

Since around 1990, following the introduction of a new doctoral degree roughly equivalent to the Ph.D. (*dr. polit.*), a doctorate has normally been a prerequisite for academic employment. Nevertheless, the point is that the now abandoned *cand. polit.* system has meant that a great number of Norwegians have "social anthropologist" as their professional title.

At the undergraduate level, anthropology has also been hugely popular, especially since the late 1980s. An anecdote illustrates this growth. Before the meeting with the new students in January 1990, I asked the very experienced Professor Arne Martin Klausen how many new students he expected. He shrugged, laughed and said "somewhere between 75 and 150," indicating that the art of prediction was not a skill given high priority among anthropologists. A few minutes later, we arrived in the auditorium to meet 340 new students. Most of them would only take a year of anthropology, but it would be enough to sensitize them to its magic and its profound insight in human affairs. Many journalists, high-ranking bureaucrats and even politicians, below the age of 50, have a background in anthropology. (Even Crown Princess Mette-Marit briefly studied social anthropology at Oslo before her engagement.)

In this way, some anthropological perspectives seep into the public sphere even without the active agency of practicing anthropologists. Moreover, all Norwegian schoolchildren are exposed to a tiny bit of anthropology in the final years of their mandatory schooling (which lasts for ten years, usually followed by three years of high school). The subject *Samfunnslære,* "social studies," includes some fragments of social anthropology, in theory making all Norwegians in their early teens aware of its existence. In high school, sociology and social anthropology is an optional subject, chosen by somewhere between 7,000 and 10,000 pupils every year.

In spite of its presence alongside many other subjects in school, there may be other reasons why social anthropology is well-known in the general Norwegian population. Hardly three days pass without an anthropologist writing in the press, debating on the radio or talking on the television. As a matter of fact, in 1995, a leading journalist in *Aftenposten,* the academically educated Håkon Harket, introduced a lengthy article with the claim that while every social commentator in the 1970s seemed to think like a sociologist, they were now "carrying an embryonic anthropologist inside": anthropological ideas about cultural difference, the significance of ethnicity, the modernity of contemporary tradition, and the sins of ethnocentrism had somehow seeped into the collective psyche. (In other countries, they might blame postmodernism for similar ailments.)

ANTHROPOLOGISTS EVERYWHERE

In a word, the presence of anthropologists in the Norwegian public sphere is exceptional. When the main liberal newspaper, *Dagbladet,* made a list of the ten most important intellectuals of the country in January 2005, followed by ten extensive interviews and a lot of noisy, but ultimately useful debate spilling into other media, three of the people on the list were anthropologists (there were none in the jury).

They appear on radio and television, write in or are interviewed by newspapers, take part in various public debates inside and outside the academic system, and publish popular books and essays. Let us therefore look briefly at some examples of anthropologists' recent interventions in the Norwegian public sphere, just to indicate the range of possible forms of participation.

The annual secondary school students' graduation involves protracted partying in public spaces, reaching a climax of sorts around 17 May, Constitution Day. The pupils, just old enough to drive and drink (although not simultaneously and certainly not in Norway), buy dilapidated old buses repainted red with risqué bon-mots and a few paid ads painted in white. Every year, concerned journalists report that "this year's partying is wilder and more irresponsible than ever before." Some years ago, an Oslo newspaper had the excellent idea to do an interview with the Argentine anthropologist Eduardo Archetti, who has lived in Norway for many years, about the phenomenon. One of his own children left school that year. Archetti explained, among other things, that for the 19-year-olds in question, this would be the first time they participated in rituals involving sex and alcohol, which was a main reason that the event was so controversial and saturated with powerful, complex symbolism. This was not exactly a message to reassure other parents perhaps, but he introduced a new perspective, and an entirely anthropological one, on a phenomenon which usually elicited predictable, worried comments from social scientists.

Some time in the autumn of 2004, on my way to giving a public talk, I happened to listen to the car radio and heard a familiar voice discoursing on the role of coffee in informal socializing. I recognized the voice as that of Runar Døving, who had recently defended his Ph.D. in anthropology, later published as a book (Døving 2004), on food and society in a coastal hamlet less than two hours out of Oslo. He described some of the typical contexts where coffee was served, adding that if you refuse someone's offer of a cup of coffee, it had better be that you are allergic or it is too late in the evening, and you are then expected to accept tea instead. He spoke at some length about the role of coffee at work (every Norwegian workplace has a semi-public space with a coffee machine) and claimed that without coffee, a great number of social encounters would simply not take place. In another program in the series, Døving described, drawing on Mauss' classic analysis of reciprocity (Mauss 1955), the typical outraged reaction if a houseguest politely refused coffee, tea, beer, soft drinks, and so on, insisting that she "just wanted a glass of water."

Yet another anthropologist, Unni Wikan, has for years argued passionately for human rights and the right to individual choice among minority girls. In her book *Mot en ny norsk underklasse?* (Wikan 1995, 2001), Wikan argues that muddled thinking informed by wishy-washy multiculturalism and misplaced cultural relativism has deprived many second generation girls of rights that would have been self-evident for ethnic Norwegian girls. She has often written in newspapers and appeared in other media to express her views, has advised political parties, and has encountered both support and criticism from others, including anthropologists and minority researchers. The many thousand Norwegians who follow minority issues with an above average interest have over the years got the distinct, and correct, impression that the anthropologists in this country represent differing views about the group–individual relationship, and accordingly hold different views regarding policy.

Again, as I was collecting material for this book,[1] anthropologists were in the national media at least three times in as many days. First, a couple of prominent sport executives proposed that one should pick out the talents at a younger age than presently occurring, in order to improve the country's competitive edge. Anthropologist Jo Helle-Valle was interviewed in this context, and later cited by commentators. Helle-Valle, who was then carrying out research on children's sports (and had himself been a children's football coach), argued that there is no indication that talent in a sport like football is evident before puberty. He also had a few things to say about the role of sport in children's social life. Second, a Ph.D. student who had just defended his thesis about transnational football fans, Hans Hognestad, was interviewed on a full page of a Saturday daily, by a journalist who clearly understood what his research was about. Hognestad could point out, among other things, that it was a curious fact that the international fan club of Liverpool had more members in Norway than any Norwegian fan club; and that this might tell us something about the flexibility of group allegiance and the transnational potential of sport loyalties. Thirdly, on that same day, I had an op-ed article about ethnicity and "human nature" in Norway's largest daily newspaper.

It is not considered a professional duty for Norwegian anthropologists to engage with the public. Some raise their voice only rarely, to comment on issues where they are specialists or where they deem that important values are at stake. Thus, in the early days of the 2001 US-led invasion of Afghanistan, Fredrik Barth appeared on radio and wrote a newspaper article discussing what the Western powers might realistically expect to achieve if they tried to impose a Western-type democracy on Afghanistan. He was one of the few people in Norway with the professional authority to do so, and although Barth rarely appears in the media, he has a perceptible impact when he does. In fact, Barth was, in his day, something of a pioneer for public anthropology in Norway. In the late 1970s, a TV series was made featuring Barth, where he spent most of the air time sitting behind his desk at the Ethnographic Museum, showing slides and talking about his fieldwork. The series was utterly captivating, it was swiftly transformed into a bestselling book (Barth 1980), and converted many young spectators to the magic of anthropology—in its way doing the same kind of work as Granada's "Disappearing Worlds" series did in the UK.

However, in the recent history of Norwegian public anthropology, the one person who stands out is Arne Martin Klausen, who was a professor at the Oslo department until his retirement in the late 1990s. Klausen's first field of intervention was development assistance, where he criticized—both in academic and in public forums—the tendency among donor organizations to neglect the cultural dimension. He would later publish studies of Norwegian society, and the book he edited in 1984, *Den norske væremåten* ("The Norwegian way of life"), had a decisive impact on public debate about "Norwegianness." The chapters dealt with topics such as the local community as totem, equality as a key value, and conflict avoidance. Tellingly, there was nothing about hybridity, creolisation or immigrants in the book. A decade later, such an omission would have been perceived as a mortal sin.

Klausen, who led a group of researchers studying the 1994 Winter Olympics as a ritual celebrating modernity (Klausen 1999), always maintained in his lectures that anthropologists should be relativists away and critics at home. He sees anthropology as a generalist's discipline opposed to the fragmenting specialization typical of knowledge production in fully modern societies. In a word, Klausen tried to teach a generation of anthropologists that they should be quintessential intellectuals: their job at home consisted in approaching society from a slanted angle, saying unexpected and sometimes unpopular things, adding width and depth to society's self-reflection.

Moreover, anthropologists are routinely contacted by organizations and media, asked about their opinions or invited to give public talks on some topic of general interest. This is not the case, for example, in the US. A few years ago, on a visit to Norway, Michael Herzfeld mentioned that he would like to reach a greater audience with his work, but alas, anthropology books sold poorly. Fredrik Barth suggested that he give a few talks to associations or organizations outside the university, in order to get to know his potential readership better. Herzfeld saw the proposition as being entirely unrealistic. How on earth should he get in contact with such associations? (Gullestad 2003).

THE EGALITARIANISM OF NORWEGIAN ANTHROPOLOGY

Some years ago, I asked a British colleague, who now worked in a non-anthropology department, how she felt about not working as an anthropologist any more. Slightly annoyed by the question, she said with great emphasis that she was relieved to have left anthropology, maintaining that social anthropology, at least in the UK, was incredibly snobbish, turning its nose resolutely up at anything smacking of populism or "not proper anthropology," and saturated with an ancient Oxbridge spirit totally out of tune with the contemporary world. The media are regarded with a great amount of condescension, she intimated, and popularization and "impure" engagements with the outside world (which might compromise one's integrity as one of the selected few) were viewed with deep suspicion.

These remarks led me to recall the situation in Norway, where social anthropology has enjoyed a reputation as an anti-elitist kind of activity, an unruly anarchist science of great-coated, ruffled men with unpolished shoes and strange views, since the mid twentieth century. In many nonacademic observers' view, it compares favorably with the humanities, where the western canonical traditions still tend to be reproduced in an almost monastic way, and even with subjects like sociology, where the reverence for ancestors like Weber and Durkheim ("the classics") can sometimes make lectures sound like sermons. Norwegian journalists contact anthropologists for comments on current affairs every day of the week—be it a royal wedding, a sport scandal or recent political changes in a third world country—and the anthropologists play an important part in public debate.

However, what struck me at the time of the conversation was not this difference, but the fact that although many Norwegian anthropologists now study aspects of their own society, the vast majority of us know much more about contemporary African witchcraft and sacrifice in Eastern Indonesia, than about the way of life typical of the domestic working class, which could easily be observed by a twenty minute tube ride from the leafy, bourgeois environment of the university campus. No anthropologist stepped forward and tried to explain, on the basis of ethnographic research, why, for example, a substantial part of the working class had recently changed its political alignment from Labour to the populist, anti-immigration Progress Party.

The fact is that there is a certain otherworldliness about academic anthropology virtually everywhere. Therein lies its charm for the wider public, perhaps. While a sociologist or political scientist might deal with, say, Olympic Games in terms of the global economy, power abuse in the IOC or domestic nationalism, an anthropologist would be more likely to see it in the light of Western individualism and the cult of modernity, and would presumably interpret it as a ritual, drawing on a century of research on rituals in nonliterate societies. Anthropology can offer slanted and skewed, unexpected and thought provoking perspectives on apparently pedestrian and mundane matters. This has made some anthropologists darlings of the media in Norway, but the very same quality of the subject has led its practitioners to withdraw elsewhere. To put it differently: in spite of its considerable growth, anthropology still cultivates its self-identity as a counterculture, its members belonging to a kind of secret society whose initiates possess exclusive keys for understanding, indispensable for making sense of the world, but alas, largely inaccessible for outsiders.

Jonathan Spencer (2000), in an account of British anthropology in its main period of demographic expansion from the 1960s to the 1980s, points out that the dominant figures of the discipline shuddered at the thought of introducing anthropology in secondary schools (see also Shore 1996). Leach argued: "It could be very confusing to learn about other people's moral values before you have confident understanding of your own" (quoted in Spencer 2000: 3). As a result of the anthropologists' refusal to adapt their subject to "A"-level requirements, thousands of young Britons have learnt the rudiments of sociology and psychology in their late teens, while hardly anybody has been exposed to anthropology.

The anthropologists simply did not want their subject to become too popular. Fearing the influx of former colonial officers and young idealists who were interested in applying anthropology to non-academic pursuits, the establishment reacted by purifying the subject even further. At the main British universities there were no curricula, but instead very extensive reading lists. Textbooks were rarely used. Again, Leach expressed a dominant sentiment when he stated:

> It must be emphasised to such potential students [who were interested in nonacademic employment] that the prospects of ever being emplyed as a professional social anthropologists (*sic*) are extremely small ... I would personally be horrified if it became apparent that the "syllabus design" ... was slanted towards "applied anthropology." (Leach quoted in Spencer 2000: 7)

In the USA, causes of the diminished engagement with the outside world differed. For one thing, anthropology has always been much larger, both thematically and in terms of demography, in the USA than in any European country. The Association of Social Anthropologists in the UK has a membership of slightly over 500, while the American Anthropological Association has nearly 12,000 members (Mills 2003: 13). In other words, although the population of the US is only six times that of Britain, there are 24 times as many organized anthropologists.

Yet anthropology fails to make significant inroads in the general intellectual discourse on the other side of the Atlantic as well. Popularization and refraining from minding one's own professional business are not activities that add to one's academic credentials. In a situation with fierce competition for few jobs, it pays more to write journal articles in the style of one's teachers than to popularize or enter into general discussions with non-colleagues. More generally, there is a deep abyss between academics and the general public in the US and, as argued by Russell Jacoby (1987), there nowadays seem to be few public spaces available for American intellectuals outside the academy itself.

WHAT DO THE MEDIA WANT?

One of the few metropolitan anthropologists who has a regular media presence is Micaela di Leonardo, who writes for *The Nation* and is occasionally contacted by mainstream media for comments on various current issues. She takes a less rosy view of the anthropologist–journalist relationship than I have done so far in this chapter. So when does "the fourth estate" contact di Leonardo? With almost audible exasperation, she lists some of the occasions when she has been rung up by journalists (di Leonardo 1998). One TV producer wanted her views on why some men are sexually attracted to very obese women. Another wanted her to take part in a Valentine's Day show on love and courtship ritual, and she has also been asked for her views on why "symmetry" seems to arouse people sexually all over the world. Yet another journalist wanted a capsule antropological analysis of why women were buying Wonderbras. (As a non-American non-woman, I do not have a clue as to what Wonderbras are, and I do not think I am going to find out.) She has also been asked for her thoughts on why, "despite so many decades of feminism, American women still enlisted the aids of hair dye, makeup, plastic surgery and diets. Didn't that prove that we were genetically encoded to attract men to impregnate us and protect our offspring?" Finally, "a Good Morning America producer begged me to appear on a show with the theme 'Is Infidelity Genetic?'" (di Leonardo 1998: 354).

These examples reminds one of Johan Galtung's term "pyjama sociology," coined after he had been contacted by a journalist who wanted the sociologist's explanation of the decline in pyjama use in the Western world (Galtung, personal communication). The trivialization of serious knowledge entailed in the examples is obvious, and in addition, all the examples mentioned by di Leonardo indicate the prevalence of a pop version of genetic reductionism, which is incidentally less widespread in Europe than in the US—not that it is entirely unknown on this side of the Atlantic either. The now retired anthropology professor Arne Martin Klausen once served on an expert panel in a popular science magaine in Norway, but he resigned after only a few months. The only questions he received, as a "scientific expert in anthropology," were of the generic kind "why do the Negroes (*sic*) have kinky hair?"

However, I must say that my own experience is different. Whenever I am contacted by the Scandinavian media for comments on current affairs, they typically ask for comments on social and cultural issues. During the last week, journalists have phoned or emailed me for comments on national differences in leadership styles, following an international survey which indicated that such differences might be consequential, on the cultural changes that took place in the 1980s following the worldwide political turn to the right, on the roots of contemporary Norwegian nationalism in 19th century romanticism (this was an Italian journalist visiting), on the new, proposed university law which threatens to remove the last remnants of democratic governance in universities, on the images of Norway projected abroad by the Foreign Ministry—and finally, I was asked to review the Indian author Arundhati Roy's latest collection of critical interventions. Sounds like heaven? Well, not quite. The agenda is set by the media, and our job largely consists in filling in a few details or offering a soundbite or two—or deciding not to, in which case they sooner or later find another academic who is willing to do so. Now, it would not be a self-serving or even relevant view that newspapers are evil incarnate. Granted, they are not peer reviewed journals, but anthropologists can still often contribute a drop of complexity, a hint of doubt or a subversive remark. Given that our existence depends on our licence to quote from others and indeed to describe their lives, we should not be above allowing others to quote us.

This ought not to be taken to imply that there should be no limits whatsoever. Anthropology can, for example, easily be reduced to a form of light entertainment by the media in what di Leonardo speaks of, disparagingly, as "the anthropological gambit": "The attribution of 'our' characteristics to 'them,' and vice versa, is always good for a laugh in popular culture" (di

Leonardo 1998: 57). This facile juxtaposition of "us" and "them," in her view, obliterates concrete power relations, context and tormented histories, and serves only to trivialize cultural differences. In this spirit, she attacks Lévi-Strauss' speech given at his admission in the Collège de France, where the revered master compares that ritual of admission with a similar ritual involving symbolic power among a group of Canadian Indians. In di Leonardo's harsh words, this "droll likening of a powerful, state-sponsored intelligentsia to a powerless group of North Americans is an example of chutzpah as obscenity" (1998: 66). I fail to see the obscenity and do not think, as a rule, that there is too much humor and laughter in the attempts by anthropologists to communicate to outsiders. Comparison can be stupid, superficial and misleading, but at the end of the day, even Gary Larson-type comparisons can bring us slightly closer to each other. Audiences are not uncritical receptacles, and "the anthropological gambit" can help them to laugh not just at the follies of their leaders, but even, occasionally, at themselves.

A number of contrasts can be posited between academic research and journalism, making for an unruly and frustrating relationship. Foremost among those is the contrast pertaining to speed: academic work is slow, while journalism is fast. Associated with this is the contrast between complexity and simplification. Journalists typically present issues in everyday language, work under serious constraints regarding both time and length, and are usually expected to tell stories with a simple message.

In most societies, moreover, the craft of journalism is not highly regarded. In the rich countries, journalism is increasingly associated with the sensationalism and commercial bias of the tabloid press. Surveys about public trustworthiness indicate that in North Atlantic countries like Britain and Norway, journalists are to be found near the bottom, along with politicians.

Media frequently ask academics to contribute, to allow themselves to be interviewed, and to furnish journalists with relevant facts. Many academics routinely refuse to cooperate with the media, given the very considerable differences in aims and methods between research and journalism. It can often be appropriate for academics to remain aloof from the media world. Their views are likely to be represented in simplistic ways by the journalists, and the kind of research they are committed to is often irrelevant to the media anyway. It nevertheless occasionally happens that the fields of interest between the two professions converge. In the case of social anthropology, this is increasingly the case in so far as the growing numbers of anthropologists study contemporary modern societies, on topics where there is already considerable media interest, such as multiethnic society and migration, national cultures and cultural change, changing kinship structures, so-called new work, tourism, consumption, and so on.

So anthropology does have a strong media presence in Norway, where anthropologists regularly comment on current events, write op-ed articles, debate minority issues on television, write polemical books for general audiences, and so on. In this engagement, it is easy to see the predictable dilemmas: the academic qualities of the anthropologist's work disappears, and only his or her opinions come across. The anthropologist's views appear in a context defined by other considerations than those which initially motivated his or her intervention, and the outcome may be frustrating to the academic, who feels betrayed and misunderstood.

On the other hand, several anthropologists have become highly skilled at using the media to influence public opinion, some of them functioning as public intellectuals with their own political agendas and the ability to explain them. The relationship between media and academics should thus not be seen as a form of one-way parasitism, but as a complex relationship where there is a struggle over the definition of the situation. Mainstream mass media may even have an untapped potential as vehicles for complex ideas.

ANTHROPOLOGY AS SPEED BUMP

Engaging in fast-paced media debate can nevertheless be compromising: one may be tempted to oversimplify, and besides, academics rarely win media debates with journalists, who know the ins and outs of fast communication better than we do. The lengthy, widely publicized debate between anthropologist Marianne Gullestad and journalist Shabana Rehman in late summer 2002, which I have analyzed elsewhere (Eriksen 2003), shows that the swirling world of the fast media is not always compatible with meticulous, calm argument. Characteristically, Rehman at one point jeered at academics for being busy discussing racism in Norway instead of demonstrating against enforced marriages. Gullestad responded that she had been working on the book in question (Gullestad 2002) for four years. Yet anthropologists can have an important role as agents of slowness, contributing their drop of complexity and a more complex, elaborate way of communicating than that which is common. Sometimes, this necessitates switching to another medium.

Following a controversial television documentary about female circumcision, which documented that the practice existed among certain immigrants to Norway, a journalist with the largest Norwegian newspaper, *VG*, decided to write an opinion piece on the issue. She duly contacted Aud Talle, who had done fieldwork in Kenya, Tanzania, Somalia, and among Somali women in London. Talle faxed her an article describing the social and

cultural embeddedness of the practice, as well as explaining the practice on
the phone. Soon after, *VG* published an article on female circumcision illustrated by an image of a veiled, chained woman trotting behind a brisk and
confident female anthropologist. The story objected against the "cultural
relativism" of the anthropologists, who preferred to study circumcision as
an exotic rite rather than trying to combat it.

At first, Talle was uncertain as to how she should react. Eventually, she
decided not to write a response in the newspaper itself. The fast media, she
reckoned, were simply unable to accommodate the kind of detail necessary
in an account which had to take all the relevant factors into consideration.
So she wrote a book instead, *Om kvinneleg omskjering* ("On female circumcision," Talle 2003). The book was published a year after the newspaper
commentary, and it is written in a popular style. It ends with a few policy
recommendations, where Talle makes an interesting comparison between
North-East African female circumcision and Chinese footbinding, suggesting that the successful campaign against the latter practice a hundred years
ago might inspire similar strategies today. Her main arguments are the ones
we expect from a social anthropologist, and which are, incidentally, rare in
general public debate: circumcision has to be understood as an individual
experience, but also in terms of cultural meaning and social interests.

Predictably, Talle's book was not reviewed by *VG* nor by any of the other
mainstream media. But it had its share of attention in the small elite media,
and—more importantly—it began to be used by health workers and public
servants, who are often reminded of their need to understand why certain
immigrants do certain things. This example shows how anthropologists can
function as speed bumps in the public sphere, why it sometimes pays to be
patient. Talle's book has an expected longevity which exceeds *VG* newspaper
articles by years.

Yet, it cannot be denied that there are some genuine dilemmas here.
Since the late 1980s, I have taken part in more radio and TV programs
than I care to remember; I have done short, long, and portrait interviews
with all kinds of media, written a great number of columns, book reviews,
and longer op-ed pieces in nearly all the major newspapers in Norway, and
contributed frequently to national newspapers in Denmark and Sweden as
well. Obviously, if it were possible, I would have deleted some of these media
appearances, especially on television, from the historical record. For years,
I would defend the view that if you were given one minute on national television to tell your fellow citizens that say, terrorism has nothing to do with
Islam, that "traditional" Norwegian culture is a modern invention with a
commercial face and a political one, or that it is a widespread feeling among
immigrants that they get the worst from both worlds; then that single min-

ute would still be better than nothing. Experience now tells me that this is not necessarily the case. Far too often, I have felt co-opted by the entertainment industry after initially entering the studio expecting a serious debate. Yet, the condescending attitude displayed towards the mainstream media *as such* among many academics, is too crude, categorical, and misinformed to be helpful. It is also ultimately undemocratic. If people who see themselves as enlightened do not try to shape opinions in their environment, who would they rather leave the task to? There is a great difference between talking to a journalist on the phone about why it might be that adults no longer wear pyjamas in our part of the world, and taking part in a forty minutes long radio program about the 2004 tsunami, risk, human rights, the Lisbon earthquake, and vulnerability. Trivialization should not be conflated with interventions that might make a difference. And there is an important qualitative difference between writing a 1,000 word op-ed article about the shortcomings of genetic determinism and talking for thirty seconds about the same topic on television. In other words, for those who fear the loss of their academic virtue, the question ought not to be for or against public interventions, but rather which kind of intervention through what kind of media. Besides, if we take a large view of things, it is probably better both for the subject's reputation and for the quality of public discourse if some practitioners occasionally make simplistic statements in the media, than if they all remained silent in the wider public sphere. It is easy to blame the contemporary media—shallow, sensationalist, profit-oriented—for the relative absence of anthropologists, but the argument can go both ways. Perhaps the unchecked superficiality and trivialism of contemporary mass media (especially television), where every issue, no matter how serious, seems to be turned into some form of entertainment, has been able to progress without meeting serious resistance, precisely because intellectuals have been busy talking to each other for the last few decades.

Real dilemmas nevertheless remain. Recently, a political scientist was contacted by a journalist writing a feature story about the situation in Chechnya. The researcher was a regional expert who thought it important to tell the public that the Islamic character of the Chechen uprising was a recent invention; that the Chechen movement was rooted in nineteenth century anti-imperial political nationalism. Getting this message across might not just influence citizens' views of the Chechen conflict, but it could also in a small way mollify the growing resentment against Islam and Muslims generally. However, it was a busy day, and the researcher had already made her point several times on radio and television during the last weeks, and so she told the journalist that she was not keen on talking about it right now. His reply was, "All right then, s'pose I'll just write something then," implying that without her expert comments, he would have to make his own amateur inferences. She acquiesced in the end, allowing herself to be blackmailed by the journalist for the sake of the public good.

Possibly, she was aware of the double-edged reward that comes from engagement with the public sphere is the possibility that one's own short-comings and weaknesses are illuminated by relevant criticism from unex-pected quarters. There is real danger in exposing oneself in this way, but if anthropology is going to influence the dominant patterns of thought in the anthropologist's own society, there is no other way.

CONCLUDING REMARKS

What's so special about Norway then? It is not easy to see why it should be there and not in Sweden, Denmark, Finland or the Netherlands, that anthro-pology should have such a powerful public presence. The explanation is unlikely to be elegant, and it is bound to involve several factors, including fortuitious coincidences. Firstly, schoolchildren are exposed to a little bit of anthropology (although this is a fairly recent development). Secondly, we were lucky to have individuals like Gjessing, Barth, and Klausen, who went out of their way to engage a larger public. Thirdly, the egalitarianism of the subject in Norway—unlike in Britain or Germany—created a space for the anthro-pologist as eccentric, which could be performed without provoking negative sanctions from the academy. Fourthly, the media pluralism of Norway (nine newspapers are published only in Oslo) offers a varied mediascape with many opportunities to express oneself. Fifthly, these four factors have created an awareness in the media, in the public service, and in organizations, of the exciting potentials inherent in the anthropological perspective. The fact that many Norwegian anthropologists now carry out research in Norway itself adds to their perceived social relevance (cf. Rugkåsa and Thorsen 2003).

NOTE

1. The material for this chapter is based on my recent book (Eriksen 2005).

REFERENCES

Barth, Fredrik. 1980. *Andres liv – og vårt eget* [Others' lives—and our own]. Oslo: Gyldendal.

Bouquet, Mary. 1996. *Sans og samling* [a bilingual history of the Ethnographic Museum]. Oslo: Universitetsforlaget.

Di Leonardo, Micaela. 1998. *Exotics at Home: Anthropologies, Others, American Modernity.* Chicago: University of Chicago Press.

Døving, Runar. 2004. *Rype med lettøl* [Grouse with light beer]. Oslo: Pax.

Eriksen, Thomas Hylland. 2003. "The Young Rebel and the Dusty Professor: A Tale of Anthropologists and the Media in Norway." *Anthropology Today,* 19, 1: 3–5.

——. 2005. *Engaging Anthropology.* Oxford: Berg.

Gullestad, Marianne. 2002. *Det norske sett med nye øyne* [Norwegianness in a new perspective]. Oslo: Universitetsforlaget.

——. 2003. "Kunnskap for hvem?" [Knowledge for whom?]. In *Nære steder, nye rom: Utfordringer i antropologiske studier i Norge,* eds. Marianne Rugkåsa and Kari T. Thorsen, pp. 233–62. Oslo: Gyldendal.

Jacoby, Russel. 1987. *The Last Intellectuals: American Culture in the Age of Academe.* New York: Basic Books.

Klausen, Arne Martin, ed. 1984. *Den norske væremåten* [The Norwegian way of being]. Oslo: Cappelen.

——, ed. 1999. *Olympic Games as Performance and Public Event: The Case of the XVII Winter Olympic Games in Norway.* New York: Berghahn.

Marcus, Geoge E., and Michael M.J. Fischer. 1986. *Anthropology as Cultural Critique: An Experimental Moment in the Human Sciences.* Chicago: University of Chicago Press.

Mauss, Marcel. 1954 [1924]. *The Gift.* London: Cohen & West.

Mills, David. 2003. "Professionalizing or popularizing anthropology?" *Anthropology Today,* 19, 5: 8–13.

Rugkåsa, Marianne, and Kari T. Thorsen, eds. 2003. *Nære steder, nye rom: Utfordringer i antropologiske studier i Norge* [Close places, new spaces: Challenges for anthropological studies in Norway]. Oslo: Gyldendal.

Spencer, Jonathan. 2000. "British Social Anthropology: A Retrospective," *Annual Review of Anthropology* 29: 1–24.

Talle, Aud. 2003. *Om kvinneleg omskjering* [On female circumcision]. Oslo: Samlagen.

Wikan, Unni. 1995. *Mot en ny norsk underklasse?* [Towards a new Norwegian underclass?] Oslo: Gyldendal.

——. 2001. *Generous Betrayal.* Chicago: University of Chicago Press.

Chapter 11

Anthropology with No Guilt—
A View from Brazil*

Mariza G.S. Peirano

INTRODUCTION

A new divide seems to be going on in anthropology: while in the metropolitan centers it appears either doomed to extinction or bent into "studies" (feminist, cultural, science and technology, etc.), in other locations anthropology is well and thriving or, if not thriving, at least providing a positive and constructive edge or approach. Renowned scholars in the 1960s warned their colleagues that anthropology might become a science without an object because of the physical disappearance of whole populations following contact, and because of the rejection of anthropology by newly independent nations. Anthropology's past sins and malpractices would lead former "natives" to turn anthropologists down. A decolonization of the social sciences was in order.[1] Indeed, time has confirmed these expectations, but something not anticipated happened—due to the guilt associated with colonialism, anthropology is being devalued even by the descendants of those who first crafted the idea of overseas fieldwork, i.e., the anthropologists from the centers.

In this chapter, I will confront this apparent puzzle by examining the Brazilian case in the context of the larger global picture. I start by looking at some of the past sins attributed to anthropology, and then turn them upside down to detect possible values and virtues. I propose that, in Brazil, anthropology's values and virtues are more stimulating than its sins; I also suggest that exoticism has been acculturated as "difference" (whether social, cultural or territorial) and that guilt has not prospered in a context which has always demanded social scientists' commitment to the objects of their study. I then examine the plurality of otherness, as found in anthropology in Brazil, and conclude the paper with a brief discussion on the implications of the label "national anthropologies."

SINS

The following is a retrospective list of past sins which have come to disturb today's "international" anthropologists (as per Gerholm & Hannerz 1982):

(i) The first sin tells of power relations. For a long time, anthropology was defined by the exoticism of its subject matter and by the distance, conceived as both cultural and geographic, that separated the researcher from the researched group. This situation was part and parcel of a colonial context of domination, anthropology being "the outcome of a historical process which has made the larger part of mankind subservient to the other." This quote from Lévi-Strauss (1966: 124) illustrates that since the 1960s, there has been no illusion that the historical relationship between anthropology and its subject matter was anything but inequitable and domineering. Yet, this awareness has not kept anthropologists from continuing their own work back then, as is the case now.

(ii) The second sin relates to field researchers. Being very few in number, until the mid century, anthropologists took "ownership" over the places and regions they studied, giving rise to area studies fraught with exoticism. It is in this context that "Americanists," "Africanists," and experts in the Pacific Islands or in Melanesia appeared on the scene. The further combination of these geographical areas with topics such as kinship, religion, law, and economics, besides fragmenting anthropology, made it almost impossible to replicate experts. As a result, each anthropologist became an institution unto him or herself, in many cases inhibiting further fieldwork in their areas of specialization.

(iii) "Salvage anthropology" was another sin. Acting like archaeologists gathering live debris, it was anthropology's task to rescue and store, for the enlightenment of future generations, remnants of "primitive" cultures and artifacts facing inevitable extinction. From this perspective, the anthropologist would go to areas of the world being conquered by Western mores with the "mission" of rescuing and bringing back the "evidence" of different (and oftentimes *previous*) forms of social life.

There was a special urgency related to the task, since whole cultures and societies were disappearing in the blink of an eye.

(iv) Last, but not least, we have the problem of funding. Here the misdeed refers to the lack of ethical principles in accepting labeled money. A good example was the support of the Rockefeller Memorial during the 1930s to provide the bulk of grants for research and fellowships to the London School of Economics. The goal of training experts who would later dominate African anthropology carried a price tag: the enlightenment of administrators and officers working for imperial regimes. (Although this pragmatic use has been contested as an unfulfilled goal, the experience remains.)

Today's Western guilt is a political statement deriving from recent awareness of power relations inherent in fieldwork. Alternative proposals have been put forward during the past decades, including outlines to recreate anthropology, attempts to bring anthropology home, ideas for new ethnographic experiments, concerns with writing (and with sites and audiences), and invitations to foreign (sometimes considered "indigenous") professionals to discuss the discipline. In short, since the 1970s, anthropologists have been immersed in self-reflection and a quest for new awareness.[2]

In Brazil, things materialize in a different way. Although we perceive ourselves as part of the West, we do not assume that anthropology's past is essentially a sinful one. Of course, when the centers put anthropology's flaws on display, this trend echoes in Brazil and elsewhere.[3] But the general idea is that, if sins exist, they are relatively distant, faraway experiences, committed elsewhere, in the past, and by other anthropologists. If there is no room here for sins, then there is no space for guilt either. In relation to the points raised above, for instance, in Brazil (i) otherness has been predominantly found within the limits of the country; (ii) research by a group of ethnographers has been quite common, especially in the case of Indian populations; (iii) salvage anthropology was never an issue—rather the study of "contact" between Indian and local populations was considered more relevant than preserving intact cultures; (iv) funds for research have come mainly from state agencies for advanced research. In looking at the history of anthropology, emphasis goes primarily to *theoretical history*, i.e., the past as a spiral movement of production, the probing and expansion of inquiries, and the questionings and problems deemed to be "anthropological." In such an endeavor, history is not judgmental, its character is not presentist, the past is not to be condemned by today's standards. Rather, the past is seen through the insights it generated and, as a living force, is brought back as values and principles.

VALUES

One may read the history of anthropology in many ways.[4] One way is to look for past sins. Another is to search for values, and perhaps virtues. In the latter mode, values are detected mostly in the sociogenetic moment when anthropology became socially recognized and accepted as a discipline, i.e., the first half of the twentieth century. I list some of them in a candid way:

(i) One important aspect of the anthropological enterprise from its beginnings was to acknowledge the diversity of cultures, societies, and peoples along with the "psychic unity of mankind." Caught in the challenge of combining these apparently polar goals, anthropologists did fieldwork in remote parts of the world, in which they had to become competent in the natives' language—fieldwork was an encounter that was supposed to last a long time (at least two years). Initially conceived as research on how "primitives" lived, successive fieldwork experiences ended up conveying to anthropologists that these peoples had different, but equivalent, categories or domains of social life. Comparison has thus always been at the heart of the anthropological enterprise, whether implicit or explicit.

(ii) The confrontation between Western categories and a different but equivalent phenomenon had one simple result: the West became "just one case" in the whole human experience. A form of relativism prevailed. From this perspective, anthropologists neither judged their subjects nor defined what was best for them—empathy was the order of the day, and priority for "the native's point of view" was mandatory. Whether they encountered witchcraft, head-hunting, peculiar forms of marriage or any other phenomena inimical to Western mores, understanding in context was the ethnographer's task.

(iii) A byproduct of this project was that Western fields of knowledge, which by that time were in the process of being consolidated (economics, sociology, law, psychology), came to produce an array of subfields, such as "legal anthropology," "economic anthropology," "social anthropology," "psychological anthropology," "anthropology of religion," indicating that the discipline could respond to different areas of inquiry. (Though both relativism and subfields have been under criticism in the past decades, their sheer existence at one point in time is inevitably part of our present understanding of the world.)

(iv) Another point relates to the nation-state. While nation-states were also being transformed into the model of the true "world culture of the times" (Dumont 1994: 14), anthropologists did not study national units;

anthropologists were studying "peoples," "cultures," "societies," "tribes" *situated* in nation-states, but not nation-states *per se*. Originated from nation-states—and anthropology being one of their offspring—anthropologists were interested in different units and milieus: the Trobrianders, Tallensi, Zande, Tikopia, Maku, Bororo, Xavante, and so on.

(v) Generally these units were smaller than nation-states—but not always so. Oftentimes anthropologists found themselves crossing national borders, either because "their" group did so and/or because other experts' findings matched or combined with their own in a specific region. (Of course, Leach's *Political Systems of Highland Burma* was *the* classic study in this direction, contesting the concept of "tribe" and forcefully denying that the boundaries of society and the boundaries of culture should be treated as coincident—an important lesson to this day.) The anthropologists' cosmology was thus of a world made out of "areas," and not of countries or nation-states.[5]

IN BRAZIL

Values often produce an inspirational scenario; in Brazil anthropology's thrill exceeds its possible past sins. Sins, if there were any, are not part of our present day; they are allowed to rest. In this context, yesterday's exoticism and today's guilt—the main grounds for the sense of crisis in the field—are locally "acculturated": exoticism becomes (familiar) "difference," while guilt is stopped in its tracks by the ambience of political commitment towards those under study. Against that backdrop, I will bring up a few of the aspects that deserve highlighting:

i. Except for its Indian populations, Brazil has hardly attracted the attention of metropolitan anthropologists. As a result, it has never experienced that historical outrage of those who have been the object of anthropological curiosity by metropolitan centers, as was the case in the first half of the century with Melanesia, South and Southeast Asia, and Africa. It is well known, for instance, that Lévi-Strauss was only interested in isolated Indian populations and not in the country as a whole. Until very recently, Brazilian anthropologists would rarely do fieldwork outside the country's territorial boundaries.

In brief: colonialism's sins were all far away; no resentment or guilt is in sight.

ii. Anthropology in Brazil was institutionalized as a social science in the 1930s, along with sociology. At that time, the social sciences were expected to devise a better future for the country as part of a movement towards modernization. They should enlighten (or even help create) a modern political elite, and identify relevant topics for investigation. But part of this grand modernization project was also represented by a timeless quest for theoretical excellence—which would then make the social sciences in Brazil attain the same level as Europe, for instance. Ever since, an aspiration for quality plus a political "mission" became a strong component of social scientists' self-identity. In this context, sociologists (and not the usual cohort of archaeologists, biological anthropologists, linguists of the center) have been anthropologists' long-established contenders for theoretical accomplishments and political relevance, particularly since the 1950s, when sociology's theoretical accomplishments received full recognition. For the following two decades, up until the 1970s, sociology was the hegemonic field in the social sciences, with anthropology representing a kind of Eve's rib.[6]

In brief: Anthropologists outwardly, at home sociologists are their alter ego.

iii. A *sui generis* picture emerges: while for sociologists a long term agenda has always involved the study of oppressed sectors of the population, guided by an implicit project for change and development, anthropologists have focused on differences and their political commitment leads them to defend those studied (in particular from the state's domination). Anthropologists thus profited from the freedom allowed by the discipline's tradition of separating "peoples" from the "nation-state" (but only partially; more later). As sociologists thus work within the parameters of a macro-sociological or historical perspective, anthropologists work with "the natives' point of view"—a byproduct of the strong imprint left by relativism.[7]

In brief: Acculturated as difference, exoticism's negative bend is replaced by a (positive) scrutiny of the native's point of view.

iv. Fieldwork has been regularly undertaken at home (though the expression "anthropology at home" is not used), following a configuration of different projects amongst which we may distinguish, though not exclusively, attempts at a more "radical" otherness, the study of "contact" with otherness, "nearby" otherness, and a radicalization of "us." (More on these ideal types, soon.) Even indigenous peoples—the prototype of a "radical alterity"—were investigated within the boundaries of the national territory. This situation reveals less a problem of funding—although this aspect needs to be considered—than the choice of an object of study which includes, or is mixed with, a concern over differences. It can certainly be argued that indigenous groups represented the "available exoticism" in Brazil, but since otherness was not predominately radical, the demand for theoretical excellence took hands with the moral force that defines the social sciences as dominated by (Weberian) "interested" knowledge.

In brief: Otherness assumes relative undertones and is directed to social and cultural aspects.

v. The emphasis on difference and alterity may be related to the dominant influence of a French perspective (over a German one, for instance). Playing down a strict interest in peculiarities or singularities (the basis for exoticism, for that matter), the predominant interest has been to study different "others" within a totality represented by Brazil.[8] Indeed, Brazil is the ultimate ideological reference. Social responsibility is fundamental, but the idea that prevails is that knowledge of different viewpoints, especially the viewpoints of (whatever) "natives," amounts to a strong enough political statement. Moreover, in contrast to contexts where anthropology today becomes a "voice" (see Fischer 2003), anthropology in Brazil is a field (as sociology used to be for Durkheim) and a discipline, whose social recognition has increased in recent decades. (One is tempted to say that, in Brazil, anthropology stands for the modern values of individualism and universalism, and respect for differences.)

In brief: While the sociologists' main "mission" is represented by projects of change and development, the anthropologists' task is primarily based on the understanding of differences (even when mostly within the nation-state).[9]

ALTERITIES (IN THE PLURAL)

For a brief overview of what has been produced in Brazil under the label of anthropology, I propose to identify four ideal types: "radical alterity" involves the study of indigenous peoples, but also of peoples abroad (both are territorially distant); "contact with alterity" focuses on the relationship between the indigenous with local populations; a sort of "nearby alterity" is represented by urban studies; "minimal alterity" refers to the investigations in the social sciences themselves. Ideal types are models in relation to which empirical examples can be measured in order to elucidate some of their relevant characteristics.[10]

Radical alterity. In contrast to canonical fieldwork overseas, "radical" alterity in Brazil has never been far-reaching. A first case is the classic study of indigenous populations located within the geographical limits of the country; a second one is represented by the more recent project of going beyond Brazil's territorial limits. While ethnological fieldwork is well established in the country and has produced a considerable amount of literature on Tupi and Gê Indian groups, for example, fieldwork abroad is more recent and takes researchers to the United States, looking for immigrants, or else to Africa or Asia, in search for fellow Portuguese-speaking peoples, once colonial subjects of Portugal (such as Mozambique, Cape Verde Islands, Guinea Bissau, East Timor). In both cases, an ideological link to Brazil is in order; there is no "free" otherness, indeed no exoticism in sight.[11]

Contact with alterity. Contact between Indian groups and regional populations became a legitimate academic concern during the 1950s and 1960s, particularly after the introduction of the notion of "inter-ethnic friction." This concept resulted from a bricolage of indigenist concerns and sociological theory, revealing "a situation in which two groups are dialectically put together by their opposing interests."[12] Inter-ethnic friction was proposed in a context where the theories of contact, both British (Malinowski) and American (Redfield, Linton, and Herskovitz), had proven inadequate. This hybrid combination became the basis for many long term projects, and it proved fundamental in the consolidation of several graduate programs in the country.[13]

Nearby alterity. Since the 1970s, anthropologists in Brazil have carried on research in large cities, making urban studies a case of "nearby alterity." Given that the teaching of anthropology is part of the social sciences curriculum, it is common for anthropology to become a counterpoint to sociology. Under the political authoritarianism of the 1960s, anthropology was seen by many as an alternative to challenges coming from sociology, in a more or less silent dialogue that has persisted ever since. The attraction to anthropology rested both on its qualitative approach and on the promise of answers to understand both the country's diversity and, eventually, its ideological unity. Topics of interest range from immigrants to race relations; religion, messianism and Afro-Brazilian cults; popular festivities; kinship and family; party politics; violence; peasants and industrial workers; workers' unions, etc.[14]

Us as others. Since the early 1980s, the study of the social sciences themselves has become a distinct field of inquiry. In general, these studies propose to understand science as a form of modernity, with topics ranging from historical contexts to biographies of social scientists and investigations into classical (European) sociological authors. (Apparently it is here that recent movement at self-reflection finds shelter in Brazil.) Trends such as the "anthropology of anthropology," "ethnography of anthropology" and "history of anthropology" live side by side, as do studies on the teaching of anthropology. A comparative perspective with Europe is often implicit, thus prompting the difficult question of the audience for whom they are intended, and consequently, of the language of enunciation, given that Portuguese is not a world language. Of course, simple translations are not satisfactory given the different audiences being sought.[15]

CONCLUDING REMARKS: "NATIONAL ANTHROPOLOGIES"?

In recent decades, references abound to "national anthropologies." Although this is not a well-defined term, academic common sense has it that this expression refers to the discipline as developed in non-Western, or "peripheral," countries. Recent international conferences (such as the EASA conference in September 2004, for instance) have added to this recognition in many panels.

Over two decades ago, Gerholm and Hannerz edited a special issue of *Ethnos* dedicated to "The Shaping of National Anthropologies" (1982). For the organizers, the important divide was between an "international" anthropology, comprised by American, British, and French disciplines, and "an archipelago of large and small islands" in the periphery, where "national anthropologies" are found. The idea of "national anthropologies" seems to have caught on since then. Recently, in discussing alternative styles for fieldwork, Gupta and Ferguson (1997) found them "in strong and long-established 'national' traditions as those of Mexico, Brazil, Germany, Russia, or India" (1997: 27); similarly Clifford (1997) suggested that traditional fieldwork would certainly maintain its prestige, but that the discipline might come "to resemble more closely the 'national' anthropologies of many European and non-western countries, with short, repeated visits the norm" (1997: 90).

In this context, I close this essay with two brief comments, one on the "national" component of the expression, and the other on the plurality of "anthropologies."

First, "*national* anthropologies" seems to denote a residual category, for those not included in the "international" mainland. To gloss over possible negative overtones, adjectives like "strong" and "long-established" may be used. It is true that, historically, anthropology's development (as with other sciences of the social) coincided with the formation of European nation-states, a process which has always allowed the ideology of nation-building in its many forms to become if not an exclusive, then at least a powerful parameter for the characterization of these sciences. The expansion of anthropology, however, also coincided with the building of empires, a fact that poses serious problems for former and present hegemonic powers as to how to deal with the troubling question of whether anthropology may survive in a post-colonial era (and, for many, a post-nation-building era as well). In this scenario, either *all* possible manifestations of the discipline are (or were) in some sense "national," or we should add the label "imperial anthropologies" to contrast to the "national" breeds.[16] Granting that no explanatory value is attached to any of them, perhaps we should recall that anthropologists do have a place in the world. Fortunately, though, wherever social theory is socially produced, it is relatively autonomous from its immediate contexts of production and therefore capable of attaining desirable levels of communication.

Second, "national *anthropologies*" suggests that there are as many "anthropologies" as the contexts in which they develop. What, then, is left of the universalist promise of anthropology, in which comparison is a major stanchion and source? It is a fact that anthropology manifests itself in many versions, varieties, and contexts. Its multiplicity, however, does not deny its universality; the awareness of its multiplicity just makes self-reflection and communication more complex. The picture of the three "others" with whom we must converse, i.e., our immediate peers of the same local community (be they fellow anthropologists, historians, literary critics, sociologists), the peoples studied (whether overseas or just across the hall), and the colleagues from other traditions and other places, past and present, is not new. Rather, it is in this context that anthropological theory–this rich and always open-ended outcome of successive fieldwork experiences which contest both common sense notions and previous theories–stands in the role of a (Peircean) Third: a full convention to allow dialogues across cultures to be in fact between equals (we all have the same monographs in our private libraries; field anecdotes are socially shared; similar ethnographical stories are used as productive metaphors). Why not value among ourselves what we grant all natives? We may breathe in the idea of comparison beneath a universal umbrella, in which different manifestations of our own discipline are rich examples of diversity. Anthropology is one and many.

NOTES

*   This paper was written as a communication to the panel "Other Anthropologies: Regional perspectives on transnationalism and globalisation," organized by Aleksandar Bošković at the EASA Conference in Vienna, 2004. I want to thank Sasha for the invitation. I am indebted to Antonádia Borges for a keen reading and for excellent suggestions.

1.   See, for instance, Lévi-Strauss (1961) and Goody (1966).

2.   See Peirano (1998). Latour (1996: 1) comments: "It is a strange fact that, exactly when the discipline reaches the peak of its power–having overcome the period when cultures of the world were robust and vigorous and anthropology weak or barely existing, and the following one in which anthropology had gathered momentum (chairs, journals, field sites, endowments) but traditional cultures

weakened and began to disappear—guilt-ridden anthropologists began to denigrate their own achievements in postmodernist vogues."

3. Barth (1996: 1) comments: "American cultural anthropology today dominates the international scene, both in mass and quality, and is largely trend-setting for what we all try to do."

4. On different approaches to the history of anthropology, see Peirano (2004), for a comparison between the historiography of anthropology, an "anthropology of anthropology," and "theoretical history".

5. Thus, for instance, groups could be put together in ecological/sociological areas such as "lowland South American Indians" or "Amazon region Indians"—but *not* "Brazilian Indians," or "Colombian Indians."

6. See Peirano (1981) for an attempt at developing an "anthropology of anthropology" using social sciences in Brazil as a case study.

7. As a result, to this day sociologists see anthropologists as "soft" empiricist social scientists, less socially and politically committed, less methodologically rigorous, interested in peculiar differences, and always content with their discipline. On the other hand, anthropologists censure their colleagues for their hidden agenda about "how things ought to be."

8. The significance of Durkheim's sociological project for anthropology in Brazil may be succinctly recognized in the opening paragraphs of *The Elementary Forms of Religious Life,* where the author explicitly denies that curiosity about mere exoticism is appropriate by affirming that sociology did not intend to study a very archaic religion "just for the pleasure of recounting its oddities and singularities." Durkheim emphasizes that sociology's goal is first and foremost to explain a current reality, "something close to us and consequently capable of affecting our ideas and actions." It is no coincidence that many anthropological studies in Brazil contain the term "sociology" in their titles. (See, for instance, Cardoso de Oliveira 1978; DaMatta 1981).

9. At a time when the social sciences are concerned with "methodological nationalism" (Beck 2004), anthropologists may feel exempt from these entrapments—anthropology studies groups, societies and tribes, not nation-states. Indeed, it may study "ideologies" of nation-states. See Peirano (1992).

10. For a comprehensive bibliography according to the four ideal types outlined here, see Peirano (in press).

11. See Viveiros de Castro (1999).

12. See Cardoso de Oliveira (1963).

13. See Pacheco de Oliveira (1998).

14. See Velho (1994); DeMatta (1981); Fry (2005).

15. Good translations, such as Viveiros de Castro (1992) and Vianna (1999), required the help of anthropologists themselves (Catherine Howard for Viveiros de Castro, John Charles Chasteen for Vianna).

16. It goes without saying, for instance, that Africa could be considered "home" to the British, who exported the idea of totality to their colonies in the early twentieth century, leaving England itself critically unquestioned by its frail sociology.

REFERENCES

Barth, F. 1996. The Practice of American Cultural Anthropology: A View from the Margins. Paper presented at the panel "How Others See Us," AAA, San Francisco.

Beck, Ulrich. 2004. "Cosmopolitical Realism: On the Distinction Between Cosmopolitanism in Philosophy and the Social Sciences," *Global Networks* 4, 2: 131–56.

Cardoso de Oliveira, Roberto. 1963. "Aculturação e 'fricção' interétnica." *América Latina* 6: 33–45.

——. 1978. *A Sociologia do Brasil Indígena*. Rio de Janeiro: Tempo Brasileiro.

Clifford, James. 1997. *Routes: Travel and Translation in the Late Twentieth Century*. Cambridge, MA: Harvard University Press.

Clifford, J. & G. Marcus (eds.). 1986. *Writing Culture: The Poetics and Politics of Ethnography*. Berkeley and Los Angeles: University of California Press.

DaMatta, Roberto. 1981. *Carnavais, Malandros e Heróis. Por uma Sociologia do Dilema Brasileiro*. Rio de Janeiro: Zahar.

Dumont, Louis. 1978. "La communauté anthropologique et l'idéologie." *L'Homme* 18, 3–4: 83–110.

——. 1994. *German Ideology. From France to Germany and Back*. Chicago: University of Chicago Press.

Durkheim, Emile. 2001 [1912]. *The Elementary Forms of Religious Life*. Oxford: Oxford University Press.

Fischer, Michael M.J. 2004. *Emergent Forms of Life and the Anthropological Voice*. Durham: Duke University Press.

Fry, Peter. 2005. *A Persistência da Raça. Ensasios antropológicos sobre o Brasil e a África Austral*. Rio de Janeiro: Civilizaçao Brasileira.

Gerholm, T. and U. Hannerz . 1982. "Introduction." In *The Shaping of National Anthropologies*, *Ethnos* 42 (Special Issue), pp. 5–186.

Goody, J. 1966. "The prospects for social anthropology." *New Society,* Oct. 13, pp. 574–76.

Gupta, A. & J. Ferguson. 1997. "Discipline and practice: 'The Field' as site, method and location in anthropology." In A. Gupta & J. Ferguson, eds., *Anthropological Locations: Boundaries and Grounds of a Field Science*. Berkeley: University of California Press.

Latour B. 1996. "Not the question," *Anthropology Newsetter* 37, 3: 1, 5.

Lévi-Strauss, C. 1961. "La crise moderne de l'anthropologie," *Le Courrier* (UNESCO) 14, 11: 12–17.

——. 1966. "Anthropology: its achievements and its future," *Current Anthropology* 7, 2: 124–27.

Oliveira Filho, João Pacheco. 1998. "Uma etnologia de 'índios misturados.' Situação colonial, territorialização e fluxos culturais." *Mana* 4, 1: 47–78.

Peirano, Mariza. 1981. *The Anthropology of Anthropology: The Brazilian Case*. Unpublished Ph.D. dissertation, Harvard University. <http://www.unb.br/ics/dan/Serie110empdf .pdf>

——. 1992. *Uma Antropologia no Plural. Três Experiências Contemporâneas.* Brasília: Editora da Universidade de Brasília.

——. 1998. "When Anthropology is at Home." *Annual Review of Anthropology* 27: 105–29.

——. 2004. "'In this context': as muitas histórias da antropologia," in H. Pontes, L. Schwarcz & F. Peixoto, eds., *Antropologias, Histórias e Experiências,* Belo Horizonte: Editora da UFMG, pp. 99–123. (English version in: <http://www.unb.br.ics/dan/Serie352empdf.pdf>)

——. In press. Otherness in Context: A guide to Anthropology in Brazil. In D. Poole, ed., *Companion to Latin American Anthropology.* Oxford: Blackwell.

Vianna, Hermano. 1999. *The Mystery of Samba. Popular Music & National Identity in Brazil.* Edited and translated by John Charles Chasteen. Chapel Hill: University of North Carolina Press.

Viveiros de Castro, Eduardo. 1992. *From the Enemy's Point of View. Humanity and Divinity in an Amazonian Society.* Translated by Catherine Howard. Chicago: University of Chicago Press.

——. 1999. "Etnologia brasileira." In S. Miceli (org.) *O Que Ler na Ciência Social Brasileira (1970–1995),* pp. 109–223. Volume I. São Paulo: Editora Sumaré & Anpocs.

Postscript

Developments in US Anthropology Since the 1980s, a Supplement

The Reality of Center-Margin Relations, To Be Sure, But Changing (and Hopeful) Affinities in These Relations

George E. Marcus

INTRODUCTION

This collection, in addition to the *Ethnos* special issue published more than two decades ago, provides not only a valuable understanding of the diversity of anthropologies, but also how, wherever it has been institutionalized, anthropology has served as a screen or projection, from a marginalized cosmopolitan perspective, of the national histories and dramas in which it has grown up. This is no less true of the anthropologies of the so-called "center" (imperial anthropologies? those of the United States, Britain, and France) as of the anthropologies of the so-called "margins." One of the advantages of understanding the histories of the anthropologies of the latter is to realize more consciously how much the anthropologies of the former have also been entwined in their own national dramas.

The essays of this volume provide accounts primarily of the institutional evolution of anthropology in various states and nationalisms, and this is an indispensable contribution in an already globalized world of instant, fluid communication. But I have found fascinating the reading between the lines of these essays for the personal stories and more intimate histories of anthropology in each of these settings. For example, in places like Russia (the former Soviet Union) and Argentina, the history of anthropology has been tied to both complicity and struggle with authoritarian, mercurial, and sometimes brutally censoring political regimes. In Kenya, the opportunities that anthropology provided for inquiry were entwined first with colonial rule and then nation-building under the ideology of development. I was also interested in the actual histories of contact between anthropologies of the center and those of the margins. These are somewhat legible in the essays of this volume, but perhaps, it remains a separate volume to produce—a crucial one for a fuller understanding of what the anthropologies discussed here became, or could become, in their own national contexts.

In reading these essays, I often wondered what kinds of persons would pursue a career in anthropology, a self-consciously marginal discipline not well or immediately understood by the publics, as opposed to, say, a career in law, medicine, or economics. The biographies of leading anthropologists in these places must be as interesting as are the stories of the insitutionalization of anthropology themselves.

I also tried to think across these cases with three dimensions in mind that seem especially to have defined the character and possibility of anthropology in diverse national settings:

(1) The character of the practice of fieldwork as the research modality that seems to distinctively define the ethos and identity of modern social/ cultural anthropology in all of the places where it has been established. Rarely elsewhere (except for, say, Japan, Brazil, and Norway), it seems, have resources been available for prolonged periods of fieldwork that became definitive of anthropologies of the "center." How fieldwork has taken shape in these anthropologies in itself would be an excellent index of their special epistemological dimensions of how they defined their subjects, how they understand objectivity, how subtly they define the political and ethical commitments, typical of anthropology generally.

(2) The extent to which these anthropologies have pursued and fulfilled the comparative goals which have historically been at the heart of anthropology, or the extent to which comparison has been at the service of, and a supplement to, the nation-defining project—that is, the extent to which comparisons are produced on a universalizing canvas, or are at the service of a narrowly nationalist project of sorting out diversity within a particular historic project of nation-building.

(3) The extent to which these anthropologies view themselves as having been involved in a project of modernity as well as nationalism. Do they remain across the boundary from the modern in their distinction as

experts of the traditional, or even still, the primitive? Or are they free to enter the historic preserves of the modern and the contemporary, allowing themselves to pursue their curiosities wherever they take them—even if this means moving beyond the confines of the "other" as different according to *ethnos*, culture, or level of development (civilization)? Does anthropology have uses in these various places beyond peculiar forms of diversity management or explaining the margins relative to their own centers and mainstreams of contemporary life?

Indeed, the very same questions about the limits and unfulfilled potentials of anthropology could equally be asked of anthropologies of the so-called "center" as well as of those of the so-called "margins." Rather than to continue to pursue a commentary on this valuable volume as if I were producing a review of it (which I do not intend), it might be a useful contribution instead to provide, as a supplement, a personal view of recent developments in social/cultural anthropology in one of the anthropologies of the center—that of the US—to place alongside (on the margins of) the accounts of the other anthropologies of this volume. I would not suggest doing so if I did not think that there have been certain changes in anthropologies of the center (in the US, anyhow) occurring mostly since the 1982 *Ethnos* issue appeared that have made them and the anthropologies of the margins, if not more equal, then more alike in ways that matter to the practices of each.

Even though it is homologously marginal in its own context of hierarchies of disciplines and university institutionalizations of expertise, the vastly greater wealth invested in anthropology in the US as well as the numbers practicing it make all the difference in shaping its relations with anthropologies of the margins. Prestige, status, and influence move along with the sheer weight of numbers in justifying the center-margin distinction characterizing the way in which US anthropology exists in relation to other anthropologies. But especially since the 1980s, social/cultural anthropology in the US has become disorganized (or rather more diffusely reorganized) through seminal critiques (the so-called "Writing Culture" moment, Clifford and Marcus 1986) and the trends that followed them. Not only was US anthropology at its center cut from its historical moorings in traditional research agendas (e.g., who studies kinship or mythology now?—topics once at the center of the discipline), but its best work since has been produced in transcultural and thoroughly interdisciplinary movements and research programs (represented in the US university by such conglomerates as media studies, ethnic studies, cultural studies, science studies, postcolonial studies, women's studies, etc).

I believe that this development has both nominally and substantively brought the agendas of US anthropology closer to those of the other anthropologies discussed in this volume. No longer, for example, do US anthropologists arrive in place X to do their kinship studies while local anthropologists are concerned with issues of poverty. There is now likely to be a much greater affinity of concern and interest in a globalizing and relativizing world between anthropologists of the center and anthropologies of the margins even though that distinction is still held in place by the prestige of relative wealth and status enjoyed by the former. But in a world of fluid information and access, it is less theory, concepts, and models of "how to do it" that the center has to offer, but differently inflected curiosities shared with anthropologies elsewhere. As I suggested above, this different nature of relation and affinity cutting through and across the center-margin distinction is worth a successor volume to this one.

To give a sense of this, I offer a supplemental account of developments in US anthropology since the critiques of the 1980s, with special attention to the nature of those controversies that have occasionally preoccupied the discipline. These have moved from concerns with the paradigms of anthropologies of the center as such—rather academic controversies—to controversies that are truly transnational in scope and identification. In these terrains, one can see the making of a substantial world anthropology, so to speak, which despite differences of power, have more to do with the affinities that create a common ground, effectively defining and focusing periodic major controversy across the center-margin divide. It is my hope that this supplement will provide a useful complement and hint of new possibilities of conversation beyond the center-margin divide brought about as much by changes in US anthropology itself as by changes among the other anthropologies that are chronicled here.

THE 1980s AND AFTER: NO TURNING BACK

Through the 1960s and even before, there was a counter-discourse emerging regarding mainstream social and cultural anthropology ... in the US Anthropology was part and parcel of colonialism, and could not escape this past in the present. The positivist language that has defined anthropology in the academy was not supported by the kind of method that fieldwork is, especially after the publication of Malinowski's diaries in 1967. The construct of the human, or the idea of culture, is flawed as the justification or rationale for a distinctive and rigorous line of inquiry. But anthropology in the US had always been reflexively self-critical and healthily skeptical about its own foundations, and this has been constructive. What happened in the 1980s is that many other disciplines, especially humanistic ones, like history and literary studies, in an effort to renew themselves with a social relevance, became passionately interested in many of anthropology's established framing concepts and postures. In literature, history, and art, interest in the nature of cultural difference and the expressions and exercise of power through cultural innovation and production became the fashion in a far less parochial manner. In intent, at least, the non-West, and difference that creates identity for ethnicities, women, and gays and lesbians became the subject of sympathetic interest among influential scholars in literary studies and history. At the same time, the Western polities were in a post 1960s conservative reaction, and the largely left/liberal academy, particularly in the US, did not have much of an outlet for political expression or activist energy. The cultural left in the academy, as it came to be called, bore this weight through styles of critical research that moved in designation from the rather apolitical character of so-called postmodernism to the Marxist inflected cultural studies, inspired by its established British expression. Fine-grained observations, narratives from everyday life, and testimonies in the voice of otherwise anonymous subjects—also the basic material of ethnography—were in fashion rather than big theories or visionary narratives of society and culture.

By the early 1980s, the gathering internal critiques of anthropology intersected with this strong wave of critical thought in the humanities in the form of a critique of the ethnography as text and genre, and then as research process. The key work in this event was the volume *Writing Culture* (Clifford and Marcus 1986), but there were many others, and there was an entire literature of feminist revision of traditional anthropology that predated and paralleled the Writing Culture critique. The critique of anthropological rhetoric and representation unlocked and focused all of the other evolving internal critiques and led to the hope for alternative practices, invested for a time in the notion of ethnographic experiments. There was a strong opening to the influences of sources of critical thought new to Americans—especially that of the French poststructuralists—flowing through literary studies. Also, there were new ways of writing history and culture history into work that was basically ethnographic and ahistorical in character. The scholarly and literary production around postcolonialism produced by an elite of largely South Asian scholars of literature and history in U.S., British, and Australian universities had perhaps the greatest effect on shaping what is now mainstream social and cultural anthropology today.

During this same period from the early 1980s onward, there was a marked increase in scholarship of professional quality on the history of anthropology, especially its twentieth century history. The importance of the availability to teachers and students in anthropology of a rich and critical history of the discipline cannot be overestimated. To my knowledge, these newer works are widely read and used in teaching. The availability of such a growing twentieth century history of the field has thus in itself had a profound effect on how anthropology can be practiced now—thoroughly demystifying once authoritative practices, but also giving the resources for revisionist histories that fit quite well with the way the discipline is in fact evolving.

The book *Anthropology as Cultural Critique: an Experimental Moment in the Human Sciences,* written by Michael Fischer and myself, and published in the same year as *Writing Culture* (1986), was a comprehensive statement and argument about the implications of the wave of 1980s critiques specifically for the dominant traditions of styles and topics of research in social and cultural anthropology in the US. Through the 1980s, ethnography addressed both new topics and topics that it had addressed before, regarding its core focus on cultures and identities in change, but the conditions and styles of ethnography changed dramatically. The multiplicity of methods and perspectives that was characteristic of works coming out of comparative literature and cultural studies characterizes the most innovative, and now even standard, ethnographies. Conditions of collaboration in fieldwork became a more explicit aspect of ethnography. The subjects of ethnography could no longer be constituted in objective terms as previously done. These changes came about not only because of the effectiveness of self-critique within the academy of the 1980s, but also because of changing realities on the ground, so to speak: the subjects of anthropology have never been primeval; they have always been in a state of change even during the artificial stabilization of the colonial period; but it can also be persuasively argued that the world in which anthropology defined its traditional subjects changed as dramatically during the last quarter of the twentieth century as did the practice of anthropology's traditional, emblematic method.

In terms of intellectual fashion, the world of postmodernity transmuted by the late 1990s into a world dominated by globalization. For cultural analysis, under a regime of globalization, what was postmodern in the 1980s remained postmodern, only more so. Studies of identity processes and politics focused many of the critical cultural theories in fashion in the US and came to dominate anthropology's traditional constitution of its subjects as peoples and places. Now culture in the latter was non-essentialist, fragmented, and always penetrated by complex world historical processes mediating the global and the local as it is found in ethnographic research anywhere. Following the *Writing Culture* critiques of the 1980s, the *Public Culture* initiative, associated with Arjun Appadurai and a journal of the same name that he and others founded, was perhaps the major expression of the changing forms of analysis of anthropology within its traditional area specialties. At the same time, anthropology developed ambitious research in topical arenas new to it that dealt with institutions such as media, science, technology, markets, advertising, and corporations, irrespective of the habitual peoples and places mode of defining traditional subjects, and by the late 1990s, with a legitimacy and prestige at least equivalent to this habitual mode.

So, at present, while the schematic lines of anthropology's traditional interests remain constant, and appear so to its publics, its practices of research, its relations to subjects, and the substance and structure of its characteristic diverse array of topics are all very different than just two decades ago. Indeed, since the *Writing Culture* critiques of the 1980s that centrally affected the discipline, it can be fairly said that there has not been another equivalent central tendency, or competing central tendencies as metadiscourse, since that time to suggest an agenda for a discipline in its new and revised terrains of research—nothing like structuralism, cognitive anthropology, Marxism, or symbolic/interpretativist approaches of a couple of decades ago, or classic topical debates about kinship, religion, ritual, and belief before that.

Just because the old centers no longer hold does not mean that anthropology is disorganized or dissolving. Rather, it does not have a disciplinary sense of itself in the many topical arenas to which it is drawn and makes substantial contributions. Like so many other disciplines concerned with analyses of contemporary culture, anthropology's entry into certain terrains is inevitably belated or derivative in relation to other discourses and practices already on the scene. For example, there is virtually no topical interest that anthropology addresses today where contemporary journalism is not likely to have been first, or has dealt with the descriptive task of classic ethnography more quickly and often just as effectively. Though inevitably derivative, anthropology's entry into a certain topical arena still leaves the question of what is distinctive about what its emblematic ethnographic inquiry offers. And it is a question worth answering. This is precisely the task of disciplinary metadiscourses about its new and revised projects that anthropology, in all of its present curiosities and centrifugal engagements, has yet to address. In any case, there is for the foreseeable future no turning back to the archival function of ethnography in the old peoples and places domain of inquiry. The bodies of theory, practices, and topics which established this interest are in abeyance; in some instances, played out; or simply not able to be pursued because the conditions in many places under which the fieldwork must be undertaken will not permit it.

NOTABLE CONTROVERSIES

It is perhaps worth tracking the changes in US social and cultural anthropology, which I have outlined by a brief iteration of a series of controversies,

approaching scandals, that have at certain moments gained widespread attention, not only among anthropologists, but also breaking out in the old
(pre-Internet) national public sphere as defined by major print and electronic
media (for example, all of these controversies, but one, gained prominent attention in the *New York Times*). It is interesting that in the 1960s, the major
public controversies involving anthropology had to do with its complicities
in American geopolitics, its siding with neocolonial causes on occasion,
most prominently the assistance that anthropologists working in Thailand
gave to the US in its wars in Southeast Asia. By the 1980s, these controversies were about the modes and effects of anthropological representations
of traditional subjects and the real social stakes involved in representation
itself. In the following brief discussions, I have selected those controversies
that have not only been prominent in public, but that are instructive as
symptoms which systematically track the major path of change in social and
cultural anthropology since the 1980s.

*1. The attempt (in 1983) by Derek Freeman to expose Margaret Mead's youthful and
perennially influential work,* Coming of Age in Samoa.

The Australian anthropologist Derek Freeman attacked the most widely read
early work of Margaret Mead, several years after her death, and decades
after this work had any relevance to ongoing discussions among US anthropologists. Still, for a broader educated public in the US this work epitomized
"what anthropologists do" and also the truth of the doctrine of cultural
relativism that anthropology contributed to American thought. Freeman's
heated and very public attack on this work as a caricature and on Mead as
naïve created mischief and embarrassment for anthropology, which caused
it to defend a work long ago out of date, but still at the heart of the ideology
of the field, in order to retain its authority in relation to its most important
and broad public. And this controversy emerged just as anthropology was
undertaking its most searching self-critique challenging that very same ideology through a highly sophisticated analysis of its own habits of representation, as evidenced not only in its classics, but in its most current work.

*2. Gananath Obeyesekere's critique of Marshall Sahlins' account of the murder of
Captain Cook in the Hawaiian islands, and Sahlins' Refutation (early to mid 1990s).*

The distinguished anthropologist Gananath Obeyesekere, influenced by the
styles of postcolonial argument originating largely with the work of South

Asian scholars in history and literary studies (but opening in 1978 with the landmark work, *Orientalism,* by Edward Said), moved from his scholarship in Sri Lanka to take on the premier anthropologist of Polynesia, Marshall Sahlins, in his interpretation of the fatal visit of Captain Cook to Hawai'i, through which he introduced his influential approach to structuralist history. This was a classic controversy over the minutiae of ethnographic material and interpretation, of the sort that had focused the attention of the discipline in previous generations. But it was also about an argument that took representations as the main object of critique (was the deification of Cook by the Hawaiians an expression of their mode of thought, or was this just a European myth, a representation consistent with beliefs about the nature of primitive, in this case, Hawaiian, thought?).

This is not a controversy that reached the broader public realm. But while, as noted, it was a candidate for a riveting controversy of the classic sort within the discipline, it also failed to hold prolonged attention or generate much of a literature of debate even within anthropology. This failure to function as a focusing controversy in anthropology indicates that the concerns of the discipline had moved considerably beyond the important but traditional issues that were debated over in the minutiae of the ethnographic material, which is the form that the exchanges between Obeyesekere and Sahlins took. Or else the discipline in its diversity had become too fragmented to pay much attention to this controversy, beyond the attention that the prestige of the participants, as among the most senior and distinguished of anthropologists, had attracted.

Indeed, while the controversy was motivated by the issues animating cultural studies in the 1990s (that is, Obeyesekere's critique of representing the Other), it was fought out, to Sahlins' advantage, over older disciplinary questions requiring depth of ethnographic expertise. At that point, the disciplinary audience acknowledged Sahlins' achievement, and then lost interest.

3. The anthropologist David Stoll's exposure of inaccuracies in the powerful testimonial work by the Guatemalan Maya and Nobel Peace Prize recipient, Rigoberta Menchu.

I, Rigoberta Menchu, a testimony of oppression and genocide perpetrated against the Guatemalan Maya, had great influence in the US when it was published in 1987. It was received as an eyewitness, powerful document, and therefore the truth, of gross human rights violation at a time when multiculturalism and struggles over identities of various ethnicities and subject positions were at the forefront of humanistic and political discourse on the liberal/left in

the US. David Stoll, an anthropologist with long experience in the same places and areas that were the scene of Menchu's writings, published in 2000 a massive case against the accuracy, and therefore the documentary truth, of her influential work. Once again, it was a representation at stake in this controversy: a kind of traditional sense of anthropological truth, based on accurate, objective reporting, and "native" truth, based on complex situations of life engagement and genres of truth-telling. It was anthropological truth (of an unreconstructed sort, little affected by the *Writing Culture* discussions) against the truths of "natives" who speak in their own terms and genres. This can thus be seen as a mature controversy of the era in which representations were the object of critical cultural analysis, and the political stakes of contesting the sense of truth in representation were apparent. Anthropological representation of a conventional sort (valuing Western standards of accuracy) had come face to face with independent representation of its classic "Others" in a world where the traffic in representations is unpredictable and promiscuous. This controversy produced fascinating reactions (Arias 2001) that gauged the tension of representations between the authority of the academy and others in communities which the former had made its object of study.

4. The critical exposure by the journalist, Patrick Tierney, in his book, Darkness In El Dorado *(2002), of the ethnography of Napoleon Chagnon on the Yanomami and the larger context of biomedical research of which his research was a part.*

In 2002, Patrick Tierney published an indictment of long term research on the Yanomami. The Yanomami had become an emblematic "primitive" people in US anthropology due to the writing of Napoleon Chagnon, whose early monograph (1968, but revised many times), *The Yanomamo: The Fierce People,* had become a staple in the university teaching of anthropology. Chagnon's research had long been contested, debated, and considerably revised within anthropology, but its broader research context had never been clearly documented. This is what *Darkness In El Dorado* did, clarifying Chagnon's research as part of an ambitious long term project of biomedical research that allegedly resulted in harm to the Yanomami. This controversy, which had existed before in terms of a critique of anthropological representation like the other controversies that I have documented, also went well beyond this toward conceiving Chagnon's work as part of techno-science and its assimilations of the worlds that anthropology had classically defined for the West. As the most recent, symptomatic public controversy marking the reception of anthropology in the broader public sphere, it has gone far beyond the truth of its science based on the critique of its representations—a preoccupation from the 1980s *Writing Culture* era, marking a shift in anthropology's inter-disciplinary participations—back toward a concern with changing modalities of culture contact in a postcolonial, globalizing world. The issues of the ethics and purposes of anthropological research suddenly transform when an instance seen in the tradition of a classic work that suffered mere critique of representation is seen in larger instrumental context and design.

Through the symptom of controversy, one understands the production of anthropology as embedded in a far more complex set of relations in the contemporary world that goes beyond its colonial past and its Malinowskian paradigm. One could say that whatever their specific concerns, this is what all contemporary projects of ethnographic research in social and cultural anthropology are mapping and exploring: the web of their own conditions of producing knowledge about specific others.

Taken together, these controversies are interesting because they illustrate a certain progression in the development of US anthropology over the past two decades, where its most pressing issues of collective self-definition have moved in the reach of their discussion from the relatively unconscious boundedness of the society and national context in which the discipline developed to a fully engaged global theater of participation and enactment of events which might have been previously only academic affairs, and narrowly circumscribed US ones at that. It would seem that the realm of active accountability for US anthropology has expanded markedly over the past two decades, and this shifting and more diverse and complex context of US anthropology's reception, is bound to be changing the nature of the center-margin relations between US anthropology and its professional "others." This was more than evident in the scope of participation in the "Rigoberta Menchu" and "Yanomamo" controversies. In these instances, at the very center of US anthropology's self-concerns, was a multiple, varied, and indeed global discourse in which the relevant anthropologies of the "margins," among others, were powerfully heard.

THE CURRENT ENTHUSIASM FOR A PUBLIC ANTHROPOLOGY

If there has been a present central tendency within social and cultural anthropology amid all of its recent diverse curiosities and research pursuits, it has been the call for a public anthropology, an anthropology whose primary *raison d'être* and prestige lay in the direct and tangible contributions that it is making to certain issues and events of the world, drawn from the wisdom of the accumulated tradition of past work and applied in the present (there are many expressions of this tendency: for example, the popular collection edited by MacClancy, 2003). US anthropology has always been public-minded; this is the embedded cultural critique side of the discipline that has constituted the very motive that has propelled it to study other societies. And there has been an applied or practicing anthropology for decades (albeit in its own terms it has occupied a "second-class citizen" status in the discipline). But the desire for a public oriented, citizen anthropology is much more open and mainstream.

The desire for a public anthropology implies a discipline more concerned with its accountabilities, its ethics, and its obligations to diverse others in its research efforts than with a guild-like, enclosed preoccupation with debates, models, and theoretical traditions that drive it as a discipline. This development is interesting and distinctive, but there is still the need for the discipline to inform itself reflexively about how the call for public anthropology changes the character of its research agendas in a systematic way. This leads from a consideration of the desire for recognition from the most prestigious of its potential publics, the mainstream national and international press and media, to a consideration of the varied kinds and constituencies that it faces—its many local and more intimate publics, that range from the other agencies and disciplines that find anthropology useful or important, to the social movements with which anthropology wishes to affiliate in an identity of activism, and finally to the publics within the realms of the fieldwork itself, that is, the reception of subjects and clients within the bounds of particular projects of research. And these of course include its special reconfigured relationships with anthropologies of the "margins."

ANTHROPOLOGY'S PUBLICS

Every project of anthropological research constitutes a specific public sphere of reception that also corresponds to a politics among the diverse constituencies that come into existence with any project of research. In this sense, the very reception of anthropological research while it is being performed from inception, through fieldwork, and written product is crucially engaged with a specific theater of receptions or publics. The recognition, theorization, and incorporation of this level of reception into disciplinary method and practice is perhaps the key task facing US social and cultural anthropology in its current state

By its searching curiosities and new positionings, to some extent made available to its by its relative wealth compared to other anthropologies, US anthropology conducted in traditionally unconventional settings—transnational, science and technology arenas, the so-called arena of the multisited process engendered by globalization—has discovered unique reception classes or publics for itself. In these venues, the most exciting publics for anthropology are neither the traditional imagined "Public" of American life, nor its patron and collegial constituencies, but the publics that are accessed by the complex paths of contemporary ethnographic research itself.

Traditionally, this public for anthropology would be its subjects, and there has been a longstanding desire among anthropologists—really a hidden standard for their ethnography—of response and validation from their classic subjects. What, for example, would have the Trobriand Islanders, or the Nuer, or the Samoans thought of anthropological work on them? This could be asked for any community, people, or place that anthropology made its subject. Equally, anthropologists have wondered how they could mediate or participate in the relations of the generally encapsulated subjects that they have studied with dominant entities and authorities such as states and corporations. This has long been an imagined or virtual constituency of anthropological research, which in most cases of ethnography has never really been actualized. With the emergence of indigenous movements in recent times, these imagined or desired publics for ethnographic projects have become actual. So activism is more than just an academic posture of left-liberal academia for US anthropology. It is an imperative of most projects in the traditional mode whether ethnographers in their personal convictions are particularly "political" or not. Thus, the politics of fieldwork have now circumstantially actualized responses from the most important local publics as subjects that have long been a potential and a desire in US anthropology. It also, as I have noted, changes its relationships to the other anthropologies.

But there are publics in this mode that are not conventionally conceived in terms of this longing for the response of, and collaboration with, one's circumscribed indigenous subjects in the course of ethnographic research. Most contemporary ethnography is played out on a broadly multi-sited canvas of cross-cutting communities, or at least locations, of subjects who may or may not be in active relations with one another. Ethnography these days emerges from a configuration or network of relations encompassing both institutions and communities, elites and sites of ordinary culture in everyday life. Ethnographic designs forge not only constituencies for research projects in these domains, but also the publics of reception to which anthropologists have very specific and enduring relations beyond the bounds of conventionally conceived fieldwork. When such anthropologists produce work to be presented to professional communities, this is often cast as "a report to the academy," a partial exposure of a terrain of multiple constituencies in which the academic constituency is only one, but of course, an authoritative one. The norms for evaluating and creating anthropological knowledge that incorporates such publics as integral to defining fieldwork has yet to be established or articulated. These publics within the bounds of fieldwork are perhaps anthropology's most important contexts of reception.

The question of a public anthropology is not so much how the work of a professional guild will be disciplined and used by others (of course this sense of the public to which it will appeal remains), but how in its very modes of presenting results, it already reports an engagement with, and a participation in, public spheres encompassed within the fieldwork itself. It is as if the meta "public" of anthropologists is invited into research that is challenged to make something of anthropology that is already engaged out there in the situations of fieldwork. This is the outcome of the much vaunted reflexivity in ethnographic production so emphasized in the 1980s critique. In the complex, multisited terrains of contemporary ethnographies, anthropology itself is the final meta-public for its own best and most innovative work. In this position, it has only to redefine what its stakes are in this modality of research which is public at its core.

WHITHER SOCIAL-CULTURAL ANTHROPOLOGY IN THE UNITED STATES?

The critical anthropology that Fischer and I argued for in 1986 (Marcus and Fischer 1986) has become far more pervasive than we expected. We started with the premise that there was an embedded critical rationale, reflecting back on its society of origin, in much outward directed ethnography; that this critical tradition, while somewhat repressed, was still quite strongly motivated; and that with the general vision for anthropology then in disarray amid the enthusiasm for critical theory and reflection sweeping the human sciences, this was a propitious time (during the 1980s) to focus upon and develop this marginalized potential for critique within the practice of social and cultural anthropology. By the mid 1990s, the passion of this general critical trend in US academia had abated, but not without powerful and lasting effects. As I argued, critical purposes and approaches became the rationale for much of cultural and social anthropology with regard to its styles of practice, its topics, and its politics in the environments in which it is produced. We have gone far beyond the heritage invoked at the beginning of *Anthropology as Cultural Critique* to a critical rationale for a diversity of projects and curiosities about the contemporary that do not yet have a clear and specific disciplinary meta discussion or sense of purpose.

By no means has anthropology become sociology now that its interests come entirely within the framework and conceptual categories of modernity. Its history, its sensibilities, and methods remain distinctive. But in its characteristic diversity, anthropology is less clear in its own reflexive understandings of what remains systematically distinctive about its present interventions in domains of research that are rather crowded with other styles and disciplines of inquiry. In my view, these new interventions have been more shaped by the legacies of the powerful influences from the period of interdisciplinary fervor during the 1980s and 1990s than by what remains of or is adapted from the distinctive tradition of inquiry that anthropology developed from in the early twentieth century through the 1970s.

Indeed, anthropologists have a firm intellectual compass in relation to the interdisciplinary spheres and communities to which their work relates and appeals. Anthropological research participates in a much more exciting interdisciplinary world after the 1990s that blurs genres and sometimes those beyond academia; it makes strange bedfellows in the best sense; it is driven by a passionate interest in describing emergent contexts of change, where new norms and forms of social and cultural life are becoming. Anthropology has much to contribute in these terrains, and fuels itself on a disciplinary slogan of public anthropology at the moment.

Yet, how research, on a project to project basis, is substantively received in the rather disorganized, or perhaps centrifugally organized, community of anthropologists in the stew of new interests and old and evolving specialties in which they are involved, is much less clear. What is perhaps neglected in the contemporary enthusiasms for public anthropology is what is at stake for a discipline with a certain distinctive past that experienced a rupture in the 1980s, leaving both continuities and changes which have not been digested in terms of what is distinctive about ethnographic research in its anthropological tradition. For many anthropologists, there is little present concern for rethinking its present research practices in terms of a distinctive, but limited disciplinary past; the eclectic, multimethod posture imported as a style from cultural studies prevails at the heart of the ideology of anthropological research in its new terrains.

The task remains then to rearticulate, and in a sense, to reinvent for US anthropologists themselves their sense of doing anthropology in the present, so that the very desire for a public anthropology can be pursued among the discipline's many publics with a clarity and understanding of purpose. In my view, this is a task that could benefit and be informed by more open discussions of affinities with various other anthropologies in their shared but very differently received disciplinary traditions across the "central-margin" divide. Now, more than ever, as US anthropology becomes world anthropology, though certainly not one among many, but thoroughly open in its accountabilities, it needs to learn from the experiences of other anthropologies, to which this volume gives valuable access.

REFERENCES

Arias, Arturo. ed. 2001. *The Rigoberta Menchu Controversy.* Minneapolis: University of Minnesota Press.

Clifford, James, and George E. Marcus. eds. 1986. *Writing Culture: The Poetics and Politics of Ethnography.* Berkeley: University of California Press.

Freeman, Derek. 1983. *Margaret Mead and Samoa: The Making and Unmaking of an Anthropological Myth.* New York: Pelican.

MacClancy, Jeremy, ed. 2002. *Exotic No More: Anthropology on the Front Lines.* Chicago: University of Chicago Press.

Marcus, George E., and Michael Fischer. 1999 [1986.] *Anthropology As Cultural Critique: An Experimental Moment in the Human Sciences.* 2nd edition. Chicago: University of Chicago Press.

Menchu, Rigoberta. 1987. *I, Rigoberta Menchu: An Indian Woman in Guatemala.* London: Verso.

Obeyesekere, Gananath. 1994. *The Apotheosis of Captain Cook.* Princeton: Princeton University Press.

Sahlins, Marshall.1996. *How "Natives" Think: About Captain Cook, For Example.* Chicago: University of Chicago Press.

Stoll, David. 2000. *Rigoberta Menchu and the Story of Poor Guatemalans.* New York: Westview Press.

Tierney, Patrick. 2002. *Darkness in El Dorado: How Scientists and Journalists Devastated the Amazon.* New York: W.W. Norton.

Afterword

Anthropology's Global Ecumene

Ulf Hannerz

INTRODUCTION

Sometime by the late 1970s, after I had seen a fair amount of the American and British varieties of anthropology, as well as a little of some others, and had been observing at close hand the commitments and peculiarities of Swedish anthropology in its first decade or so of serious growth, I suggested to a colleague with interests in intellectual history and the sociology of knowledge, Tomas Gerholm, that we should try and put together a journal issue on "The Shaping of National Anthropologies." It turned out to be a somewhat complicated enterprise, but materialized in the journal *Ethnos* a few years later (Gerholm and Hannerz 1982).[1] Sadly, Tomas is no longer with us. No doubt he would like me have enjoyed following the burgeoning study of national anthropologies since then.[2] By now there is perhaps hardly a country where anthropology exists where the history and current characteristics of the discipline have not been chronicled and/or scrutinized, briefly or at length, by insiders or outsiders, and thus there are rich materials for comparative study. It is hardly surprising if European anthropologists, in a part of the world with great historical diversity, a turbulent recent past, and increasing internal interconnectedness, have taken some special interest in identifying their respective heritages, and comparing their present situations (see Dracklé, Edgar, and Schippers 2003). As the present book shows, however, with its contributions out of Africa, Asia, Latin America, and the United States as well, the anthropology of anthropology has become a worldwide reflexive effort.[3]

In these comments, I will mostly not go into great detail in inspecting the particular national anthropologies described in other chapters of this book, or elsewhere, but offer some comparative notes, and also consider their interconnections—to see what they tell us about the discipline of anthropology as a global ecumene. A volume like this, I believe, can serve us as a tool, in the words of Richard Fox and Andre Gingrich (2002: 8), for "overcoming retrospective provincialism—that is, by introducing valuable elements from divergent national anthropologies and by expediting an international conversation for an anthropology 'of the present'." It may even help us raise a few questions about the future.

ACADEMIC LANDSCAPES

The first thing to note must be that somehow, something that can be called "anthropology" now shows up just about everywhere, in the scholarly landscape of almost every country.[4] In some places, it is a long-established presence. Among the anthropologies discussed in this book, in Japan, the Netherlands, and Russia, the discipline can be traced back at least into the nineteenth century, if not further; and in each of these cases, the early establishment and growth had something to do with colonialism, of internal or external varieties. Although the chapter on American anthropology deals only with recent history from the 1980s, it is true that its early origins are similar. Only the comparably extended, internally diverse Ottoman Empire does not seem to have supported an academic enterprise now to be claimed as pioneering anthropology; Turkish anthropology, according to Tandogan, began in the 1920s. (Yet it is interesting to learn that when Turkish field workers have recently gone abroad, their studies have taken them on the one hand to wherever there are now compatriot migrants, but on the other hand to the Balkans, and to Azerbaijan, Turkmenistan and Uzbekistan—ancient connections seem to play a part in such outreaches.)

Whatever may have been its time of origin, we learn in these chapters, that anthropology has then in several places gone through some difficult, hazardous times. In Turkey again, in later decades of the twentieth century, military regimes caused an academic brain drain. In Argentina, the struggles between soldiers, Peronistas and others have shaped an uncertain academic environment. The loss of empires surely had an impact on the political premises of Japanese and Dutch anthropologies. In Kenya and Cameroon, the stigma of association with colonial power affected anthropology at least in the early period of national independence. During the 1930s Stalinist terror, Kuznetsov points out, the leading Leningrad anthropologists were accused of anti-Soviet activity, arrested, and executed. Even so, anthropology survived or could be resurrected, and in some other places it has shown up on the scholarly scene much more recently. In eastern Europe, as both Bošković and Elchinova suggest, "anthropology," at least as an academic label, has been a part of the post-socialist transition, without the taint of compromised past orthodoxies. One may sense that a little earlier, in certain southern European countries coming out of periods under other kinds of authoritarian regimes, anthropology similarly arrived with the favorable connotations of intellectual liberation—not least the pleasurable sensation of new comparisons, and more countries heard from.

In any case, again, by the beginning of the twenty-first century, anthropology is present as a recognizable, and more or less recognized, entity in the academic landscape just about everywhere. In the last third of the preceding century, even (perhaps especially) in countries where the living conditions of anthropology have over time been least troubled, we intermittently came across speculations about of an impending "end of anthropology," but still the discipline seems alive and reasonably well. Although many African universities have been through particularly hard times, Fokwang and Ntarangwi appear reasonably optimistic about the future of anthropology in their respective parts of the continent. The material and organizational circumstances of academic life may be constraining, but colonialist origins no longer matter so much, and anthropological knowledge is valued both for its practical uses and as a value in itself. From her vantage point in Brazil, Peirano discerns that the discipline may indeed be doing better in places which have not traditionally been seen as its centers.

The academic landscape has had some conspicuously stable features from one country to the next. Its internal boundaries and its division of labor also show some variations, however, referred to in the chapters. The nearest neighbors, "significant others" for local anthropologists, are not everywhere, and have not always been, the same. In the Netherlands, according to Vermeulen, an old Indology with close connections to Dutch colonialism was somehow exchanged for a new postcolonial "non-western sociology" without immediate counterparts in other national academias. But there had also been a close early affinity with geography, resulting in, if not quite another discipline, at least a distinctive research orientation known as "sociography." Russian anthropology, even in Czarist times, another chapter notes, also had more direct links to geography than was typically the case elsewhere. Yet later, of course, as historical materialism became the reigning understanding of the world, Soviet anthropology was subordinated to history. In Africa, anthropology may find itself somewhere between history and archaeology, on the one hand, and development studies on the other, and may itself turn into "African studies." In Bulgaria, *trakologiya* (Thracian studies) could be a part of the scholarly background of some anthropologists, and in Turkey, Tandogan tells us, cultural studies arrived to claim its space on the scene in the 1990s. Marcus argues that much of the best work in American anthropology now comes out of interdisciplinary contexts such as media studies, science studies, and post-colonial studies. And then in a number of places, the scholars who identify themselves as anthropologists seem to struggle to define their relationships to what may in their respective habitats be "ethnology," "ethnography" or "folklore" (not to mention sociology). This is the case in Bulgaria as well as in the republics of what used to be Yugoslavia, but also in Japan. To a degree, this is just a matter of dealing with the old distinction between what in German used to be *Volkskunde* and *Völkerkunde,* which in some national contexts, such as in Scandinavia, can be a mostly rather benign puzzle, although confusing even to compatriots elsewhere in the local academias.[5] In other places, however, the scholarly labels and boundaries in question are not so innocent, as one or other of them may have become associated with disliked past regimes, whether of the right or the left.

Would all these particular divisions of labor, and these boundaries, reappear if the order of academic disciplines were invented afresh at the beginning of the twenty-first century? Probably not, but then disciplines (not only those now somehow sharing a terrain with anthropology) are perhaps not entirely rational task oriented organizations, but rather like tribes, with identities, traditions, ancestors, and charter myths. They are historically entrenched, and may have vested interests in an existing setup. Redrawing the academic map, consequently, is probably a project which would have many obstacles in its way. Whether we approve of them or not, we may be juggling with these blurred classifications for some time yet. And perhaps, after all, something of value in one or other existing research traditions could be accidentally lost were some other newly made up organization of scholarship to be imposed. In any case, one may suspect that the existence of a standard international academic pattern, including a set of more or less universally recognized disciplines, has so far been an important source of legitimacy when it comes to introducing disciplines previously not present in a national setting, and maintaining them thereafter.

IN THE METROPOLES AND AT THE MARGINS?

Conceivably, one could try to write about a national anthropology as if it were hermetically sealed, with an entirely autonomous path of development. No author here has really done that. The story of a national anthropology tends in no small part to be about its linkages to other anthropologies elsewhere. In our 1982 introductory essay, Gerholm and I devoted much attention to center-periphery relationships in the world of anthropology, and when that essay has been referred to by later commentators, the concern is often with such matters.

For one thing, we suggested that there was an "international anthropology," made up largely of the American, British, and French versions of the discipline, which we contrasted with the national anthropologies our journal issue dealt with (India, Brazil, Poland, Sudan, Canada, and Sweden). That was a way of referring to their general strength, and in particular to their influence across borders. Yet in a way, of course—as Peirano notes—such a formulation could be somewhat misleading, and we did not entirely stick to it. American, British, and French anthropologies are national anthropologies as well, and they are certainly marked by their national contexts in different ways. Let me from here on refer to them as metropolitan anthropologies—a term which we also used, and which is still a way of acknowledging their wide influence. (I take Marcus' alternative, "imperial anthropologies," to be more than half facetious.) We may at the same time note that they are perhaps the most purely national anthropologies, insofar as they can be those least influenced by the varieties of anthropology existing elsewhere—others tend to be rather more hybrid, creolized varieties of the discipline, open to the influence of one or more centers.

It is good to have Marcus' chapter in this volume, identifying American anthropology as one national anthropology among others, and Marcus himself is undoubtedly someone who takes a keen interest in the diversity of anthropologies. He may be right, too, in arguing that the differences between anthropologies in the centers and at the margins are no longer quite what they were, say, a quarter century ago. Nevertheless, it remains true that his chapter has less to say about influences from "other" anthropologies on "his" than the other chapters generally do. (When he notes the influence of French poststructuralists, he sees it as an influence flowing through literary studies, and it does not seem as if French academic anthropology is directly involved.)

One should certainly not conclude, however, that American anthropology is closed to the outside; it is not, and it is perhaps uniquely open in one particular way. Let me bring in one personal experience here. When in the late 1990s I took on the task of editing sociocultural anthropology for the new *International Encyclopedia of the Social and Behavioral Sciences,* I and other section editors were asked to keep in mind that the work was indeed supposed to be "international" not only in terms of readership, but with regard to contributors as well. By the time my editorial work was completed, I was rather pleased to have lined up highly qualified anthropologists from 25 countries as entry authors—but then as the encyclopedia appeared, I could note that a number of them from elsewhere had already joined the ranks of American academia. The US academic job market is, and has long been, unusually open to foreigners and newcomers, and it offers living and working conditions which are attractive by most standards.[6] Certainly it is through immigration to American campuses that some external intellectual influences are, selectively, absorbed. Perhaps postcolonial studies would not have been such a prominent field in (and adjoining) US anthropology recently if the American academic community had not successfully recruited a number of the leading representatives of the post-colonies?[7] Marcus also suggests something along such lines. One could look at this, too, as a matter of brain drain, but that is perhaps another story.

But let us get back to … well, those "other anthropologies," whatever we shall call them, and the relationships with the metropoles as seen largely from their perspectives. The terminology here by now seems a bit ambivalent, and tongue-in-cheek. For Marcus, "margins" are "so-called"; I would still be reasonably satisfied with "center and periphery," but most of us may be unhappy with "provincial." Perhaps the category is really residual, meaning "other than metropolitan." Another term not used in this book, Krotz's "anthropologies of the South" would be a more restricted category, perhaps replacing what in the past might have been described as "Third World anthropologies," including among those covered in this book the African and Latin American instances, but certainly not Japan, Russia, Norway, the Netherlands, or the Balkans.

No doubt a center-periphery vocabulary remains in some ways relevant. In 1982, Gerholm and I suggested that if, say, a Scandinavian anthropologist meets an Indian colleague for the first time, "quite possibly they will try to place one another by way of common acquaintances at Chicago or Cambridge, rather like Australian Aborigines identifying each other by searching for kinship links when they meet as strangers." Some decades later, there are certainly still at least traces of such old asymmetries. On a personal note again: out of the first eight chairpersons of the European Association of Social Anthropologists (EASA), between 1989 and 2005, four were British (one of South African origin), one was Danish, one Swedish, one German (although teaching in the Netherlands), and one Portuguese—but I was the only one among them without a doctorate from the United Kingdom. Just possibly there were in the early phase of the life of the association some protectionist overtones of keeping European anthropology in the intellectual sterling zone, as the late Ernest Gellner put it, and safe from postmodernist and other unsavory influences from the other side of the Atlantic. Yet, I believe one could also discern here some of the efficacy of old, established networks.

If any contributor to this volume comes close to portraying a national anthropology as autonomous vis-à-vis other anthropologies, it may be Kuznetsov—hardly surprisingly, as Russian anthropology no doubt was rather isolated from international influences during much of the twentieth century. But then perhaps in the Soviet era, more especially during the decades after the Second World War, this was again the particular self-sufficiency of a metropolitan tradition, a center with a periphery of its own? At the Department of Ethnography of the Moscow State University, Kuznetsov points out, there were students from "East Germany, Vietnam, Spain, China, Mongolia, Peru, Romania, Czechoslovakia, Ecuador, Yugoslavia and many other countries." What happened to them? Where are they now? It would be interesting to know more about the relationships and practices of the international anthropological community behind the Iron Curtain, and to get some sense of whatever traces of it may still be discernible. There may be some salvage anthropology of anthropology to do here, as soon as possible, while many of the informants are still around.

The Soviet instance as well as those of the more continuously recognized metropolitan anthropologies show, as Gerholm and I also noted previously, that relationships within the world of anthropology to a degree reflect the geopolitics of the wider world. Metropolitan anthropologies are or have been those of past or present great powers. Yet their influence is worked out through smaller-scale connections, and then occasionally these smaller-scale linkages may also happen to come about in ways which do not so immediately reflect macro-political realities.

Returnees and field workers have been recurrent kinds of actors on the ground as anthropology has expanded internationally, and as connections between old and emergent national anthropologies have taken shape. The scholars returning to their countries of origin after training elsewhere may not always turn out to become such bridge builders: Ntarangwi reminds us that Jomo Kenyatta, returning from Malinowski's seminar to Kenya, could conceivably have turned into one, but he found other things to do. (Coming back to China, on the other hand, the recently deceased Fei Xiaodong, a member of the same seminar, could engage in pioneering scholarship, although the Cultural Revolution interrupted his work.) Expatriate field workers as bridge builders are exemplified in the Cameroonian case as Fokwang mentions Phyllis Kaberry, the Ardeners, and the historian-anthropologist Sally Chilver as foreign visitors with a strong local involvement. Tandoğan points out that Paul Stirling was a key figure as several Turkish students were trained in Britain. And that, of course, points to a connection between expatriates and returnees—more generally, Krotz suggests that the first native anthropologists were likely to seek their academic training, and continued scientific legitimization, in that country from which the first fieldworkers came.

Clearly in the past, such ties frequently remained within the frames of empires. Fieldworkers in British colonies came from Oxford and Cambridge, those in French colonies from Paris, and the promising young native of one of these colonies was sponsored as a student in the "mother country." It is true, too, that these old empires may continue to exercise a certain soft power in past dependencies: in Cameroon, British scholars have been prominently active in the Anglophone West, whereas Fokwang notes the French dominance at the main university of the Francophone East. Yet more recently, Cameroonian graduates have proceeded to further study in the Netherlands, the United States, South Africa, and Switzerland, and Ntarangwi refers to American, German, Danish, and Indian as well as British strands in Kenyan anthropology.

Perhaps it is more generally true that connections between national anthropologies have been diversifying at the same time as the relative weight of metropolitan anthropologies has been changing? In Europe it would seem that EASA, as well as various EU exchange programs, have gradually spread personal encounters with other anthropologies more evenly across the continent. At EASA conferences, one will now find workshops co-organized by anthropologists, say, from the Netherlands and Portugal, or from Austria and Sweden; such redistribution of contacts and collaborations may be one of the significant consequences of the growth of the organization. Eriksen bluntly describes Norwegian anthropology, since the 1950s, as largely a branch of British social anthropology. I am not sure every observer would agree. In any case, the overall international influence of British anthropology is hardly any longer what it once was. In a recent historical overview, Eriksen's countryman Fredrik Barth (2005: 56–57) concludes that relative to American anthropology, the balance has shifted; but he also notes a suggestion that a confluence between these two into a wider Anglophone anthropology may be taking place. (Marcus, for his part, in this volume, is hardly in much doubt about the influence of American anthropology on the discipline as practiced elsewhere.)

Occasionally the preceding chapters also reveal historical connections which may not be entirely obvious. Guber, writing about Argentine anthropology, acknowledges the history of American influence, somewhat ambivalent in a way which appears partly to reflect political debates within the metropolitan discipline itself in the times concerned. But then she also refers, intriguingly if rather in passing, to various intellectual and academic links to

Italy, in earlier periods of the twentieth century; it is true that there was a significant stream of migration from Italy to Argentina in much the same period.

On the whole, and in principle, we may sympathize with free flow, diversified linkages, and a weakening of center-periphery structures (especially those involving the dominance of a single center, rather than the competition of several). We may then also discern, however, that it could get a bit messy. Where a diversification of linkages has occurred, more generally or at least to different metropolitan anthropologies, how are the various influences managed on the respective national academic arenas? There may be situations where the diversity of sojourns abroad can be a resource when the experiences of returnees are combined. Elsewhere, in a generally very positive account of the growth of Malaysian anthropology, Shamsul (2004: 297) thus notes that the several national varieties with which the first generation of scholars had engaged could come together in a unique "Malaysianized version" of the discipline. That sounds like a happy outcome, but not an inevitable one. The authors in the present volume mostly do not go into detail here, and one may sense that they remain rather discreet about clashes where differing styles and networks of metropolitan anthropology become the social and cultural capital of particular academic returnees. (Should we make our anthropology four-field or not? How much critique or how much postmodernism is enough, or too much? "In Oxford ..." "Not at Berkeley ...") Simultaneously, of course, these may be clashes with whatever is present as homegrown, more or less established anthropologies, perhaps of types which may until recently have gone under some other academic brand name. Boskovic and Elchinova are among those who refer to such intricacies. Possibly some Bourdieuesque interpretation of the games played in national anthropologies would occasionally be illuminating?

TURFS AND VOICES

If I may come back once more to our line of argument in 1982, let me note that Gerholm and I suggested somewhat in passing, at the end of our remarks on center-periphery relationships, that there could at times also occur a certain reversal of such relationships, insofar as a field area becomes a kind of center of attention in itself. Brazil, say, could be a center for ethnographers from the United States, France, Japan, the Netherlands, Sweden, Poland or wherever; they, then, would turn into a sort of periphery, a diaspora of Brazilianists.

Such an argument raises more general questions about the worldwide distribution of anthropologists and their field involvements. In an increasingly

distant past, perhaps, the kind of center just identified would have to be seen
in one way as a mostly empty center. Those were the days when things were
simpler, when fieldworking anthropologists were expatriates, from the metropoles, and natives natives. Now things get more complicated, as that center
is populated by local colleagues, as well as perhaps temporarily by other visitors from elsewhere. In fact, some variety of relationships may result here.

Some expatriate anthropologists may largely ignore the fact that those
local colleagues are there, and avoid contact with them, for practical or intellectual reasons. They want to spend the time at their disposal in the field
rather than in another set of academic corridors, or they want to maintain
their own perspectives unadulterated. Those local anthropologists, for their
part, may be unaware of such expatriate passages through the territory, or
may resent the fact that the incoming researchers do not bother to make as
much as a courtesy call or find out what related research is going on.

Then it is also possible that those visiting scholars do seek contact—and
find that their local colleagues are people like themselves, who prefer to go
abroad for field work. Something like this may happen for example in Japan,
or for that matter in Scandinavia: those colleagues who happen to be in their
offices may try to be generally helpful and hospitable, but their anthropological minds may be elsewhere. Perhaps the scholars whose knowledge about
local conditions turn out to be more helpful are then people elsewhere in the
academic corridors, like sociologists, or if the *Volkskunde/Völkerkunde* distinction is in place, the ethnologists or folklorists. But their disciplinary points
of view may of course be different.

There is now a good chance, however, that a sizeable proportion of
those local anthropologists are mostly engaged in anthropology "at home"—
indeed an internally diverse category, but one which can usually at least be
understood as "in the home country." By now it may appear that outside the
metropoles, and a few other more or less affluent countries such as Scandinavia, the Netherlands, and the German-speaking countries, this has in fact
become the dominant practice. What relationships between expatriates and
natives will develop here? If we want to understand the organization of the
global ecumene of anthropology, it seems to me, these are relationships that
deserve more organized attention. Conflicts over ethnographic turfs and
challenges to ethnographic authority may arise. Anthropologists at home
may claim more subtle local knowledge. Since on the other hand the expatriate anthropologists often come from the prosperous international centers
of the discipline, they may not only be better funded, but also have easier
access to the latest in theoretical debates and fashions, and to publishing
channels. In different ways, several of the contributors to this book—for example Sugishita and Tandoğan—point to such factors. One can sense the

potential for conflicts, and one can identify instances which reach at least to the discipline's gossip circuit, where they are too often construed as personalized little scandals rather than as examples of a tension increasingly built into the discipline.

Perhaps the strongest chance that a non-metropolitan anthropology can at least situationally, as a field region, turn into a center in its own way may be found in those places which indeed do attract expatriate scholars, but where there is a reasonably large local/national scholarly community, with an intellectual tradition tending toward some autonomy. Among the national anthropologies discussed here, Brazil seems to me to provide an example. Center-periphery strains are apparent here as well, but I note Peirano's argument that Brazilian anthropologists may feel themselves rather distant from some of the recent political, moral or epistemological problems and weaknesses preoccupying colleagues in the metropoles. Just possibly a similar disinclination to engage more actively with certain of the particular burdens of metropolitan anthropology can be discerned for example in Scandinavian and Central European anthropologies, without much in the way of a colonial past, without present great power status, and without many immigrant scholars from the postcolonies around? In these settings there may be other issues, closer at hand, to anthropologize.

This takes me to the intricate problem of voices. What anthropologists, and anthropologies get heard, where, and by whom? There are questions of international relationships here, as well as of the public presence of anthropology.

To a fairly high degree, center-periphery relationships in the global anthropological community seem structured in part also by the world system of language. At present only those scholars who write in English can really count on being reasonably accessible to colleagues everywhere. This means that whether they are actually aware of it or not, only those living in countries of (more or less) native English-speakers can count on reaching a wider local audience and an international audience at the same time, with the same piece of writing. Others have to choose, and the choices can affect the international visibility in their own way. On an individual basis, the alumni and alumnae of Anglophone academic institutions are probably more likely to continue doing at least some of their publishing in English, wherever they come to reside later. For scholars in smaller countries, with modestly sized national anthropological communities, it may seem to make little sense to publish more strictly academic work in the national language, so quite possibly they will habitually choose to use English for such works. Writing in the national language then becomes the choice for particular genres, such as more popular works, or textbooks.

Under such circumstances some national anthropologies may have a greater international visibility than their sheer numerical size would seem to warrant—this may be the case of Scandinavian anthropologies. In contrast, and rather more importantly, where the national community of anthropologists is large, the scholar may take the national language to be the natural choice for all writing and publishing. Sometimes this choice is also supported, or even enforced, by an explicit public policy to cultivate that language even internationally as a scholarly language—a policy which may not be particularly realistic, but which may effectively contribute to restricting circulation.

For reasons of such kinds, some national anthropologies become less known elsewhere in the world than one would perhaps have expected. Of the anthropologies discussed in this book, this seems true of those of Japan, Brazil, and to a degree probably even the Netherlands. The tendency is intensified when the anthropological community in question conducts a great deal of expatriate research. Japan specialists from elsewhere in the world may well learn enough Japanese to find out what their Japanese colleagues are writing about their own country. European or North American Africanists or Southeast Asianists, on the other hand, are not so likely to know the work of the Japanese colleagues with whom they share a field.

It is true that some Japanese anthropologists, and expatriate bridge builders, are sensitive to the situation, and that there have been recent initiatives to publish in English, in book series and periodicals. But that opening is still very limited, and again, the linguistic limitation of access involves other major national anthropologies as well.

A more concerted, generous and well-informed effort to offer anthropological writings of varied origins in translation would certainly be useful in decentering the global flow of anthropological knowledge and ideas. We should realize, however, that the obstacles to communication are not entirely linguistic, but have to do with the organization of publishing as well. It is clear that some non-metropolitan English-language publications—Canadian, Australian, Indian—do not really reach out as widely as those of established American and British publishers either.

If non-metropolitan anthropologies are variously visible, or audible, internationally among colleagues in the discipline, how strong is their presence at home, on more public arenas?

Several of the contributors to this book are concerned with this question, and come to quite different conclusions. Tandoğan describes Turkish anthropology as a "silent discipline," with little impact on public debates or in the media. Eriksen, on the contrary, emphasizes the high public profile of Norwegian anthropology. Fokwang describes the Kaberry Research Centre as an intriguing venture in involving a range of non-academic, more or less amateur participants in local research in the Cameroonian Grassfields region. Marcus' argument about the outward, public orientation of American anthropology does not really seem to match Eriksen's Michael Herzfeld anecdote, but then Texas may be different from Massachusetts.

The Norwegian case is indeed striking, and as Eriksen suggests, it can be used for comparative purposes. I would be inclined to emphasize the implications of scale. No doubt there is something to Marcus' claim for the public involvements of many American anthropologists. Nevertheless, I believe it is important that American anthropology especially, and the other old metropolitan anthropologies a little less fully, have been large enough and well-organized enough to have a certain intellectual autonomy, for some time at least with a sufficiently large job market and publishing market to live by its own internal rules, standards, and fashions. Careers and reputations have in considerable part been controlled by peers in the discipline. Under such conditions, it is feasible and reasonable to turn in large part inward. If Norway has a thousand anthropologists, that is a truly remarkable number for a country of its size. But of the four regular university anthropology departments, the two largest only have about thirty permanent staff members between them (still sizeable numbers, it should be pointed out, by European standards). Norwegian anthropology has reached its mass and its public presence only by reaching into (some might say "infiltrating") diverse research institutions, presumably developing special skills of communicating and making itself relevant at interdisciplinary and public interfaces.

Undoubtedly it is also partly a matter of scale that the orientations and talents of some small number of individuals can also make a real difference here—Eriksen mentions some of them, although it should be clear that he must also be included in their number. I would also, however, want to suggest that a feature of the Norwegian academic landscape has also mattered. Those Norwegian anthropologists who have been so inclined seem to me to an unusual degree to have had the field of more or less public and popular social and cultural commentary to themselves, as far as the academic division of labor is concerned. The disciplinoid of "cultural studies" does not really seem to be present. Moreover, while the distinction between *Volkskunde* and *Völkerkunde,* ethnology and anthropology, is in place in Norway as in much of Northern and Central Europe, it appears that ethnologists have remained longer with a more traditional definition of their discipline, and concern themselves less with current issues.

When so inclined, anthropologists in Norway have thus found a place as experts and commentators "at home" (not least on questions of cultural diversity and immigration); and as far as a comparison of national anthropologies is concerned, I think it is noteworthy that when these produce anything like "public intellectuals," it is when the latter engage in large part with national issues. In the Netherlands, Vermeulen notes somewhat in passing, the veteran André Köbben has derived his public reputation more from his involvement in Dutch minority affairs than from any of his more strictly academic work, which has mostly been related to fields elsewhere. In large part, the public presence of anthropology, and individual anthropologists, may indeed have been strongest where the discipline is less of an expatriate pursuit, and more a matter of remaining within the nation—which is to say less in the metropolitan anthropologies, and rather more in some of the "anthropologies of the South." I would think of examples in India and Brazil. This should not just be taken as a plea for more anthropology "at home." More reflectively, it may be seen as an indication of the continued strength of national frameworks even in times of globalization. This is evidently where the public is still most engaged, most curious, most inclined to listen to new opinions. We seem not yet to have really come up with working formats for a more fully cosmopolitan public commentary, of a kind where the wider perspectives of anthropology toward humanity can come into their own.

That may be one project for our common future. But I wonder what other questions, less noticeable in accounts of national anthropologies and their development until now, although perhaps hinted at, could also emerge as foci of further international conversations in the anthropological ecumene? Are we on our way, after all, into a period when that standard international academic pattern referred to above may no longer be quite so stable?

Most of the chapters here depict or assume a landscape of universities, or sometimes museums and other institutions, which are parts of a state apparatus. Even the successfully expansive Norwegian anthropologists seem to remain mostly public employees. In the United States, it is true, academia has long had a rather stable mixture of state institutions and others. But now the habitats of anthropologists may be changing in various ways, in the metropoles and at the margins, and we see occasional hints of it in the preceding pages. In Turkey, new private universities—developing there and elsewhere as an ingredient in globalization—seem to emerge as pivotal academic milieux. In Kenya, we learn in another of the preceding chapters, anthropology may flourish in the years to come, but less as an anthropology of thick descriptions, and more as one of short term consultancies; a struggling community of scholars will be "for hire to any one with a paycheck." National and international NGOs will feature significantly in the professional anthropological habitat. In the academic heartlands, we find arguments, sometimes heated, about changes between modes of knowledge production (often away from disciplines, toward the interdisciplinary). Perhaps as a part of the long march of a neoliberal culture complex through state machineries, we face the ubiquitous demands of audit cultures affecting styles and rhythms of research as well as training.[8] And as a consequence of supranational integration, we may be reshaping courses and degree systems to make scholarship more mobile.

Pessimists could be inclined once more to see such scenarios as spelling the end of anthropology, at least as we have known it. Optimists, and activists, may prefer to see challenges rather than problems. In any case, we do not seem to lack topics for future conversations.

NOTES

1. The *Ethnos* issue, I should add, was not based on a conference, which would no doubt have been enjoyable, but under the circumstances hardly feasible.
2. Our journal issue has been widely and generously recognized as a pioneer effort, but I would want to acknowledge that there were related efforts before ours, or more or less simultaneous with it: Fahim's (1982) volume on "indigenous anthropologies," for example, or Diamond's (1980) big, but uneven and rather anachronistic book.
3. I would also especially want to draw attention to Yamashita, Bosco and Eades (2004) and Kuwayama (2004), for highly illuminating discussions of certain Asian anthropologies.
4. Bošković mentions that as far as he knows, there has been no attempt to establish anthropology in Macedonia.
5. This is a familiar distinction in much of Europe; in the United States it is distantly reflected in a handful of folklore programs or departments spread among major universities. Academic life in the United Kingdom seems to be the deviant along this dimension, as there is no *Volkskunde* strongly institutionalized there, and this shows in the frequent unawareness, and insensitivity, of Anglophone anthropologists with regard to the significance of this split in intellectual traditions and academic identity politics in much of Europe.
6. To what extent this may be affected in the long term by restrictions on international mobility related to "the war on terror" and considerations of "homeland security" remains to be seen.
7. For some insights into this, see the volume on the South Asian intellectual migration edited by Assayag and Bénéï (2003).
8. Clearly there is a growing awareness of such issues in European as well as American anthropology; see, e.g., Strathern (2000) and Brenneis (2004).

REFERENCES

Assayag, Jackie, and Véronique Bénéï, eds. 2003. *At Home in Diaspora*. Bloomington: Indiana University Press.

Barth, Fredrik. 2005. "Britain and the Commonwealth." In Fredrik Barth, Andre Gingrich, Robert Parkin, and Sydel Silverman, *One Discipline, Four Ways*. Chicago: University of Chicago Press.

Brenneis, Don. 2004. "A Partial View of Contemporary Anthropology." *American Anthropologist* 106: 580–8.

Diamond, Stanley, ed. 1980. *Anthropology: Ancestors and Heirs*. The Hague: Mouton.

Dracklé, Dorle, Iain R. Edgar, and Thomas K. Schippers, eds. 2003. *Educational Histories of European Social Anthropology*. Oxford: Berghahn.

Fahim, Hussein, ed. 1982. *Indigenous Anthropology in Non-Western Countries*. Durham: Carolina Academic Press.

Fox, Richard G., and Andre Gingrich. 2002. "Introduction." In Andre Gingrich and Richard G. Fox, eds. *Anthropology, by Comparison*. London: Routledge.

Freedman, Maurice. 1979. *Main Trends in Social and Cultural Anthropology*. New York: Holmes & Meier.

Gerholm, Tomas, and Ulf Hannerz. 1982. "Introduction: The Shaping of National Anthropologies." *Ethnos* 47: 5–35.

Kuwayama, Takami. 2004. *Native Anthropology*. Melbourne: TransPacific Press.

Shamsul, A.B. 2004. "Anthropology, Identity, and Nation Formation in Malaysia." In Shinji Yamashita, Joseph Bosco and J.S. Eades, eds., *The Making of Anthropology in East and Southeast Asia*. Oxford: Berghahn.

Strathern, Marilyn, ed. 2000. *Audit Cultures*. London: Routledge.

Yamashita, Shinji, Joseph Bosco, and J. S. Eades, eds. 2004. *The Making of Anthropology in East and Southeast Asia*. Oxford: Berghahn.

Name Index

General Index

Lightning Source UK Ltd.
Milton Keynes UK
UKHW02f0932030718
325148UK00011B/898/P